Why Can't We?

Why Can't We?

The Story Of THE CRANBERRIES And The Band's Iconic Frontwoman DOLORES O'RIORDAN

Curated by Stuart Clark

AS TOLD THROUGH THE PAGES OF *HOT PRESS*

Why Can't We?

CREDITS

Published by *Hot Press* Books,
100 Capel Street,
Dublin 1
Ireland.

First published 2021
Copyright © *Hot Press*, 2021
The moral right of the author has been asserted.

ISBN: 9780957611467

A ◉HOT PRESS original title
To subscribe to *Hot Press:* write to subscriptions@hotpress.ie
To order more copies of this book, email orders@hotpress.com or visit hotpress.com/shop

◉HOT PRESS BOOKS

Why Can't We?

The Story Of THE CRANBERRIES And Their Iconic Frontwoman DOLORES O'RIORDAN
(As told through the pages of Hot Press)

Curated by STUART CLARK

Production Director: Máirín Sheehy
Design and Art Direction: Eimear O'Connor
Archive Research & Production: Karen Kelleher
Photo & Editorial Research: Jess Murray
Photographic Retouching: Miguel Ruiz, Eimear O'Connor
Cover Design: Eimear O'Connor
Cover Photo: Matt Anker
Publishing Director: Duan Stokes
Editor: Niall Stokes
Commercial Team for this project: Mark Hogan, Catherine Madden, Ellen Gough, Katie Harrington

Photos used with kind permission.
Every effort has been made to contact the original copyright holders of the photographs, but one or two were unreachable. We would be grateful if the photographers concerned would contact us.

SPECIAL THANKS

• To Noel Hogan, Mike Hogan and Fergal Lawler of The Cranberries; Eileen O'Riordan, PJ O'Riordan and all of Dolores' family; the tireless Nollaig Hogan; Alan McEvoy, Sebastian Davey, Kieran Kelly; Lindsey Holmes, for all the help down the days; Siobhán Hegarty for the proof-reading and wise counsel; the *Limerick Leader* for their generous assistance; Mark Crossingham and everyone at Universal Music; Professor Eoin Devereux; Rowena and Richard Parry for their unwavering support.

• To all of the photographers, who took such brilliant shots of The Cranberries and of Dolores over the years – your work is very special.

• To the *Hot Press* journalists and writers, who collectively made and continue to make the magazine what it was, and is – and contributed so many great stories over the past 40+ years, including those which are included here on The Cranberries.

• To those who participated enthusiastically in providing new material to us for this book, including Matt Anker, Kevin Barry, Dan Brodbeck, Andy Earl, Graham Keogh, Olé Koretsky, Jim Leatherman, Simon Le Bon, Kellie Lewis, Melodie McDaniel, Lisa McGee, Javier Patón Melgarejo, Phil Nicholls, Mark Prendergast, Mick Quinn, Andy Rourke, Michael Stipe, and Stephen Street.

• To the fans across the world who contributed photographs and memorabilia.

The Cranberries are managed by Helter Management
www.cranberries.com

Why Can't We?

CONTENTS

FOREWARD

BY NIALL STOKES

There has never been a book that covers the story of the globally celebrated Irish rock titans The Cranberries, and the band's iconic frontwoman, Dolores O'Riordan. That thought had been preying on our minds in *Hot Press* for some time. We knew that we had, in our vaults, the makings of a great way to tell a story that was dramatic and inspiring – but also, ultimately, and unavoidably, heartbreaking.

Hot Press Deputy Editor Stuart Clark had been there from the start. Literally. Based in Limerick, he was writing for a local newspaper when the first line-up of a band then calling themselves The Cranberry Saw Us coalesced. As a man who knew how to string a few words together, he was commissioned to write the group's first ever press release. Anyone who has been there, at the fledgling moment in any band's career, knows how intoxicating that can be for a nascent bunch of rock superstars. In this case it was made all the more so – intoxicating, that is – when Stuart received his lavish payment in the form of a bottle of what has always been a favourite tipple among a certain class of rock 'n' roller, Jack Daniel's. Discretion ensured that he never enquired exactly where the bottle had come from!

Then came the inevitable split. Luckily for the world, it should be added. Out went the venerable Niall Quinn, a fine songwriter who was also committed to a band called The Hitchers. In came a waif straight out of secondary school – a 'country girl' by the name of Dolores O'Riordan – who, as it turned out, could sing like an angel. Which she did. And the rest is 'theirstory'.

We spent some time sifting and calibrating, and thankfully, the *Hot Press* vaults proved to be as well-stocked as we had imagined. The magazine had always enjoyed a great working relationship with The Cranberries, and their publicist Lindsey Holmes, who also works with U2. Whenever anything was happening, we got a call – and, in general, the kind of quality access that makes all the difference to the journalistic outcome. But that was only the half of it. As the band developed artistically, and became enormously successful commercially, they grew in confidence. From the outset, Dolores – who undertook most of the media duties – had always been true to herself. Gradually she became even more voluble and, when the occasion demanded, outspoken. Our approach was always to give artists who genuinely have interesting things to say the space to say 'em. With Dolores, it was always a slam dunk.

We talked to the Cranberries guitarist, Noel Hogan, frequently too, and to Fergal Lawler, and the enigmatic Mike Hogan, when we got the opportunity. But it was usually Dolores who stepped to the fore. And she gave a brilliantly honest account of herself every single time. In 2001, we did a special issue on the band when the *Dreams* compilation album was released to mark the end of their first decade – and everyone in the band pitched in to help. By any standards, flicking through

To the memory of
Dolores Mary Eileen O'Riordan
(1971–2018)

"THE STARS ARE BRIGHT TONIGHT..."

Why Can't We?

the back issues, you could see that therein was editorial gold. And so, with the impact of the Covid pandemic biting hard, we decided to talk to the band and see if they'd be up for the adventure. If they were, we'd put together the first ever career-spanning book about the band, taking in Dolores' solo work as well, and a bit more besides – including the desperately sad part of the story that we are all still grappling with emotionally. As it turned out, there wasn't a whole lot of persuading to be done. Fans of the band needed something good to hold onto. The Cranberries understood that. The idea quickly got the green light.

It has been a labour of love since then for the team here at *Hot Press* – and especially for Stuart Clark, who has curated the book that you are holding in your hand with great dedication and finesse. Our Art Director, Eimear O'Connor, has also gone way beyond the call of duty. And so too has PJ O'Riordan, Dolores' brother and manager of her estate, in helping to steer the ship home.

To ensure that there would be original material in the book, we sought out musicians, videographers and producers who had been there at key moments in The Cranberries' career, or when Dolores was doing her solo recordings. We also made a call-out to fans, thereby uncovering some fantastic images that had never seen the light of day before. Not everything would fit. There was nipping and tucking to be done and a narrative shape to be orchestrated. The more ground we covered, the more we fell in love again *("Impossible not to do!")* with the marvellous qualities that made The Cranberries, and Dolores O'Riordan, so special.

They were a unique group, who delivered an Irish indie masterpiece with their debut album, *Everybody Else Is Doing It, So Why Can't We?* That record gave us a name for the book: *Why Can't We?* And from there, it was a deep dive into the ebb and flow of a career that saw them sell well in excess of 40 million albums and rack up over a billion YouTube views for the video accompanying 'Zombie' alone. And here we are, a year later, more or less, hammering the final pages into shape, making them ready to entertain, enlighten and beguile – and hopefully to move readers, on occasion at least, to tears.

There is now – and forever will be – a deep and enduring sadness at the heart of the story of The Cranberries. But there is nothing whatsoever we can do to change that. What we can do, instead, is to put on the records and listen again with open hearts. We can hear the music jangling and surging and then that voice – Dolores O'Riordan's extraordinary, beautiful, evocative, ethereal, emotional voice – ringing through like a sweetheart from another planet, telling us perhaps that she has us wrapped around her finger, and leaving us with auguries of intimacy and immortality that linger long after the record has ended.

This then is herstory, history, theirstory. I hope you love reading it as much as we did putting it all together. *"And now I tell you openly,"* Dolores O'Riordan sings on 'Dreams', *"You have my heart don't hurt me."* And she has ours. Amen.

· Niall Stokes is founder and editor of *Hot Press* magazine

⦿HOT PRESS

Music City – not Stab City

U2 were the biggest band in the world when, on November 18th, 1989, a quartet calling themselves The Cranberry Saw Us played their debut live gig in the Flag Café, on Limerick's Broad Street. With at a push forty people there to see them, and bum notes aplenty – Noel Hogan described it afterwards as "a shambles, totally mortiftying" – it didn't feel like we were witnessing the future of Irish rock 'n' roll. As the troubled 1980s ground towards an end, the likelihood of four scruffy indie kids from Limerick joining the chart-topping, globe-trotting band from the Northside of Dublin on the global stadium circuit hovered somewhere between zero and none.

Opposite photo: Matt Anker

You had to go all the way back to January 1978 to find the last time anybody from Munster's second city had appeared on *Top Of The Pops*. And that didn't really bear thinking about: Terry Wogan's crooned version of 'The Floral Dance' was lots of things – but a call to arms for the next generation of Limerick rock 'n' rollers wasn't one of them. In fact, the Treaty City didn't have much of a modern musical pedigree at all. Prior to Wogan's crimes against brass bands, the mood in local muso circles had been one of optimism followed by crushing disappointment. True, the legendary Ennis Road actor Richard Harris had gone Top 5 on both sides of the Atlantic in 1968 with the first recording of the Jimmy Webb song 'MacArthur Park', but that too was essentially a one-off.

There were some nearly stories. Trippy psychedelic soulsters Granny's Intentions – they'd started life as The Intentions and later became Granny's New Intentions – had promised much during the late 1960s. With a feisty Johnny Duhan on lead vocals, they established a strong foothold on Ireland's thriving beat scene, before shifting base to London. They recorded a handful of singles, signed a record deal with Decca, released a debut album, *Honest Injun*, in March 1970 and almost achieved commercial lift-off. But it didn't happen and the band petered out. Johnny Fean, who grew up in both Limerick and Shannon, was also active on the beat scene, and made an early impression in a local power trio called Jeremiah Henry. But when Declan Sinnott left then-burgeoning Celtic Rock heroes Horslips, Johnny was invited to replace him, ending the immediate hope that a band formed and bred in Limerick might make the big time.

Reform, an ebullient pop-rock three-piece led by Don O'Connor, also looked like contenders during the 1970s and into the '80s, but they too fell short. Future *Riverdance* composer Bill Whelan left the city to go to UCD in the late 1960s, playing in a number of jazz rock outfits and joining the successful, pioneering folk group, Planxty, in 1980. But that didn't last, and it would be the mid-'90s before he would ascend to a very different kind of superstardom.

There were moments during the early-to-mid '80s when it seemed that things might be looking up. Taking their cue from the UK's 2 Tone movement, The Outfit served up a bona fide classic in the rocksteady shape of 'El Salvador' before splintering and giving birth to Toucandance and The Groove whose respective 'Green Eyes' and 'Blue Blue Monday' singles are rightly regarded as Limerick classics.

"The mood in local muso circles had been one of optimism followed by crushing disappointment."

Opposite: Dolores and the guys star-gazing, by Matt Anker.

Above: The *Hot Press* ad for The Cranberry Saw Us' March 14th, 1991 show in The Attic, a Dublin venue that was bursting with sixty people in it. Zrazy were Ireland's first-ever openly gay female duo. The Franks and the Sultans both went on to enjoy UK chart success.

Tuesday Blue, whose drummer just happened to be Johnny Fean's baby brother Ray, looked like they had the potential to develop into a serious proposition. Adam Clayton of U2 was a fan. They signed a one-off single deal with U2's Mother Records for the release of 'Tunnel Vision'. *Hot Press* writers were lavish in their praise. In 1986, they signed to EMI Manhattan in New York. On paper, the $250,000 deal seemed like a dream one.

Queen and Bowie man David Richards was brought in to produce their debut album, *Shibumi,* which earned them favourable comparisons with the likes of U2, Simple Minds and Depeche Mode. They'd made an impressive start, but it was not to be. The record sold so sluggishly outside Ireland that the bean counters in the label summarily pulled the plug on them. They were not the first Irish band to be unceremoniously dumped by a major record company, but the impact was devastating. There was dismay, bordering on despair, in their hometown when, not long afterwards, Tuesday Blue decided they'd had enough and called it a day.

As well as loving the power and majesty of their music, people had badly wanted them to succeed as a way of giving two fingers to the national media who, following an outbreak of gang violence, had branded Limerick 'Stab City'. Sober analysis of the crime figures showed that it was no more or less dangerous than any other big Irish town or city, but why let the truth get in the way of a juicy headline? It was becoming harder than ever to escape the grim truth that its bad reputation was conspiring to drag Limerick and its denizens down.

It would have been silly, and fundamentally counterproductive, to deny that parts of Limerick were blighted by grinding poverty and the social divisions that accompanied it. Come from what was deemed to be the 'wrong' neighbourhood and good luck getting a job interview. Nor were you likely to be admitted into a nightclub where the doormen's "regulars only" refrain was code for something far more insidious.

The queues outside the city's dole offices were long, and emigration remained the best career option for many. All of these factors combined to make Limerick one of the last places a record company talent scout from Los Angeles, New York or even Dublin would want to come with their expense accounts.

Despite – or perhaps *because of* – this, there was a vibrant, close-knit local music scene that Mike Hogan, Noel Hogan and Fergal Lawler were desperate to join.

The first issue of *Night Times* magazine hit the streets on March 1st, 1990. Emblazoned across its front cover was the headline 'Music City – Not Stab City!' Inside, there were mentions of They Do It With Mirrors, Preacher's Story, World Spirit Mood, Private World, A Touch Of Oliver, Up The Downstairs, Utopian Puppets, The Drive, X-It, a fledgling outfit calling themselves The Cranberry Saw Us – and The Hitchers, who are pivotal to this tale.

Having originally messed around together in a band called Rothmans And A Stolen Barrel Of Heineken, singer Eoin O'Kelly, guitarists Daragh Twoomey and Hoss Carnage (possibly not his real name), bassist Mark Coleman and drummer Niall Quinn made their live debut as The Hitchers on January 20th, 1989 in The Oasis Club, an alcohol-free disco that was part of the Limerick Youth Service Centre.

Still at school, and peddling the idiosyncratic pop-punk anthems that would end up on their *The Streaking Chicken From Mercury Who Exposed Himself To Everything* EP, The Hitchers were soon playing to 300 kids who were as young as themselves, in local Limerick venues like The Glentworth and The Granary.

They'd created enough of a buzz to bag a spot on *The Reindeer Age,* the now seminal Limerick compilation LP, which featured most of the bands that were active on the scene at the time. Unlike Terry Wogan and 'The Floral Dance', the album – recorded in Pearse Gilmore's Xeric Studios – *did* lead to an upsurge in band equipment sales at Savin's Music Centre on O'Connell Street.

Despite The Hitchers' burgeoning rock star status around town, Niall Quinn wasn't entirely happy. He enjoyed hitting things very hard, sure, but he also wanted to write and sing his own songs, which was beyond the ken of most drummers, with a few honourable exceptions like Phil Collins and Karen Carpenter.

Niall was therefore all ears when three fan boys, who were always down the front at Hitchers shows – he knew them only as Ferg, Mike and Noel – solemnly informed him that they wanted to start a band. Their problem was that they couldn't find a singer. Would he be interested? Niall was tempted, but he was hardly going to abandon the Hitchers ship for a start-up group. Quick on his feet, he said that he would – but only if he could hold onto his existing drumming gig.

They shook on it, and since punny names seemed to be in vogue – The Sultans of Ping FC had already started to make an impression in Cork – decided to call themselves The Cranberry Saw Us. It could have been worse, with The Crandoodles and The Cranberry Doodles among the other names considered. The newly-minted four-piece quickly cobbled together a half-hour set that included the predominantly Niall Quinn penned 'I Was Always All Ways', 'Throw Me Down A Big Stairs', 'Good Morning God', 'Sixty-Niner' – Niall usually performed that one with his trousers round his ankles – and the hilariously titled, unashamedly satirical 'My Granny Drowned In A Fountain At Lourdes'.

Everything was going splendidly – or so it seemed – until, just six Limerick shows in, Niall dropped a bombshell. He needed to devote more time to The Hitchers. He was leaving.

For many young bands that would have been it, over, finished, *kaput*. But the remaining three members of The Cranberry Saw Us had experienced the adrenaline rush of playing to crowds – and they liked it, liked it, yes they did! They had heard a song of theirs on the radio and they liked that too. Bruised but not broken, Ferg, Mike and Noel regrouped. They weren't going to settle for college or, even worse, a 9-to-5 job.

For his part, Niall Quinn was feeling guilty. He hadn't planned to leave the lads in the lurch, but that was the net effect. One way of assuaging his guilt was to see if he could help them find a replacement singer. A moody Morrissey clone might have fitted the bill. Or even a mushroom-haired Robert Smith lookalike: there were a few of them around Limerick alright. But Quinn had something entirely different up his sleeve. A friend of his, Kathryn Hayes, had told him about a girl in her sister's class at Laurel Hill Secondary School who had a brilliant voice.

Enter Dolores O'Riordan. Leaving Cert exams soon to be completed, the dark-haired county Limerick girl was up for a spot of musical adventure herself. She was happy to audition as Niall Quinn's replacement.

What happened next is one of those great rock 'n'roll rags-to-riches stories, which manages to weave Princess Diana, George Clooney, Michael Stipe, Suede, Pavarotti, Duran Duran, the King of Norway, Woodstock, Calvin Klein, The Rolling Stones, Adam Sandler, Zucchero and not one, but two Popes into its narrative. And that really is just for starters!

As the editor of *Night Times*, the entertainment man at the *Limerick Tribune* newspaper, and presenter of the Radio Limerick One rock show, I was there to witness the birth of The Cranberries. I wrote their first press release and got

The Cranberry Saw Us

+ A TOUCH OF OLIVER. AT THE SPEAKEAY. SAT. 10th NOU.

Above: Flyer for The Cranberry Saw Us' double-header with fellow Limrockers A Touch Of Oliver whose 'Carousel' track Dolores later guested on.

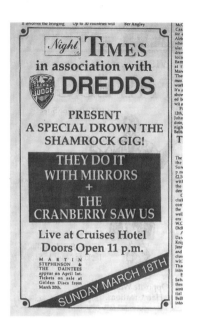

"A band of this stature comes along perhaps once in a generation."

paid with a bottle of Jack Daniel's. One of the press releases, and the demo it accompanied, found its way to *Hot Press*. The magazine also became early champions of the band and – a short time later – offered me a job. And so it's through its pages that we accompany The Cranberries on their journey from those early DIY days in Limerick to superstardom and beyond.

Along the way there was fun, friendship, triumph, adversity, controversy and, ultimately, the gut-wrenching tragedy of Dolores' death in January 2018 in London.

Across those thirty years, I had regular catch-ups with Noel, Mike, Fergal and Dolores – who, we gradually learned, had an extraordinary, instinctive ability to sing beautifully and to conjure emotions of a kind that we all struggle to understand or express in mere words. She also developed the ability to connect with fans, even those located way back in row Z. In so many ways, she fulfilled the potential, which local admirers like myself spotted at the outset. But there was also so much that her loss deprived us of.

Dolores O'Riordan was smart, loving, loyal, dedicated, complex and as funny as fuck. Hers truly was a unique and special talent. Alongside her three brothers-in-arms in The Cranberries, Noel, Mike and Ferg, she gave Limerick what it had always craved – a world-beater of a band who proudly represented the city wherever they roamed.

From my conversations with her, I'm not sure that Dolores ever fully appreciated how much she was loved locally, and indeed abroad – or how many people she inspired to express their own innermost personal thoughts and emotions through song.

This book is dedicated to Dolores, to The Cranberries, to Limerick, and to the magic of rock 'n' roll. I thought of signing off with the line: *'If the Cranberries did it, why shouldn't you?'* But to do so would be to forget something fundamental, which is that a band of this stature comes along perhaps once in a generation. The stars may have aligned for the four-piece from Limerick, in the way they had a decade previously for U2: the good fortune of finding the ideal creative foils plays a part. But without the raw materials The Cranberries possessed – the talent, the work ethic, the ability to write marvellous tunes, and to perform them so beguilingly – we'd still be looking to Limerick more in hope than expectation.

Either way, theirs is an inspiring tale: so please sit back and enjoy it... as it happened.

Stuart Clark, Dublin, October 2021

Above: *Night Times* ad for the last Cranberry Saw Us gig with Niall Quinn fronting the band.
Opposite: Early shot by Brendan O'Halloran, a Limerick fireman who moonlighted as a rock photographer.

THE CRANBERY SAW US

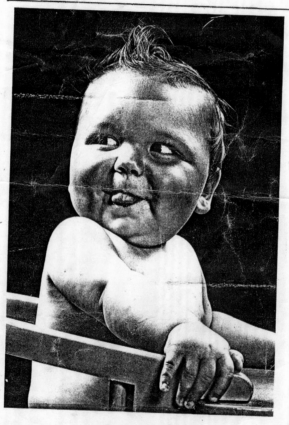

THE OASIS CLUB FRI 23rd FEB

£2 + INDIE DISCO DOORS OPEN 9 p.m.

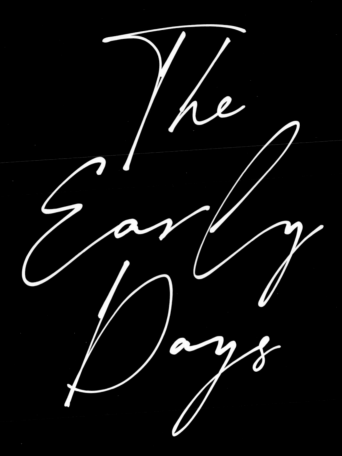

A Year In The Life Of A Baby Rock 'n' Roll Band.

It began with a demo tape, cooked up in the final days of 1989 in Xeric, a Limerick studio run by Pearse Gilmore that was quietly establishing itself as a Mecca for local rock 'n' roll talent. It was there that the compilation album *The Reindeer Age* was also recorded. But from the start, Stuart Clark had spotted that The Cranberries were potentially made of The Right Stuff. That crucial first full year – recounted here in a series of six tell-tale episodes including some early reports by him for the *Limerick Tribune* – found The Cranberry Saw Us shape-shift into the far more organic-sounding The Cranberries. The portents were indeed good.

HOW'S IT GOING TO BLEED?

THE CRANBERRY SAW US are a foursome who, as far as I know, have not yet played live. Instead they've headed straight for the sound-proofed environs of Xeric Studios and have managed to cook up a nicely varied four-track demo tape.

It opens with 'Throw Me Down A Big Stairs', a quivering guitar song that smacks of a good idea. A brooding intro latches onto a catchy melody and it's a good, competent effort.

'How's It Going To Bleed' is deadly serious in tone and its measured moodiness flows nicely alongside a delicate refrain.

'Storm In A Teacup' on the other hand, sounds like The Monkees – bright, playful pop with its heart in the right place and you almost forgive them for the truly awful rhyming couplets. Finally, 'Good Morning God' displays a Cure-ish guitar riff and a Stunning-type line in lyrics. If they give it a bit of time, who knows?

***Anything* demo review by Stuart Clark, January 1990**

 IT SHOULD NOT BE FORGOTTEN that in the past Limerick has produced some of Ireland's better musical talents, Reform and Granny's Intentions being the two that come most readily to mind. Against that backdrop *The Reindeer Age*, a beautifully packaged piece of work released by Xeric Records, is designed to show that, as a centre of musical activity, Limerick can live with the best of 'em, and – in the main – it succeeds in this regard rather better than most albums of its type.

Many of the bands on this record, from The O'Malleys to Tuesday Blue, have attained success to a greater or lesser degree, and their achievements having been quite well documented already. In the context, I found myself being drawn towards the lesser lights herein, and while not everybody on this 14-tracker will be world-beaters, there's enough evidence to suggest that quite a number will make a serious dent in our consciousness in the future.

I thought that our failure to convert Private World's 'Blue Gem Sea' into hit single status last year was a major mistake. Here, with 'Change The Room', they've proved that they have both depth and adaptability. Pearse Gilmore's strong confident vocals are a huge asset, while James Hanley's keyboard work is also superb.

Up The Downstairs with 'I Fall Down' are a classic example of a band who've figured out most of the angles. The song itself is strong, they use reverb and echo sparingly and to great effect, and there's enough space left in the track for the listener to supply his or her own fills. Up The Downstairs should be kept under close observation...

The Separators on the other hand are an outfit at a more developmental stage, whose lyrics need refining and whose vocalist needs to exercise a little more control

Above: The Limerick compilation, which inspired The Cranberry Saw Us to start doing it themselves. **Opposite:** An early band shot taken by Xeric Records boss and then manager Pearse Gilmore.

THE CRANBERY SAW...

THE CRANBERY SAW...

NIALL VOCALS, GUITAR
NOEL GUITAR, VOCALS
MIKE BASS GUITAR
FERGAL DRUMS
with cameo appearances
by JIM.KEYBOARDS
ANDY...HARMONICA
MORGAN.ACCORDIAN
CLAIRE.VIOLIN
engineered by PEARSE
recorded at XERIC 24
7/1/90 (using the
rhythm method)
THIS 4 TRACK DEMO COSTS
£2.50
1990 T.C.S.U.

THE CRANBERY SAW US
ANYTHING

over those difficult top notes. A danceable tune though.

The Drive, meanwhile, have already made inroads into the national consciousness as finalists in the Carling/*Hot Press* Band Of '89 contest and 'Attitude' shows why, suggesting in the process that their name might be more appropriate than we had realised.

Side Two opens with 'The Telephone' from Toucandance, my favourite track. Production here, as elsewhere, is very tight and I love the call-and-response vocals between Eamon Hehir and Mary Jelverton. Guitar and keyboards add an effective hard edge without swamping the song. Elsewhere, Some Farmers and Surrealists have pop sensibilities well tapped, with the latter's 'Symphony' beng potentially of minor classic status. Bright and breezy, it's a track I'll return to repeatedly.

The Reindeer Age shows Limerick rock at various stages in its gestation period and as such should not be regarded as the full picture. It is nevertheless proof positive that life, with all its imperfections, doesn't end, as some people believe it to, at the exit from Dublin's Long Mile Road...

The Reindeer Age compilation review by Oliver P. Sweeney, March 1990

And Then Came Dolores...

AN N.M.E. HACK, who was admittedly rather tired and emotional, told me after last week's Lark in the Park gig that Limerick probably has the best crop of young bands in the country and, you know what, I'd have to agree with him.

The city may lack an outfit of, say, Hothouse Flowers' or Something Happens' stature but the amount of new talent crawling out of the woodwork is quite frightening. Hardly a week passes without some spotty faced individual accosting me on O'Connell Street with a demo tape and, what's more, 75% of them are very listenable.

Unfortunately, while the groups are beginning to get the recognition they deserve, one of the main catalysts of the recent explosion, Xeric Studios, remain unsung heroes. Xeric founder and resident engineer/producer Pearse Gilmore doesn't

Above: The first Cranberry Saw Us cassette demo, *Anything*. Note the misspelling of the band's name, which was to become a recurring theme. It was recorded at Xeric Studios, under the guidance of Pearse Gilmore, who was interviewed by Stuart Clark in July 1990, following the release of *The Reindeer Age* compilation.

seem in the least bit perturbed though.

"I don't mind if we're not that well-known because, as far as gig-goers are concerned, our role isn't particularly important," he reflects. "They want to go along and see bands and if they like what they hear that's what matters. I'd be worried if the musicians themselves weren't aware of the studio and its facilities, but that's not the case."

As understatements go, that ranks alongside saying Shane MacGowan could do with a trip to the dentists. Xeric has played host to virtually every young and not so young Limerick hopeful in recent years, including Tuesday Blue, Toucandance, The Hitchers, A Touch Of Oliver, They Do It With Mirrors, The O'Malleys, Up The Downstairs and The Tear Collectors. They've also worked with nationally known names like The Stunning, A House, Burning Embers and The Louise Morrissey Band, but have generally found it difficult to attract the major names from Dublin.

"We never expected U2 to start coming down to Limerick but at the same time we were hoping to get a few more high-profile groups in," Pearse admits. "It's a gradual process and I'm pleased with the work we've done recently with Philip Donnelly, who's produced and played with people like Nanci Griffith and The Everly Brothers. He's mixed a couple of tracks here that he recorded in the States and has been trying out other ideas for his solo album. He's also keen to fly somebody over from Nashville, which would really put us on the map."

Tuesday Blue demoed a lot of material at Xeric. Does Pearse regret the fact that they never managed to crack it and maybe carry the studio along on their coat-tails?

"There was never any talk of them recording their second album here but, yes, it'd be nice if one of the Limerick band's associated with Xeric did well and boosted our profile," he admits. "It's going to happen eventually because there are some very talented people around."

Just to illustrate the point, Pearse was chatting to me while mixing the latest demo from The Cranberry Saw Us, a local band who've emerged from the rehearsal studio with a new lead singer called Dolores, and a full set of fresh material. I can't give you the full post-mortem till I hear the completed tape next week, but a sneak preview of 'Sunday', a remarkable Cure meets Kirsty MacColl workout, totally blew me away.

"The Cranberries are typical of what's happening at the moment. They haven't played many gigs, but they've come in and recorded four great tracks. The Stilted Men are another band who are on their third or fourth demo and Dave Fanning seems to love them. The side of the business which needs developing now is Xeric Records – hopefully we can make a bit of money out of it! We started eighteen months ago with Private World, released the *Reindeer Age* compilation earlier this year, and since then have done the Peter O'Malley single 'Poitin' and The Hitchers' 'Fruit' cassette single."

Xeric unleash two more gems this month. The first is 'Inspiration', a new 45 by Galway-based Too Much For The Whiteman; and the second a trad collection from Clare's Micho Russell, *Under The Cliffs Of Moher*.

"Micho is a remarkable man," Pearse concludes. "He's 76, from Doolin and has been playing the flute and tin whistle since he was a kid. He's travelled all over the world – Germany, France, Holland, England, America... We're releasing the album on cassette and CD and I'm trying to tie up a distribution deal in West Germany, where they love that kind of stuff. We don't mind who we work with as long as they're good!"

Pearse Gilmore interview by Stuart Clark, July 1990

the cranberries

TONIGHTS ENTERTAINMENT
THURSDAY 5 NOV.

LATE BAR TO 1.00 A.M.

*PROMOTION : CARLSBERG
EXPORT
BUY ONE GET ONE FREE!!*

LIVE ON STAGE

THE CRANBERRIES
&
BUTTERFLY CHILD
and DISCO

STARTS :9.30   ADM: ONLY £2

Above: An early double-header with Butterfly Child, AKA Belfast singer-songwriter Joe Cassidy. who signed to Rough Trade. Fans didn't need the inducement of a free drink for very long!

IT DOESN'T HAPPEN VERY OFTEN but once in a blue moon a new band comes along, and you say to yourself: "This could be the start of something big." Latest Limerick hotshots The Cranberry Saw Us are still a long way from a record deal, but if they can develop some of the deft little touches on this, their second tape, could be serious contenders by Christmas.

The Cranberries got off to a bit of a false start last year when they were formed pretty much as a vehicle for the songs Niall Quinn didn't feel were suitable for his own band The Hitchers. The arrangement was never intended to be permanent and when Niall was forced to quit, due to other commitments, the rest of the lads were faced with the prospect of a long and often frustrating search for a new lead singer.

They weren't really sure what they were looking for – but when they stumbled across Laurel Hill sixth former Dolores O'Riordan they knew they'd found it.

A total newcomer to the local rock scene, the lass sounds for all the world like Kirsty MacColl's younger sister and has a deliciously unaffected, almost innocent style, which wouldn't seem out of place on an All About Eve record.

The opening cut on their *Water Circle* demo, 'Sunday', is the band's trump card. Boasting a naggingly infectious hookline, and lush keyboards, it's a beautifully understated pop song dominated by Dolores' multi-tracked vocals.

'Linger' is more of the same, this time showcasing Noel's Cure-ish guitar work and Fergal's sparse but effective drumming. 'A Fast One' begs comparisons with Cavan indie darlings The Would Be's, and is already one of the highlights of their live set. 'Chrome Paint' is the only disappointment. The moody, atmospheric song calls for a hint of menace, but Dolores' tasteful warblings are just far too pleasant on this occasion.

***Water Circle* demo review by Stuart Clark, August 1990**

DOWNSTAIRS AT CRUISES HAS BEEN CHARMINGLY renamed The Termite Club for a new season of alternative discos and live rock every Thursday, Friday and Saturday. A Leaving Cert double header featuring The Hitchers and The Cranberry Saw Us kicked things off last week with the O'Connell Street basement more packed than Dolly Parton's jumper and twice as much fun to get into.

Seeing as the last time any of the *Limerick Tribune* crew took an exam Jack Lynch was still Taoiseach, we did feel a *little* out of place but managed to find room for our walking frames and enjoyed a swift half before being escorted back to the home.

The Cranberries, by their own admission, still have a long way to go as a live act but are finally beginning to relax and enjoy themselves on stage. They've already shown they can deliver live and tonight, faced with a largely partisan crowd, proved they don't need umpteen takes and a 24-channel mixing desk to do songs like 'Sunday' and 'A Fast One' justice.

The Hitchers also looked like they were having fun amidst the chaos, racing through a string of tried and tested favourites like 'Streakers Of Newcastle' and 'Fruit' with all the finesse of a mating Kangohammer. They also chucked in a couple of new tunes for good measure. 'Blame It On His Hormones' sounded particularly impressive and bodes well for their next cassette single in early October.

Termite Club, Limerick live review by Stuart Clark, August 1990

 THIS SEEMS LIKE AN OPPORTUNE moment to put The Cranberries' latest four-track tape through the mincer. Blessed with a lead singer in Dolores O'Riordan who's capable of melting even an Eskimo's heart, the fruity ones have been building up a sizeable following with their

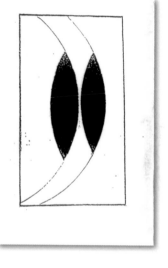

"The lass sounds for all the world like Kirsty MacColl's younger sister and has a deliciously unaffected, almost innocent style which wouldn't seem out of place on an All About Eve record."

Opposite: Dolores putting her best feet forward by Matt Anker. **Above:** The sleeve of the *Water Circle* demo was a bit of a Rorshach test – what did you see?

1. NOTHING LEFT AT ALL
2. PATHETIC SENSES
3. SHINE DOWN

All songs by Noel and Dolores.

Dolores O'Riordan — Vocals/Keyboards
Mike Hogan — Bass
Noel Hogan — Guitar/Backing Vocals
Fergal Lawler — Drums

Additional vocals on 'Pathetic Senses' by Pearse Gilmore and Miko Mahony.
SPECIAL thanks to Pearse, Mike, Sett and Ken, without whom this would not have been possible.

Engineered by Pearse Gilmore
Produced by Pearse, Miko and T.C.S.U.
Calligraphy by Miko Mahony
Inside Photo by Joe Quinn
Thanks to Edel for the photograph.

RECORDED AT LYRIC STUDIOS, LIMERICK
For further information contact:
Xeric Music
The Foundry
Edward St,
Limerick
Tel 061-40566

LOVE IS AN HARMONY

© 1990
XER 012

THE CRANBERRY SAW US
Nothing Left At All
See inlay card for details

d copying, re-recording, broadcasting or public perf

Dolores, Mike, Noel, Fergal

hauntingly atmospheric doodlings, which sound like a blissful union between The Cure and The Sundays. Part of the attraction is their youthful innocence: The Cranberries give the impression they're only just beginning to discover what life's all about and Dolores' endearingly naive lyrics are enough to bring a tear to the eye of even an old fart like me, who waved farewell to his teens when she was still in primary school. 'Nothing Left At All' kicks things off, a thoughtful song very much in the 'Linger' vein, with seductively effective multi-tracked vocals, delicate guitar work and rumbling feedback courtesy of producer Pearse Gilmore. Pearse also makes a guest appearance on 'Pathetic Senses', the interplay between himself and Dolores working a treat, and producing an end-result that's not dissimilar to something you'd find on the Cocteau's new *Heaven Or Las Vegas* album.

The Cranberries spent a lot longer on this demo than on their *Water Circle* debut and it shows. The deft touches of percussion and sparing use of synth, and other studio FX, give the cuts much needed depth and show that – in some ways rather sadly – the band are growing up fast.

'Reason', a bittersweet love song which has an overtly meaningful feel to it, possesses a harder edge. Dolores might only have left school during the summer but, judging by the lyrics, has already had her fair share of broken hearts. Either that or she's just a miserable so and so!

'Shine Down' is another delightfully melancholy tale of woe, with much gnashing of teeth and tearing of hair. Her voice has just the right degree of 'did-li-ai-dai', making it unmistakably Irish without crossing into Country and Gumboot territory. The head Cranberry tells me that the tracks are going to be released as a cassette single next month, and that they'll be playing a major headlining gig to coincide. I don't want to big them up prematurely – there's still a lot of work to be done – but methinks Britain's A&R population should get here pronto!

***Nothing Left At All* demo review by Stuart Clark, November 1990**

IT'S AMAZING THE DIFFERENCE 12 months can make.

This time last year, the prototype Cranberries were little more than a Hitchers offshoot with a natty line in snotty-nosed power pop and precious little else. Since then, they've brought in a new lead singer, completely revamped their set and produced two demos, which have had most local pundits frothing at the mouth with delight. And why are this unlikely bunch being tipped as Limerick's 'band most likely to' while some of their more established counterparts seem to be

"Her voice has just the right degree of 'did-li-ai-dai', making it unmistakably Irish without crossing into Country and Gumboot territory."

Above: The Cranberry Saw Us' first commercially-produced demo tape, *Nothing Left At All.* Copies regularly sell for upwards of €500 on Discogs.

floundering in a sea of apathy? Noel Cranberry seems a mite non-plussed.

"This line-up has only been together for eight months and we thought it'd take at least a couple of years before people in the music industry started taking us seriously," he says. "We never expected things to happen this fast, it's all been a bit of a blur! This probably sounds like false modesty, but I really can't understand why we've been singled out for so much attention: we do what we do quite well, but so do a lot of other local bands. One thing that has definitely helped is that we've worked bloody hard. We rehearse at least three times a week, myself and Dolores are continually working on new songs, and we've played live whenever the opportunity's arisen."

The Cranberries make their first foray into the commercial world this week with the three-track *Nothing Left At All* cas-single, which will be officially launched on December 27th in the Savoy Top Floor. As I said in an earlier review, it's an interesting mish-mash of styles and influences, with names like The Sundays, The Cure and Kirsty MacColl all in there somewhere.

"We've been compared to a lot of people since we started and, in the early days, I think these comments were valid," Noel observes. "Recently though, we've started to develop our own distinctive style and I can't think of anyone else who sounds like us. We're growing up; I know that I'm a better songwriter than I was last Christmas and Dolores finds it a lot easier to come up with lyrics. It's a good partnership: we're both on the same wavelength and if I don't like something she's written, I can say so without hurting her feelings, and vice versa. We've signed a management deal with Pearse Gilmore at Xeric and his input has been invaluable. He's given us pretty much unlimited studio time, which means we're 100% happy with everything we've recorded."

Having set the scene, let's give Noel a thorough grilling!

What are you hoping to achieve with the EP?
The main objective is to sell enough copies to keep us in beer over Christmas! No, we want to develop our profile locally and provide the people who've come to see us over the past year with a keepsake of the band. There's 150 tapes in the initial batch and half of those have gone to Golden Discs, FM, Stardiscs and Empire. I'm not sure exactly how many we've sold, but they seem to be shifting quite fast and we'll get rid of the rest at next week's gig. We'll also be sending out copies to people in the business who've expressed an interest already. That's part the reason we've spent so much time and money on the presentation: we want to try and fool everyone into believing we've got our act together!

The Cranberries' first handful of live appearances were – how does one put this tactfully? – rather shambolic. The potential was there for all to see, but a lot of the deft little touches displayed in the studio were lost on stage.
I can't argue with that: our first few supports were a total mess! It's all very well and fine having the songs worked out, which we did, but you can't put them across properly until you feel relaxed and in control. The best way to learn is to dive in at the deep end and the last two shows we did with A Touch Of Oliver and Cactus World News were a lot less nerve-racking. Actually, the Cactus gig was probably the best we've done so far. Pearse was in charge of the sound and, as he knows the set so well, he was able to stick in echo and other effects at just the right moment. We also had a problem earlier on with Dolores: her voice is much gentler than most singers' and if it's not mixed properly she gets drowned out.

Above: Another early Limerick run out with Dublin outfit Rex & Dino who later morphed into Blink.

So what can punters expect from next week's show?

A lot of new songs. The longest we've played for in the past is 30 minutes, so we've had to come up with a lot of new material to pad out the set, which is now over an hour long and much more varied. Miko Mahoney, who was on *The Reindeer Age* compilation, is opening for us.

One thing that worries me about The Cranberries is that you're not particularly visual. I really can't imagine Dolores turning somersaults or Ferg's drum riser flipping over *à la* Mötley Crüe! So, do you have any other Baldrick-like cunning plans to bolster your live performances?

I agree with what you're saying. We're not the kind of band that leaps around a lot and stands on the monitors! Our music tends to be quite moody and we've been talking about getting in a proper light show to create the right atmosphere. That sort of thing costs a lot of money, but we'll find it somewhere.

You mentioned earlier that a few music business types have shown an interest – has anyone made a tangible offer yet?

Put it this way, we've talked very informally to a couple of people, but that's as far as it's got. We're ready to be heard by a wider audience and I'd be disappointed if we didn't have a record out both here and in England, by the end of next year. I'm not saying we could go into the studio tomorrow and record an album, but we'd certainly be able to put together a good EP. I've never been to London but from what I've heard and read about the indie scene there, I'd say we'd fit in.

Noel, you're being very evasive!

I've made a point of chatting to some of the older bands and they've all said the same thing: don't get excited about record company interest until they actually sign you. Even then, there are no surefire guarantees you're going to be successful. Look at Tuesday Blue – one minute they had a nice juicy deal with EMI America and the next they were back in Limerick playing the pubs.

Why do you think The Cranberries will succeed where others have failed?

Good question. I haven't a clue! There are bands that we loved like Private World and Up The Downstairs, who were forced to break up because they weren't getting anywhere. It's easy to adopt the attitude 'If they can't do it, neither can we' – but that's very negative. One thing I've already learnt is you've got to hound people. If you record a demo, send a copy to every single company you can think of, and then ring until you're sure they've listened to it. Go to the press, keep talking to RTÉ – it eventually pays off. We've been pestering *Jo-Maxi* (on RTÉ television) for a whole year and now they've said we'll be on early in the New Year. You can't sit back and wait for people to come to you – you've got to make the running yourselves.

You can relax now, grilling completed!

The Cranberries' general approach and attitude, combined with their music, suggest that exciting times lie ahead. The *Nothing Left At All* EP certainly couldn't be described as flawless but it's a powerful statement of intent which the band, and the people looking after them, can be justifiably proud of. Judge for yourself whether they're worth the hype next Thursday. I reckon it barely does them justice!

Noel Hogan interview by Stuart Clark, December 1990

> "You can't sit back and wait for people to come to you – you've got to make the running yourselves."

Opposite: Dolores dreaming of success in The Cranberries' first UK shoot for *Melody Maker*. Photographer Phil Nicholls went on to become a good friend of the band's and toured with them in the States.

We Have Lift Off

Getting ready to conquer Ireland – and the world.

By now, Ireland's U2 were well established as the biggest band on the planet. The effect was to inject a surge of energy into the local rock scene, and to bring A&R scouts here in significant numbers. There were plenty of hot-to-trot outfits coming through, as *Hot Press* writers were quick to acknowledge, reviewing some of the big multi-band gigs of 1991. Here, we chart in seven easy pieces, the kind of bustling national scene The Cranberries had arrived into – and how (easy comparisons with The Sundays notwithstanding) they quickly lifted themselves above the pack, with the launch towards the end of the year of a mesmerising EP. But first, a local derby...

Opposite photo: Cathal Dawson

A Hurricane Is Brewing Down South

IT'S LIMERICK. IT'S TUESDAY NIGHT. And a stable full of college pop kids are wallowing in cranberries at The Stables.

The Cranberries are four-strong, a traditional pop-fit in that classic mould. The Smiths and The Sundays spring to mind, but only for an instant. You see, The Cranberries are too young and too naive to owe any debts. They just play and write and sing.

Or rather Dolores sings. At eighteen, she's glad/happy and writes about boys in the schoolyard and teen angst at the disco. Behind her, Noel strums a huge guitar, picks nimbly and shuffles briskly through the sweetest leaves of easy melody, guitar pop.

'Uncertain' opens. 'Sunday' follows, a queasy, easy, teasing swirl of jangle and pluck and then it's that gorgeous single – 'Nothing Left At All'. This is evasive melody and stirring restraint combined, all gasps and held-back drums. In years, it will be a treasure. Think of 'Hand In Glove' or 'Lions In My Own Garden (Exit Someone)'. That good. And then 'Put Me Down' finally convinces us that The Cranberries are nothing less than brilliant, building from a whisper and resisting the temptation to scream.

The Cranberries are twenty of your sweetest dreams and an unending walk down Paradise Way. Love them.

The Stables, Limerick live review by Colm O'Callaghan, February 1991

THE CRANBERRIES PLAY A SVELTE left-of-centre indie guitar pop. With the release of their debut single, 'Nothing Left At All', they have done nothing to stem a rising tide of record company interest.

The Cranberries began life as The Cranberry Saw Us, a perverted pop four-piece with current Hitchers drummer, Niall, singing and leading.

"Niall just couldn't keep both bands going," guitarist Noel explains, "so when he left, the three of us, my brother Mike (bass), drummer Fergal and myself continued writing instrumental pieces. And then Dolores (O'Riordan, singer, songwriter) heard about us, and she auditioned – and she was in."

"I'm actually from the country," Dolores says, "but last month I moved into civilisation."

To where, I ask.

"To Limerick city, of course."

Naturally.

"Limerick is a great place," Noel assures me, "if only because it's so small. You know everybody and everybody knows you. The only thing I don't like is the gig set-up, where you have some small-minded people running the venues. It's really difficult to get live gigs here in Limerick and the people who run the venues don't help. They think that all of the local young

Opposite: Striking a moody 1993 Dublin pose for *Hot Press* sharpshooter Cathal Dawson.

bands are all noise, and rubbishy. One day, we might have the last laugh on them. These people like to import their music from everywhere else – just as long as it's not from Limerick! That rubs me up the wrong way."
Noel and Dolores interview by Colm O'Callaghan, April 1991

THE CRANBERRIES HAVE BEEN TOGETHER for less than a year. Their first demo attracted much interest and they signed a management deal with studio owner and producer, Pearse Gilmore. A number of offers from record companies have followed so Cranberry offerings are expected to be heard on the airwaves this summer. Press reviews of gigs and recordings have been enthusiastic, with *Hot Press* describing the band as "nothing less than brilliant."

The *Dublin Event Guide* described them as "a band to adore and champion and idolise." A recent *NME* gig review declared: "The Cranberries are the stuff on which obsessions can be built." The Cranberries recently finished a Fanning session for 2fm and English support tours are being lined up for the summer. The Cranberries are Dolores O'Riordan (vocals), Noel Hogan (guitars), Mike Hogan (bass), Ferg Lawler (drums).

Hot Press **Newsdesk, May 1991**

HELLO AND WELCOME TO CORK ROCKS, a series of rock 'n' roll shows housed in the infamous environs of Sir Henry's music emporium on Grand Parade. As it turns out, Cork Rocks 1991 is three nights of truly remarkable Irish pop. In years to come, we'll be telling our children that we were there. Naturally they won't believe us. But, for the record, here in the Southern capital, we've got shuttle-flights full of record company people landing. We've got BP Fallon. We've got bulging houses filled with flailing pop kids. And we've got The Frank And Walters.

This band are remarkably-flared, local power-poppers, with more hooks than Herrol Graham. 'Davy Chase' and 'Fashion Crisis Hits New York' have us stomping and BP Fallon is impressed. A band who'll kick you in the teeth.

The Precious Stones, from Dublin, have lots of denim clothes and some little stadium songs on the back boiler. They're rather clever footballers too and deserve every bit of luck that comes their way.

The Subterraneans are reborn and revamped and are still stunningly brilliant. They open with 'Gameshow', they close with 'I Fought The Law' and in between they box clever, with groovy pop fists. Take them to the haven of your bed.

But keep some space too for The Intoxicating Rhythm Section, the band who once asked U2 to support them at The Baggot Inn. Sampling James Brown (again) and Kraftwerk did them no harm and this funk-laden groove-riff machine had us open-mouthed upfront.

Bird follow on, the sound of muso-pop with songs. Rare enough, that. Great voice, bundles of energy and 'Sex Control' is amazing.

Night two and we're into overdrive. The Wishing Stones, from Dungarvan, surprise with three-way harmonies and chiming guitar-pop. 'Shirley' is a corker. And then The Brilliant Trees appear and play great songs very greatly indeed. They're rather, well... brilliant, in fact.

The Cranberries are next and put us all to shame with the most beautiful girl-pop you'll hear all year. 'Put Me Down', 'Linger' and 'Dreams' are the sounds of next year's *Chart Show* right now and God, how we swoon. A Touch Of Oliver, also from Limerick, bring a touch of the unexpected to their guitar rambles. 'Golden Valley Reserve', 'Burn' and 'Candy Bottle Green' are spiffing, but we need just a tad more bollocks here and we'd be laughing.

Above: The Sunday line-up at Cork Rocks '91 was a humdinger. Opposite: Dolores O'Riordan playing a blinder at the 1991 Limerick Lark by Brendan O'Halloran.

And then it's Chelsea Drugstore, playing well-intentioned generic Deacon Blue-style music that's half-clever and slightly out of focus. The kids upfront are disappointed. Put it down to nerves and expectation. I did.

So then to the third night at the fair. Lir continue to divide and conquer. They're doing their own thing and couldn't care less. Azure Days follow with lots of moody pop songs with great tunes. 'Anything For You', 'Back Down To Justice' and 'World Junk' are pristine and liquid. The girls love them.

Toasted Heretic are utterly amazing, front-man Julian Gough shining with the huge self-belief of a young Morrissey. They take this one by the throat and throttle it halfway to delirium. 'Galway And Los Angeles' is the best song we've heard all year.

Therapy? pick it up and chainsaw their way into our bloodstreams. They open with 'Punishment Kiss' and headbutt their way through some psychotic dog-rock trashcore and it's amazing.

Finally, The Sultans Of Ping FC, who have the most incredible underpants in pop. Once in love with football, now in love with sex, this band put the rot back into erotic and kick like hell. Tonight Cork, tomorrow the universe.

Cork Rocks, amazingly brilliantly, remarkably beautiful. It could only happen here.

Cork Rocks review by Colm O'Callaghan, June 1991

AS THE HEAVENS OPENED and the press area in The People's Park began to resemble the hippos enclosure at Dublin Zoo, I have to admit the thought of nipping home for the omnibus edition of *Eastenders* and spending a relaxed afternoon with Dot Cotton *did* cross my mind. However, we hacks are made of sterner stuff and resplendent in a very fetching 'above the knee' Limerick Corporation dustbin liner, I took up position stage left for the 1991 Treaty 300/2fm Limerick Lark.

Colours were first on, a role that normally involves playing to the park keeper, a cocker spaniel and a couple of Senior Citizens out for their Sunday constitutional. The band had, however, taken the sensible precaution of bringing a crowd with them, who proceeded to go totally nuts, in response to what was, indeed, an impressive performance. Their Cult fixation may border on the unhealthy, but there's no mistaking the calibre of amphetamine-d rockers like 'I Will Fall' and 'All Right'. The gentler, semi-acoustic 'Cartoon World' showed they're starting to establish their own identity and given a bit more time, a new name, and a few extra feet of hair to bolster the image, Colors could be serious contenders.

Those Stilted Boys, on the other hand, have already attained that status by combining choice jazz influences with the better parts of Matt Johnson's The The songbook. Scowling and grimacing their way through a spirited set, these archetypal angry young men used Brian O'Grady's funky bass slapping to good effect on 'Havana', while Ian Dodson's barbed vocals dominated 'Abusing Me'. A hot-to-trot combo but, lads, do you have to be so miserable *all* the time?

By now the rain had cleared, The People's Park was filling up and They Do It With Mirrors weren't about to spoil the party. Limerick's elder statesmen have improved beyond all recognition over the past year and in 'Titan', 'Pinnochia' and 'Bucket' have a trio of songs that are capable of ripping the UK Indie charts wide open. Lead singer Kevin Brew provided the group with a much-needed focal point – his idiot dancing could spark off a whole new craze and he's no slouch in the vocal department either.

'Candy' may have been four minutes of pure pop perfection but don't for one single minute think Shane O'Neill has gone soft in his old age. The Blue Angels

LARK IN THE PARK 2

Sunday 14th July
Peoples Park, Pery Square
Presenting
AN EMOTIONAL FISH
WITH
**The Cranberries,
The Blue Angels, The Mirrors,
Those Stilted Boys, Colors.**

PLUS SPECIAL GUEST **CRY BEFORE DAWN**

Compere: LORCAN MURRAY
Time: **2.00 p.m. — 6.30 p.m.**
A DREDDS PRODUCTION
in association with
LIMERICK TREATY 300
The Treaty Press, Limerick

From top: Dolores in Celtic frock mode, and The Cranberries on a 1991 Limerick Lark bill that underlined the rude health of the city's music scene. Photo by Brendan O'Halloran. **Opposite:** The band shot that same year by Robin Grierson.

have just as many teeth as their heavenly predecessors and proved it with a searing version of 'Get On Back' that owed more than a nod and a wink to the strutting arrogance of Mick Jagger. The psychedelic blur of 'Shooting Star' rammed the point home and it was interesting to see the teenage contingent as well as the mature-r heads, looking suitably impressed.

There was a definite air of expectancy as The Cranberries took to the stage. Some extravagant claims have been made on their behalf in recent months and this was their chance to justify the hype. It's easy to see why the British press are in such a tizzy about them: the new Island signings are the missing link between the Cocteaus and The Sundays, with all the commercial possibilities that entails. Show opener 'Same Old Story' set the mood, a dreamily hook-laden song with vocals that can only be described as exquisite. 'Uncertain In Love', 'Pathetic Senses' and 'Linger' all confirmed Dolores O'Riordan to be a remarkable talent – but couldn't hide the fact that the poor girl was scared out of her wits.

An Emotional Fish have developed into man-eating sharks, grabbing their audience round the throat and steadfastly refusing to let go until they draw blood. You won't find a more demented frontman than Ger Whelan – he may ooze charisma but when he goes walkabout in the crowd you fear for their safety nonetheless! As befitted the occasion, they stuck to tried and tested favourites like 'Demon Jive', 'Grey Matter' and 'Celebrate' and were never in anything but complete control, making for a performance that was as visually thrilling as it was musically inspired.

After that sort of onslaught, Cry Before Dawn were always going to be an anti-climax and despite trotting out a workmanlike 'Best Of...' package, they couldn't stem the flow of bodies heading for the gates. It might have been a different story a few years ago but, as I'm sure the Wexford four-piece are discovering, people have short memories.

Overall it was a great day, superbly organised and proof positive that Limerick is a well happening place to be. Stab City? Nah, *Music* City?

Limerick Lark review by Stuart Clark, July 1991

I HAVE TO ADMIT THAT UP TO NOW, I'd heard more about The Cranberries than *of* them. And even having gotten familiar with these four tracks, I'm not yet entirely convinced of the band's songwriting ability. But what I am sure about is the silver-seamed singularity of Dolores O'Riordan's voice. When she sings something like 'Nothing Left At All' you can almost feel the sky closing in tight above you, getting so close that you could reach up with a broomstick and touch it. She doesn't just carry a tune, she sends it by express mail and it seems to reach your spine long before your ears. It's too early to tell what lies in store for The Cranberries. There's still another shoe to drop, on whether they can survive the maelstrom of pressures that they've just plunged into. But in the meantime, in a week when Irish singles appear to have been released by the crateload, the *Uncertain* EP is the real trophy.

***Uncertain* EP review by Liam Fay, October 1991**

> "'Uncertain In Love', 'Pathetic Senses' and 'Linger' confirmed Dolores O'Riordan to be a remarkable talent – but couldn't hide the fact that the poor girl was scared out of her wits."

Above: We're not sure what became of Hector Pickaxe & The Floating Crowbars, but The Cranberries went on to conquer Planet Rock after their Christmas 1993 homecoming show in the Theatre Royal. Photo by Des Murray.

"WHAT I *am* SURE about is the SILVER-SEAMED SINGULARITY *of* DOLORES O'RIORDAN'S VOICE."

SWEET DREAMS ARE MADE OF THESE

Formerly The Cranberry Saw Us, The Cranberries have just released their debut EP.
Mick O'Hara meets the band with the voice of an angel.

PHOTO: MATT ANKER

"I never ever went to a gig or had even heard of the term 'gig' before I joined the band," says the little girl who owns pop's most exquisite voice. "Rock concerts, that's what I used to call them. I never went to one, I'd never seen a live band that actually wrote their own stuff.

"I'd seen pub bands," she adds, "that was all. I played piano and took lessons for seven years. That was my kind of music."

So, the first gig you attended was one that you were taking part in?

"We went to one beforehand, just so I could see what it was like and what you did. I didn't even realise that these things took place or that these bands existed in Limerick."

So, what did you used to do of an evening down at home?

"Oh, I'd go up and play the organ in the church."

Dolores O'Riordan and three blokes, and me, are sitting in a van that's parked in a yard behind Charlie's Bar in Dublin where later on The Cranberries will bring tears to the eyes of grown men and ensure that all present can say "yes" when asked if their weekend was happy and filled with nice things.

The three other blokes are Noel, a guitarist, Mike, a bassist, and Fergal, a drummer. I speak with them for 40 minutes and generally have my socks charmed from my feet, the spring put in my step, and all semblance of a chill factor taken from this typical October evening.

I mention this merely in an effort to chase away any preconceptions which may have been created by the opening paragraphs. When I say that Dolores had never heard the term gig before joining the band, I am not taking the piss or ridiculing her. The Cranberries in general, and Dolores in particular, bring new meaning to words like innocence and naivete, and are honest and open and unaffected to a degree that is positively thrilling.

Born in Limerick a year and a half ago as The Cranberry Saw Us (shudder), the three boys decided that they wanted a girl to call their own.

"Myself, Ferg and Noel have been hanging around together since we were fairly young," says Mike. "We just started a band going, and put up a notice looking for a female singer, so Dolores turned up."

"A girl in my class told me about it," adds Dolores. "She knew the lads and said they were very nice, so that made it easier to audition for them."

And did the lads turn out to be very nice? She pauses for a moment and the van overflows with the sound of helpless male laughter.

"Well, they were townies you know," she finally says, "and it looked to me that when townies hung out together they all dressed the same, did the same things, went to the same places and I was really different. I wasn't like them. Every single guy I saw had torn jeans and Docs and they all had long hair.

"I met the lads and started talking to Ferg. I didn't like Mike," she says. "I strolled in and he didn't like me – he was at that age when he didn't like people if they didn't look cool so I hated him because he used to be really

"Every single guy I saw had torn jeans and Docs and they all had long hair."

sarcastic and I didn't know him well enough to realise that he was only messing.

"So I auditioned for them and they auditioned for me and we got to like each other and at that stage we didn't give a shit what each other looked like, we just realised that there was talent there. I remember the audition really well. I walked in and there were 12 fellas sitting in this room and I had to sing in front of them all. It was so embarrassing."

She winces visibly at the memory.

Are nerves a factor with The Cranberries? It's been written that you look absolutely terrified when you parade your songs in front of live audiences.

"That's definitely not true," says Fergal, the world's most talkative drummer.

"It's just that we're not a noise band," adds Mike. "We don't jump around the place but we're totally comfortable with going out on a stage."

And you're not at all nervous?

"No," they chorus, four voices speaking as one.

Even when you're playing to audiences that consist entirely of journalists, A&R men and general music biz types?

"I'm not nervous," says Dolores, "but I'm just not the type of person who goes out and can say *(adopts hysterical Lita Ford persona, clenched fists raised to the sky etc.)* 'Rock on babes!' Everybody expects you to be really loud and if you're in any way quiet they think you're nervous – but you mightn't be. The lads are the same, they're all kind of into-themselves people, not loud or anything, which I think is nice. At least it's a bit of a change."

Critical acclaim for The Cranberries has been immediate, enthusiastic and forced upon us not just in Ireland but in Britain too, in quantities so large that entire rain forests

quake at the roots, at the merest mention of this band's name.

And why not? Dolores' voice is truly extraordinary. She's been compared to everybody from Harriet Wheeler to Liz Cocteau to Madonna and sounds, not like a teenage girl from the wilds of rural Limerick, but like several teenage girls from the wilds of rural Limerick, a heavenly host of exultant angels and three hundred trembling divas singing their battered old hearts out. And all at the same time.

"We kind of take the acclaim for granted," says Fergal, much to my surprise. "I'm sure this is the way it happens for everyone and we definitely don't let it get to our heads. It's one thing that we're always really conscious of, that it must never affect us like that – because no matter how big you become you must always be the same person."

"I think," continues Dolores, "that all this, everything that's happened to us makes you say what you want to say a lot more. Before I was in the band, if I saw that something was happening that I didn't like, I'd say nothing and go along with it. It makes you a lot more confident," she adds to an accompaniment of vigorous nods and affirmative uh-huhs.

The Cranberries have recently released their debut EP. Acquaint yourself with it as soon as is humanly possible. This band is a heart of glass, flags all a flutter in a gentle breeze, beautiful babies being born into the world. And their continued existence, damn them, means this writer can no longer fall back on one of his favourite lines.

I may no longer be the best thing that Limerick has yet produced. That's why.

· **The Cranberries interview by Stuart Clark, October 1991**

When Everything Started Falling Into Place

In the early part of 1993, The Cranberries entered into a different sort of time zone.
There was a feeling out there that they had what it takes, but the band themselves were self-deprecating and almost painfully aware of their limitations. And yet – as is clear from what *Hot Press* was saying – the sweet sense that the only way was up for the Limerick four-piece would not go away as they traversed the UK and America. There was an Irish tour at the end of 1993, and in February 1994 came the re-release of 'Linger' as a single.

Opposite photo: Matt Anker

HOME OR AWAY

As The Cranberries tour in advance of the release of their debut album, Noel Hogan offers some home thoughts from abroad.

IT'S AN AGE-OLD DILEMMA: should up and coming young Irish bands base themselves at the centre of the hurly-burly of the British music biz in London, or remain at home and strive to make it big from more familiar terrain?

Preparing to release their debut album on Island next February, The Cranberries have proved to be of the home-loving variety and remain firmly based in their native city.

Guitarist and chief melody-manufacturer Noel Hogan is a little the worse for wear, as he talks to us from Newcastle, a stopover on the band's mini-tour of the UK. With the single 'Dreams' having made it into the lower reaches of the English charts and a follow-up 'Linger' pencilled in for New Year release, these are busy days for the ethereal four-piece.

A support slot with the House Of Love is scheduled for the Royal Albert Hall later this month. With such heady activity on the immediate horizon, it appears to be quite a relief to the band to have a tranquil Irish base at their disposal.

"We're definitely going to stay based in Limerick, there's no question about it," confirms Noel. "We rehearse in Mungret, just outside the city, and it's all very laid back. There's nobody about to bother us."

It's also good to have friends close at hand.

"Our mates don't exactly see us as pop stars. We have jobs the same as them: ours are just a little bit different. If we started acting like we owned the place, we'd soon be taken down a peg or two. They don't take any messing, down in Limerick."

Of course, all is not hunky dory being based outside the mainstream of the UK industry. For one thing, a couple of polished demos sent across by Sealink can lead to media types waxing too lyrical too soon about an ensemble who are just finding their feet. With The Cranberries, that's exactly what happened. The UK press were billing them as the Next Big Thing, at a time when the band themselves weren't so sure.

"When we first started playing gigs in England," says Noel, "we were being pushed as the best new indie band since God knows who. And, you know, we weren't! We just weren't ready for all the attention and it put us under a hell of a lot of pressure. We had a lot to live up to. We can do our best but no more."

An old maxim, it seems, should be writ large for emerging Irish talent: don't believe what you read in the papers.

Noel Hogan interview by Kevin Barry, December 1992

SOMEWHERE BETWEEN, I THINK, 'LIAR' and 'Linger', Dolores O'Riordan lifts her lager, dabbles fingers in it, and delicately dribbles piss-clear liquid over her brow like it's designer cologne. As the intensity builds, she not so much sweats, or even perspires, as glows. She says "Hello" in Irish, and "Thanks a million," with Limerick in each syllable.

We arrive in the Leeds Irish Centre late mid-set in P.J. Berry's solo 'Nintendo-Neil Young' thrash, fighting for bar and floorspace. It's not until the lights go up that P.J. sees the chaotic audience he's been playing to, and yells "God, but you're UGLY!". Then roadies with collapsed Brian May perms tune and pose with guitars others will play, and set out lager and towels others will use, as R.E.M. swirls around them. One T-shirt reads "WELL 'ARD" – which looks to be inviting trouble ("SO YER THINK YER ARD, DO YA!?!"). It would be great, one night, to review the roadies and ignore the band.

But not this night.

Above: The first of many *Hot Press* Readers' Poll appearances in 1992. **Opposite:** Jim Leatherman was down the front in July 1993 when Dolores got jiggy with it at Einstein A Go-Go in Jacksonville Beach, Florida.

Not this band.

The Cranberries are glittering silver-lined vocals spun out on the phased scintillations of Noel Hogan's Rickenbacker, as rich as cascading fractels. They're on the brink of charting their single 'Linger', but start slow and tasteful with 'Pretty', building through 'Sunday', gaining momentum. For each song is a page from a dot-to-dot book that grows from small clues into a total picture. Each song the seismic tick that foretells the earth tremor.

Dolores wears a formal little black number, low-cut and short. Worn with boots. Her black hair razored high over a nest of near-fetishistic ear-rings. She doesn't move too much, although she loosens up as dot meets dot, draping the mike in various pensive and impassioned poses as the razor-wire guitar high-pressure points burst around her. 'Dreams', last year's single, weaves hypnotically, as do the more powered sound-bites from the fortcoming album *Everybody Else Is Doing It, So Why Can't We?*

"Thanks a million" says Dolores as she glows.

She says it like she means it.

Leeds Irish Centre live review by Andy Darlington, March 1993

THE CRANBERRIES FINALLY get to release their debut LP, *Everybody Else Is Doing It, So Why Can't We?*, in early March. Originally scheduled for October last year, the Stephen Street-produced collection was deferred because Island feared it would get buried in the pre-Christmas deluge. Along with recent singles 'Dreams' and 'Linger', the tracks include 'I Still Do', 'Sunday', 'Pretty', 'Waltzing Back', 'Not Sorry', 'Wanted', 'Still Can't', 'I Will Always', 'How', and 'Put Me Down'. The Limerick band, who've just completed a highly successful UK support tour with Belly, play live in the Dublin Virgin Megastore at 3pm on March 3rd and then return home the following day for a 4pm appearance at Empire Music in O'Connell Street.

Hot Press **Newsdesk, February 1993**

 IT WOULD BE VERY EASY TO DISMISS The Cranberries as another Sundays: even before hearing their highly anticipated debut album, *Everybody Else Is Doing It, So Why Can't We?*, the presence of a pale--skinned, small-framed, dark-haired, cute, female singer with a pouty-mouth, signals the comparison.

At times, indeed, the album does bear an uncomfortable resemblance to the Sundays' work (funnily enough the similarity is most blatant on a song called 'Sunday'). But calling The Cranberries another Sundays would be like calling Tori Amos another Kate Bush – both unfair and highly inaccurate.

If female comparisons must be made, Dolores O'Riordan echoes Sinéad O'Connor, Sarah McLachlan and Belinda Carlisle as often as she sounds like The Sundays' Harriet Wheeler. More often than not, and some may find this hard to believe from what they've been reading, she sounds exactly like herself! Indeed 'Dreams' makes it sound as though Dolores could cut it in the Bulgarian Women's Choir and 'Waltzing Back' might gain her entrance into an international yodelling competition. Such a range should not easily be dismissed.

The songs are about love, just barely escaping the herbal tea-drinking, letter writing, potpourri-consuming quirkiness some other female-fronted bands fall prey to. On *Everybody Else ls Doing It, So Why Can't We?*, songs revolve around simple, upfront emotions with telling lines like *"This is the way you wanted it/ I didn't understand"* – or *"Never before, never again/ You will ignore, I will*

> "The Cranberries are glittering silver-lined vocals spun out on the phased scintillations of Noel Hogan's Rickenbacker, as rich as cascading fractels."

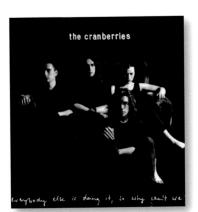

the cranberries

everybody else is doing it, so why can't we

Opposite: Dolores at the 'Dreams' video shoot by Amelia Stein.

pretend" – anchoring otherwise breezy pop songs.

'Dreams' is the album's stand-out, perfectly intermingling pure pop, lush production and vocal exoticism. 'Linger' dons a pleasant country twang and the bluesy underpinnings of 'Pretty' temper Sinéady vocal extremes.

Happily, there are no duds on *Everybody Else…* but on the downside, there are only a handful of standout cuts. One also has to wonder whether the significantly electric, keyboard-heavy, almost jazz-fusion production of the album really suits the band and their songs. Never mind. *Everybody Else Is Doing It, So Why Can't We?* is just a beginning, certainly not where The Cranberries' story will end. **Everybody Else Is Doing It, So Why Can't We? album review by Tara McCarthy, February 1993**

Just Five Months Later, Everything Had Changed…

FEW IRISH BANDS HAVE MADE A REAL IMPACT in the US. Fewer still have done it on the strength of a debut album, bugger-all hit singles, and only one US tour. And yet The Cranberries' *Everybody Else Is Doing It, So Why Cant We?* LP jumped an unheard of fifty places up the *Billboard* charts a couple of weeks ago, before nestling comfortably aroud the 120 mark. They might not have joined the ranks of Whitney and Guns N' Roses yet, but that's still a lot of records to sell at such an early stage in their career.

Fergal Lawler, eternally modest drummer with The Cranberries, puts this success down to luck. Pressed a little further, he concedes that, "College radio has a lot to do with it, definitely, and the Polygram and Island people there are really behind us. Before we went over to the States, we hadn't done much press, just one or two interviews on the phone. A lot of people had the EP we brought out two years ago, and people in the States got it on import. It was probably a mixture of word of mouth and different radio people saying, 'Have you heard about this band?', and the record company, that made it happen.

"In Ireland, there's one radio station really, and if you can get on RTÉ you're sorted. The situation in the States is very different, and it's good that the college stations really do take an interest in what's happening."

The Cranberries' first US tour, earlier this year, supporting The The, was marred slightly by the near-compulsory bout of throat trouble.

"We'd played about ten gigs in a row, as well as doing acoustic sets in shops and interviews the whole time, and Dolores' voice just packed in" Fergal explains. "She went to the doctor and he said her vocal chords were all swollen and out of shape, and that she'd have to take five days off. We happened to be in New York at the time, so it wasn't too boring. We did a few headlining gigs on our own in between the The The shows, and some in San Francisco, Los Angeles and Phoenix after the tour – and they all sold out so we went back to New York to do the shows we'd missed and they were all sold out. It was crazy."

Despite this success as novice headline band, Fergal argues that it makes far more sense for little-known bands to accept a supporting role, in order to attract attention – rather than try to tackle America single-handedly.

"You could go into some city like New York and play a club with 200 or 300 capacity, and no-one would turn up, whereas at least if you're supporting a fairly well-established band you know people will be there. It's just a case of you having to win them over, and you've got a much better production, better lights and P.A. It makes everything easier. We're going back in September for about two or three months. There've been talks of certain tours with big bands. We're going to do a headliner more than likely, although Suede have asked us to do a double-headliner

> ## "'Dreams' is the album's stand-out, perfectly intermingling pure pop, lush production and vocal exoticism."

Above: Dolores shooting the 'Dreams' video by Amelia Stein. **Opposite:** The Cranberries at King's John Castle for their 1993 Civic Reception. A stunning Dolores O'Riordan mural now graces the side of a house on adjoining Castle Street. Photo by Dermot Lynch/*Limerick Leader*.

with them. They originally asked us to support them and we said 'no'."

Does he think The Cranberries would appeal to the same type of audience as The Great Pouting Ones?

"It's hard to know. They're a great band, although I don't know what they're like as people," he says doubtfully.

Asked to offer words of advice to Irish bands thinking of taking the plunge, and crossing the Atlantic, Fergal remarks, "It's down to pure luck, really. Bands that I'd enjoy watching myself just can't seem to crack it. But so many Irish bands take the other option and get stuck in Ireland, saying, 'Ah, we're really big here'. Naturally you want to be popular where you come from, but it's the same as being popular in Holland or Denmark, Ireland is pretty much the same size."

Fergal Lawler interview by Lorraine Freeney, July 1993

ACCORDING TO OUR CHUMS AT ISLAND RECORDS, The Cranberries' debut album has now shifted a not-to-be-sneezed at 230,000 copies in the States and with the Limerick combo set to open there next month for Duran Duran, there's enthusiastic talk of the platter going all the way to the half-million mark.

***Hot Press* Newsdesk, September 1993**

CONGRATULATIONS TO THE CRANBERRIES, who this week climb to No. 18 on the *Billboard* album chart, notching up the 600,000th sale of their *Everybody Else Is Doing It, So Why Cant We?* album in the process. The lead single, 'Linger', has also gone Top 40 and with the band about to head out on the second leg of their Duran Duran support tour, cracking the million looks a mere formality. Irish fans will get a chance to see and hear what all the fuss is about when the Shannonsiders return home for Christmas dates at the Limerick Theatre Royal on December 17th and the Dublin Tivoli on the 18th.

***Hot Press* Newsdesk, September 1993**

"In Ireland, there's one radio station really, and if you can get on RTÉ you're sorted. The situation in the States is very different, and it's good that the college stations really do take an interest in what's happening."

IF SELF-SUFFICIENCY IS A BUZZ WORD in green circles, it might equally be applied to the home produce that's hogged my sound system for the past 12 months. All manner of life is there.

The alien dobro snuck its way into Gael Linn's catalogue under Frankie Lane's 10 gallon hat and charmed the pants off the legions who heard him in his myriad incarnations. Meanwhile, Cooney and Begley, that dastardly duo from the Dingle peninsula via-Port Philip Bay, spat and shuffled centre-stage on the back of a rake of crazed gigs that ran the gamut of audiences from the suave sophisticates of Whelan's to the more able-bodied hoofers of Ballinskelligs. Their hijacking of the *Bringing It All Back Home* tour sullied their reputation none either. A marriage of tradition and imagination, it proves to be an ever-more harmonious arrangement.

Cooney's fellow Yarra-siders, The Killjoys, managed to finger the dizzy romantic sensibilities with indescribable ease. *A Million Suns* has more hooks than a Japanese trawler-full of poached tuna, and G.W. McLennan proved that there is life after The Go-Betweens – and mercifully it's not as we've ever known it.

But the cherry on the cake, the jewel on the crown of the entire year has to be that beauteous virginal offering from The Cranberries. *Everybody Else...* is a pristine Prefab Sprout-ish sideways glance at love and lust and life, captured through the rainbow-bright prism of Dolores O'Riordan's chink-filled larynx and Stephen Street's considered production – music to moan, sigh and sing to (and with). It's melody to strum to. It's frankincense and myrrh in Docs and leggings. It's a beauty that's fast being beheld by many an eye and ear.

With the highs come the occasional lows. Crowded House and Tim Finn both managed to disappoint with the fruits of their studio sojourns, though Finn's *Before And After* held a few gems embedded amid the Polyfilla.

The smart money says Bob Dylan and Nick Cave were in better shape than ever. Didn't quite get the chance to lend an ear though – yet. Best of '93? Can I get back to you on the 31st?

Siobhán Long, End of Year Review, December 1993

ONE IRISH BAND WHO CAN BE EXTREMELY SATISFIED with their year are Limerick's finest The Cranberries. Their Island debut *Everybody Else Is Doing It, So Why Can't We?* received a fair-to-middling response on its European release but showed promising signs of denting the US market by early summer. Then it all went supernova for the quartet and they outshone the much-loved Suede on a co-headlining tour and sales figures surged ever upward. 100,000, 250,000, 500,000, 750,000 before finally hitting the magical million mark last week. Incredibly, The Cranberries are now true stars.

***Hot Press* Newsdesk, December 1993**

"It's melody to strum to. It's frankincense and myrrh in Docs and leggings. It's a beauty that's fast being beheld by many an eye and ear."

Above: Fergal Lawler and then manager Geoff Travis with the band's 1993 *Hot Press* Best Irish Album award. Photo by Cathal Dawson.
Opposite: The Cranberries sitting down on the job by Amelia Stein.

DOING IT FOR THEMSELVES

The Cranberries have overcome the growing pains that all young bands encounter to become one of Ireland's brightest prospects. Dolores O'Riordan and Fergal Lawler tell Stuart Clark about the new friends they've made, their first trip to America and a chance encounter with Michael Stipe.

PHOTOS: DANNY MAUGHON

This reminds me of the time I shared a bed with Maria McKee. It was fully made and we were sitting on top of it, I hasten to add, but there was a marked intimacy about the affair which you don't get when you're stuck in a record company interview room with a PR person skulking in the background and pulling faces every time you ask something even vaguely salacious.

The setting this afternoon is a suite at U2's gaff, The Clarence Hotel, where Dolores O'Riordan is peeping out at me rather blearily from underneath a king size quilt. Style watchers will be interested to note that The Cranberries lead singer is resplendent in a pair of brown and white polka dot pyjamas and matching dressing-gown, while a quick glance at the floor beside her reveals that furry Dunne's Stores' slippers are this season's de rigeur footwear.

"You wouldn't get Cher or Madonna talking to journalists if they looked like they'd just been dragged through a hedge backwards and jumped on by a herd of cows," she chuckles, "but I can't be bothered with all this image nonsense. We've done TV shows where people have thrown tantrums and refused to go on because they've got a spot on their nose, which is ridiculous.

"There's a lot of pressure on you, especially when you're female, to be 'sexy' and 'glamorous' – but if I'm not in the mood for plastering my face with make-up or doing my hair, I won't bother. I'm happy enough being myself, so why pretend to be someone else?"

It strikes me, listening to her, that even as a teenager, Dolores has already sussed what it takes most musicians a whole career to discover. And this is the girl that my British counterparts still insist on portraying as 'naive' and 'innocent'.

The reason I'm here in her boudoir, as the Limerick lass delicately puts it herself, is that she's 'completely knackered' and in need of a rest after a mad dash round the UK with Belly, and a week of laying her soul bare to the world's press in support of The Cranberries' debut album *Everybody Else Is Doing It, So Why Can't We?*

"Belly was a great tour to get," she enthuses, "because although we're very different, there are enough similarities for their fans to appreciate what we're about, and vice versa. The other thing is that they specifically asked for us – we weren't forced on them by the promoter and that meant we were able to relax and enjoy ourselves without worrying that we might be chucked off after the first night.

"For me, personally, it was wonderful getting to know someone like Tanya Donnelly, who's been in the business since she was eighteen, experienced the various highs and lows and still loves what she's doing. Her classic piece of advice to me was 'men suck' – which, I must admit, I was relieved to hear because it means I'm not the only person who feels that way every now and again."

Was she able to look at Tanya and say, "Yeah, that could be me in five or six years time'?"

"No. We got on brilliantly but attitude-wise we differ

"TYPICAL TOURISTS, we were *expecting* to get MUGGED the moment we got OFF THE PLANE, but there wasn't any HASSLE."

*

enormously. She's certainly far more cynical and hardened towards life than I am. Her parents broke up when she was quite young and she doesn't see much of her family, whereas I'm one of nine brothers and sisters. My Mam and Dad are happily married still and whenever I go home, I'm surrounded by relations.

"Tanya's biggest ambition," reveals Dolores, "is to have a kid of her own and she couldn't understand why I'm absolutely in no hurry myself to become a mother. I suppose she's looking for the closeness and sense of belonging which, in the nicest possible way, I take for granted."

When it comes to turning punters on, a *Top Of The Pops* appearance is still a powerful aphrodisiac and the surprise chart success of Belly's 'Feed The Tree' ensured that there were plenty of bums on seats throughout the tour. The Cranberries rose to the occasion by giving the headliners a serious run for their tax-free dollars and were only denied their own Thursday night assignation at the Beeb when 'Linger' stalled frustratingly close to the Top 50.

"That final night will stick in my memory for a long time," picks up drummer Fergal who's just wandered in. "Tanya invited Dolores to join her for the encore and I went into the audience to watch. She got a massive cheer when she walked on and I don't mind admitting that by the end of the song I was nearly in tears. For obvious reasons I don't often get to stand in front of the stage and watch her perform and it genuinely sent a shiver up the spine."

"When I met Ferg in the dressing-room afterwards," smiles the singer beatifically, "he was rightly emotional and that triggered me off too. The gig was a big deal for us because the record company and all the press were there, and everything fell into place perfectly. Our own set was the best we'd played in ages and guesting with Belly was the icing on the cake.

"Tanya wore a Cranberries T-shirt, I changed into one of theirs, and the roar when the crowd recognised me was deafening. It's easy to get fed up with the business side of things, but those kind of moments remind you why you joined the band in the first place."

Although they've yet to make the commercial breakthrough that Island so obviously expect, The Cranberries have laid enough solid foundations to suggest that when they do crack it, they'll get more than their prerequisite fifteen minutes of fame. Choice supports opening for House Of Love, Mike Oldfield and Hothouse Flowers have earned them a strong fan base, ranging from your standard indie kid to the chartered accountant with 2.3 children living in suburbia who thinks that The Jesus And Mary Chain is a religious order. They've also dipped their toe into that murky musical pond known as America.

"We'd heard so many horror stories concerning the States," admits Ferg, "that when we went to Los Angeles recently to shoot a video, we were shitting ourselves. Typical tourists, we were expecting to get mugged the moment we got off the plane, but there wasn't any hassle."

"We loved it there," joins in Dolores who's getting perkier

by the minute, "and they were mad for our music. Whereas the last video we made was a complete waste of money, this one turned out exactly the way we wanted it. Melodie McDaniel, who crewed on R.E.M.'s 'Losing My Religion', directed and was so easy to work with because rather than just barking out orders, she asked what you thought and involved you in the creative process.

"I nearly fainted when Michael Stipe turned up one day to see what was happening and Jean-Baptiste Mondino, the guy who directed Madonna's 'Justify My Love' and that other video where she flirts with the little boy, actually plays a part in it. We were kind of starstruck at first, but him and Michael are so down to earth and natural that we soon forgot they were famous."

It was pretty much the same story when, after an abortive first attempt, the band went into the studio with Stephen Street to record *Everybody Else...* Smiths fans will tell you that Street guided Mozzer through some of his finest moments and the producer's deft touch has worked similar wonders for The Cranberries.

"I'd never heard of Stephen before we met him," resumes Dolores, "but when he told us he'd written the music to 'Everyday Is Like Sunday' and 'Girlfriend In A Coma', I started frothing at the mouth. When I was at school, I worshipped The Smiths and suddenly to be working with a guy who knew them personally and produced their record... well, it took a while to sink in."

"Stephen's a bit like Melodie," adds Ferg, "in that he knows what he wants from you, but he's not a dictator. Before trying something, he'll bounce the idea around and he never forgets that it's your record. He told us at the end that it was the most fun he'd had since The Smiths, which was a huge compliment."

Another turning point for the band, he feels, was signing to Rough Trade Management, a company run by indie guru and former Smiths mentor Geoff Travis.

"Geoff knows the industry inside out but, in addition, he's also a music fan and that means money's not his sole motivation. He's on the phone every day going 'right lads, you've been offered this gig and that interview, do you want to do them?' We know exactly what's going on which, let's face it, is how it should be – because this is our career, our future."

At this point, the interview grinds to a halt because that swine Dawson wants to take some photos and Dolores is reticent about displaying her nighttime apparel to the whole of Ireland.

"I suppose I'm a bit conscious of the way I look," she confesses as we leave her to change, "but then again, women are entitled to be vain!"

· **Dolores O'Riordan and Fergal Lawler interview by Stuart Clark, December 1993**

While other indie-minded types worry about manifestoes, agendas and which-ism to vent their spleen against this week, The Cranberries push the bullshit to one side and – in 'Linger' – gift us a song that's as simple as it is breathtakingly beautiful. It's possible to wax lyrical all day about Dolores having the voice of an angel crying tears of warm honey, but the Limerick band's biggest asset is an adherence to such traditional values as bothering your arse to come up with a hook and melody. Even if you've already got the album, the live versions of 'Pretty' and 'Waltzing' – which are on the B-side of this global re-release of one of the highlights of *Everybody Else Is Doing It, So Why Can't We?* – make this single an essential purchase.

'Linger' single review by Stuart Clark, January 1993

Perspiring to greatness: More shots from The Cranberries' legendary July 1993 visit to Einstein A Go-Go, the Jacksonville Beach sweatbox, which had previously hosted the likes of Depeche Mode, The Replacements, Red Hot Chilli Peppers and Sonic Youth. Florida photographer Jim Leatherman liked what he saw and heard and struck up a friendship with the band.

SHOOT TO THRILL POLICY

Now an internationally renowned photographer and filmmaker, Melodie McDaniel made her directorial debut with the 'Linger' video. Drawing on her love of French new wave cinema, she created something which changed both her and The Cranberries' lives.

PHOTOS COURTESY OF MELODIE McDANIEL

"I went to school at the art center college of design in Pasadena with Tarsem Singh who had me on the crew as a stills photographer when he shot R.E.M.'s 'Losing My Religion' video.

Being on set with him taught me about casting, set dressing, putting together a really creative mood board and doing your research, which is key to making something really strong and memorable.

It's such a beautiful video. Like a lot of great visual artists and directors, Tarsem looked beyond what was trendy and of its time and made a timeless work that stands up no matter what. I love things to have a little bit more longevity myself.

The production company that Tarsem was working with saw how much creative collaboration I was doing on his projects, and that's how I ended up working with The Cranberries through a video commissioner at Island Records.

I'd observed how Tarsem had drawn little bits of inspiration from painters and famous films. I was really inspired at the time by the French black and white new wave. Even though the lyrics mightn't have matched, I felt the film noir mystery and coolness of that would suit The Cranberries.

When I eventually met Dolores and her bandmates, it was really, really great in that they didn't say, "Oh, we only want to be shot this way." They were totally open to whatever myself and the cinematographer suggested, which is so rare.

I was basing the vibe on Jean-Luc Goddard's sci-fi detective film, *Alphaville*, and the French actress in it, Anna Karina, who looked not unlike Dolores with her short hair.

Even though her own style at the time was more punky ripped jeans and t-shirt, she really embraced that 1960s French new wave look and was like, "You want me to wear a black trench coat? Sure!"

Dolores was so very sweet and giving and willing to try whatever. She really hit it off with the Director of Photography, which made a huge difference in terms of her overcoming her shyness in front of the camera.

It was The Cranberries' first time in the States and their song was taking off so they were incredibly excited.

I wasn't able to go on the trip because I was prepping the video, but my Mom took Dolores and a few others to Disneyland. I was living at home at the time and they came over to the house and hung out. You don't get that sort of interaction with artists anymore because of managers being protective and putting up walls.

There are a lot of old hotels in downtown Los Angeles where Hollywood stars would have stayed back in the '20s, which have turned into places where – how shall I put this? – a certain clientele would stay. Two of the most famous ones, the Cecil and the Rosslyn, had been used countless times before, so I found this other place a few blocks away, the Dewey, which was its own little world and across the road from this bar called Crabby Joe's, which Bukowski had drunk in. The Cecil or Rosslyn may have given me a room, but we had total access to the Dewey's three or four stories, which gave us endless possibilities.

I was really interested in the underbelly stripper culture you'd have got in old gentleman's clubs or juke joints, which is why we projected that grainy Super 8 footage above a

"Even as The Cranberries GOT REALLY BIG,
Dolores maintained her LOYAL, LOVING,
SWEET PERSONALITY."

✳

washing machine. The performer in it is Blaze Starr who was known in the '50s as 'The Hottest Blaze In Burlesque'. She had incredible presence. A few years after the 'Linger' video I did a photographic assignment called *Exotic World*, which is an outdoor strip club just outside Las Vegas in a trailer park. It was these old burlesque dancers in their fifties who came in different shapes and sizes, wrinkles and everything.

Anyway, we had Blaze on the wall and Dolores wandering along the corridors, all in black and white to give it that timeless feel.

Michael Stipe dropped by the set as did the French fashion photographer and music video director Jean-Baptiste Mondino who ended up playing one of the detectives and really looked the part.

It was my first video and the first one where The Cranberries had a bit of a budget, so there was a determination to make it as good as we possibly could. I still remember how elated we all felt when MTV put it on heavy rotation; there was no looking back after that for the band.

Dolores loved my entourage, so we got on a tour bus and went to a Cranberries gig in Arizona. Any time they came back to Los Angeles we'd meet somewhere. It was awesome.

Even as The Cranberries got really big, Dolores maintained her loyal, loving, sweet personality. She was very excited when I got her an autograph from Madonna!

I lost touch with her when she got married and had kids, which is life for you.

I was devastated when I heard about her death, but will always remember this beautiful woman who enchanted the world and fulfilled all her dreams."

· **Melodie McDaniel in conversation with Stuart Clark, July 2021**

Dewey-eyed nostalgia: The Cranberries on the 'Linger' video set with Melodie McDaniel.

"I felt the film noir mystery and coolness would suit The Cranberries."

L.A. STORY

Michael Stipe tells us about meeting The Cranberries for the first time, squeezing into Dolores' little rubber number and why R.E.M. identified so strongly with Limerick's finest.

PHOTOS COURTESY OF MELODIE McDANIEL

"It was '92/'93 and i was spending a good bit of time in Los Angeles. New York had started feeling a little tired and dirty and old and I followed my best friend, who'd rented a beach cabin in Santa Monica, out west. L.A. became my second home after Athens, Georgia, which has always been my number one base because of the band and my family. I made a lot of choices for R.E.M. based on my being there, one of the best being choosing Tarsem Singh to direct the 'Losing My Religion' video. He'd assembled this group of incredibly talented, young, fascinating, beautiful and multi-ethnic people, which included Melodie McDaniel who at the time was working mainly as a photographer and did the stills on the 'Losing My Religion' shoot. We kept in touch and worked together again on the 'Man On The Moon' video.

She got this job to work with a young band from Ireland and invited me to come on set. It was in downtown Los Angeles in this old hotel, the Dewey, that was either completely shut down or used as a flophouse. It was just a block or two away from where Wim Wenders later shot the *Million Dollar Hotel* movie with Bono,

The Cranberries were sort of jumping off the cliff hiring Melodie because for all of her undoubted talents she wasn't a proven video director. I came on set and was instantly captivated by The Cranberries. They were this vibrant, super-excited-to-be-there band making beautiful music. I was just thrilled to meet them; they were really nice, good people and brilliant songwriters. They had a great energy about them.

That's when I first met Dolores who was young but definitely not naïve and always felt very together to me. There's a storytelling tradition in Ireland that's handed down, and she wound up inheriting both that and the Irish sense of humour; she was very funny to be around. I couldn't believe that 'Linger' was the first thing she wrote with The Cranberries – what a song!

As an opening act, R.E.M. got treated very well and got treated really badly. The former is definitely preferable, so when we got big enough to have support groups ourselves we went for ones that we not only wanted to hear every night, but also had perspectives, personalities and politics we enjoyed and appreciated. Fulfilling all of those requirements The Cranberries were at the top of the list when R.E.M. decided to tour again in '95.

Dolores was a tiny woman doing a job that's not easy for women, certainly, but she never showed fear of any kind and was a natural on stage. She had that "If I'm gonna fall on my face, it's fine. I'm just going get right back up and do it again..." attitude. I loved that about Dolores.

There was a great camaraderie on the tour. I remember at one of the shows going through her wardrobe, which was full of these outrageous costumes Dolores had for going on stage, which is what you have to do if you're trying to reach Row Z. Giant video screens weren't a given at shows then so you had to project to the punters who were paying just as

Time to linger: Michael Stipe hanging with Dolores, Mike and Ferg in the Dewey Hotel.

much money, but happened to be at the back of the room. The *most* outrageous was this skirt that had rubber spikes sticking out of it. She was tiny, but I was tiny too – probably just over 130lbs – so I shimmied into her little rubber number with rubber spikes sticking out of it! We were cracking up. It probably fitted better on my head than my hips, but I owned that dress.

I don't know much about the personal dynamic between her and the band, but to me they had that same gang feel as R.E.M. did. The guys seemed incredibly supportive of Dolores as a woman who, like I say, was doing a very hard job. Allowing my insecurities and vulnerabilities to be part of who I am as a public person and performer wasn't easy for me but, still, I'm a man. I had a bit of an easier ride there than she might have.

She certainly had a command of the stage and a command of the audience, which comes back to that storytelling tradition. I'm sorry to overstate that but, as an American, it's fascinating to recognise something that is absolutely cultural.

I've never sung for a Pope... as far as I know, but she did, which I know meant a lot to her as a Catholic and is an indication of just how famous she became. Those are once in a lifetime gigs, though I think Dolores might have done it twice!

We were thrilled to have The Cranberries onstage with us, and stood and watched most of the shows from the wings. I speak on behalf of Peter, Mike and Bill too when I say Dolores and the guys brought us great joy."

· **Michael Stipe in conversation with Stuart Clark, July 2021**

"She had that *'If I'm gonna fall on my face, it's fine.* I'm just going get right back up and do it again...' attitude. I LOVED that about DOLORES."

Michael Stipe, July 2021

I Did it My Way

Despite having the might of Island Records behind it, *Everybody Else Is Doing It, So Why Can't We?* was a slow burner. But when it took off in the USA, there was no stopping it, as it lingered long in the charts where so many previous Irish bands had tended to fade away. By the end of 1993, you could say without fear of contradiction that The Cranberries had arrived. At the start of 1994, Dolores set out her stall in a powerful *Hot Press* cover story, which emphasised the band's independence of spirit and freedom from the demands of either fad or fashion. What other dramatic moments would '94 encompass? And would they get their follow-up album recorded? And how would it compare? Whatever the answers to those questions, by year end, Dolores and the rest of the band would be able to look back and definitively say: "I did it my way."

Opposite photo: Mick Quinn

FIRST THEY TOOK MANHATTAN THEN THEY TOOK BERLIN

The Cranberries turned established music industry assumptions on their head by breaking the US before the UK. Even Ireland was slower to recognise the band's unique power. But that didn't deter the band from asserting their Irishness. Also on the agenda in a thought-provoking interview with Dolores: the earning power of a rock star, sexism and the age-old question: do all men suck?

Interview: Joe Jackson

PHOTOS: MICK QUINN

Dolores O'Riordan smiles ironically, but she's not surprised. I've just been reading a *Sunday Times* article headlined "British Pop Music Slips Down The World Chart". In this elegy for the "British invasion" of '93 – "the greatest disappearing act in the history of pop" – it's claimed that the current American Top 30 features only one group that represents "the type of music that is attuned to the spirit of transatlantic youth in the mid '90s." That group is The Cranberries who are described as being "from Limerick but signed up to a United Kingdom label."

"We're signed to an American label," says Dolores, laughing. "So, even that point is wrong. And isn't it pathetic that they should try to pretend our success is a victory for British pop?"

Pathetic and predictable, perhaps. And a telling indictment of the kind of colonialist mind-set that seems to be mobilised in Britain whenever Irish artists – whether it's The Cranberries, U2, Jim Sheridan, Enya or Seamus Heaney – make a major international impact. But then Dolores O'Riordan doesn't need to be told that, as British pop music does indeed slip down the world's charts, Irish music is on the rise.

The Cranberries, after all, started out co-headlining with the so-called Band of '93, Suede, on a US tour last September and ended up stealing the show, selling more tickets and forcing Brett and the boys to abandon that particular attempted 'British Invasion' and retreat in defeat.

In 1993 The Cranberries also became the first Irish band to sell more than a million copies of their debut album in America, despite *Everybody Else Is Doing It, So Why Can't We?* , peaking at No. 18 in the US album charts. The single, 'Linger', also made its debut in the American charts in December, entering at No. 19. But The Cranberries are ground-breaking in that all of this was achieved while bypassing the traditional 'first-you-gotta-break-in Britain' strategy employed by virtually every Irish rock act stretching back as far as Thin Lizzy.

I COULDN'T HANDLE IT

Lead singer and lyric writer Dolores O'Riordan has already stated that, as a Limerick band, The Cranberries made it without needing to prove themselves in Dublin. She described the capital as "so clannish, they believed that anything that didn't come out of Dublin, wasn't worth the effort."

Does she still feel that's true?

"I don't feel it, I know it," she says, immediately displaying the irresistible self-confidence that is the hallmark of this 22-year-old from Ballybricken, in Co. Limerick. "I know they ignored us and I know they have a problem identifying with

VOL 18 NO 1 • 26 JANUARY 1994
PRICE £1.25 (INCLUDING TAXES)

HOT PRESS

THE CRANBERRIES' U.S. COUP
i did it my way
JOE JACKSON TALKS TO
DOLORES O'RIORDAN

THE BOO RADLEYS GIANT LEAP FORWARD by LORRAINE FREENEY

ALBERT THE STATESMAN by EAMONN McCANN

philip lynott • cooney and begley • pulp • vote in the only readers' poll that matters

Precious metal: The Cranberries show off a platinum disc for Irish sales of *No Need To Argue* to *Hot Press* snapper Cathal Dawson.

"Look at Elvis Presley. He came from the arsehole of nowhere and is the biggest thing that ever happened in rock 'n' roll."

anything outside Dublin. But, I wouldn't just say they are 'clannish'. They're small-minded and though some may look beyond the Pale, not enough do. But this isn't just true in terms of the music industry, it relates to all the arts.

"My boyfriend – that I used to live with – was a painter and his friend was a sculptor and, like many people who go to art college and get diplomas, they found it very difficult to be recognised outside of Limerick. They'd come to Dublin and put on exhibitions and get no support at all. Artists who live outside Dublin find it harder to get financial assistance from establishments like the Arts Council. It's the same thing in music. And a lot of that has to do with the fact that Dublin has the media on its side and it pumps out this notion that Dublin is the centre of the universe, which it obviously isn't. It definitely never was for us."

The success of bands like Therapy?, The Sultans Of Ping FC, Engine Alley, and The Frank And Walters has underlined that, shifting the focus to cities like Cork, Galway and Belfast.

"That's healthy," Dolores says. "I always knew that The

Cranberries had far more international appeal than to be content just aiming for 'We're gonna play in this particular Dublin venue for the next 20 years', and be happy to have made it in the capital city.

"So it's great for anyone outside Dublin to see we can make it despite that Dublin prejudice. But I would hope that artists in Limerick in particular — in any field — would take inspiration from our success on an international level. Look at Elvis Presley. He came from the arsehole of nowhere and he was, and is, the biggest thing that ever happened in rock 'n' roll. So, to me it's not where you come from that matters, but what's in your soul."

While Limerick gleefully celebrated The Cranberries' homecoming at Christmas, Dolores O'Riordan harbours mixed feelings about returning to her native city.

"It's strange, because I moved into Limerick city itself when I was 18 and joined the band," she muses. "But having spent most of this year on the road, I then came back and found that so much has changed for me. All my friends have gone,

"Back in Limerick people say, 'God, isn't it great? All you did was sing the few oul songs and you're famous.' What can you say to that? You say nothing and realise that you are all drifting apart."

in a sense. They're still there, but it's very hard to relate to them. And the point is that, as you travel, you make more and more new friends and they know exactly what you're going through and what is happening to you as you tour – whereas when you come back to Limerick people are talking to you about their exams or whatever.

"Or you're sitting in a pub with old friends and they're going 'Look at him, isn't he lovely looking', and you're there thinking 'Sure, but about a hundred lads a night now come up to me at gigs, so I can't look at men the way I used to, or the way youse do'. So it's kinda hard to go back to Limerick and relate to friends. That's part of the reason I could never see myself living there again."

At least one old friend from Limerick now travels with Dolores and remains one of the most important people in her life.

"Breffni and I have been friends since I was four-years old," Dolores says, "and she sees what I'm going through, because she's there all the time. She sees me getting mobbed by fans and understands exactly what I'm feeling at a time like that, which makes our relationship even closer. Whereas, back in Limerick people say, 'God, isn't it great? All you did was sing the few oul' songs and you're famous'. What can you say to that? So you say nothing. You just go, 'Yeah, it's great, isn't it?' and realise that you are all drifting apart."

What, exactly, does Dolores feel when she is being mobbed by fans?

"It's kind of annoying at times," she says. "Sure, it's great to go on stage and hear the fans screaming and all that stuff but, after a gig, I'd be dying to go out to Breff and say 'How's it going?' and have a chat with her, but I can't. I can't go near the crowd after a gig. Because all it takes is for three of them to notice you and they run over and start screaming 'Dolores, I love you. Hug me, just one hug' – and they forget I'm wrecked after a gig and just want to relax, especially if we've to journey overnight to the next gig. And those fans do take everything out of you, drain you in that way.

"So I stay backstage until the hall is empty then, sometimes, I go out. Or, other times, I stay behind the barriers and wave from a distance, which is fine. But I rarely go over and talk with them directly after a gig because physically it's draining, with sometimes ten people asking you questions at the same time. And you don't want to be rude because you do realise how much you could mean to them individually. Like, if you

meet a teenager and they tell you that a song of yours totally redeemed their head, that's lovely.

"But they also can get down on their knees, and stuff, crying and wanting more. And you can't say 'Oh go away, I'm tired' even if you feel like doing it. So it all is pressure on me. And some guys come up and claim they know you intimately because of the songs and they get all intense and scary and I have to say to the guys in the band 'Hey lads, watch him, will you?' That can be frightening at times."

It can be equally frightening when one person in an audience targets you. This happened when The Cranberries were gigging with Suede in Sun Francisco.

"Suede weren't popular on a widespread level in America: they didn't even sell one eighth of the records we sold. But their best markets were places like San Francisco, which is not surprising as San Francisco is the largest gay/lesbian settlement and Suede have that appeal. Their drummer is gay and is very open about it. But there was one guy in particular, behind all these bars and barriers, and he started calling out 'Dolores, give this to Brett'.

"He was screaming out, with his face pressed against the barrier. So I'm going 'Yeah, sure, I'll go backstage and look for Brett for you'. Then he said, 'If you don't give this to him you'll prove your anti-homosexuality'. And I looked at him and said 'Give us a break, will you?' So he started roaring 'I want to get her' and he was clawing at the barrier and I began to wonder exactly what he would have done if he could have gotten to me."

At one point Dolores O'Riordan also found that she was the object of desire for a group of lesbians, who displayed their emotions in a far less upfront manner than Brett's gay fan.

"My first major lesbian encounter took place in London, before we left to tour Europe," she reflects. "At the last gig we did in London, in The Underworld, a lesbian group came in to see us play after some meeting they'd had. And they just stood there bawling their eyes out, calling my name, saying 'Please, touch me' as if I was some kind of saviour. And I couldn't handle it at all. I was saying to the band, 'What's wrong with them?' But then I realised maybe it was the way I look or, more so, the nature of the songs, which deal with intimacy and anger and emotions that, to me, are about men, but for them could just as much be about women. It's much the same thing, isn't it?

"That experience scared me initially, because I didn't know

"One of the most amazing experiences of my life was to go into a monastery and see monks coming out at 6AM and start chanting."

too much about lesbianism. Yet since then I've met lots of lesbians and most of them are lovely girls and I'm not afraid of them anymore. They live their life and I live mine."

A NICE CAREER FOR YOU

Clearly, the popularity of The Cranberries is very much rooted in the potent appeal of Dolores O'Riordan. Listening to her speak in almost whispered tones one can't help but hear distinct echoes of the tenderness, and lyricism, that defines the music of the band. It is this, rather than any form of macho swagger, which has made The Cranberries the first Irish group to successfully follow U2 into the all-important US market.

Dolores rejects the notion that The Cranberries have eclipsed U2 in the States, but she will concede that their success has finally proven that Ireland is more than just a one-band country.

"I don't agree with anyone who says we have eclipsed U2 in any way," she argues. "People kept coming up to me after we won that National Music Award last week, saying, 'Dolores, U2 had that Best Band award for ages and now The Cranberries got it, youse beat U2!' That really sickened me, because U2 always have been a source of inspiration to a band like us.

"They came from Ireland, went off and broke internationally and showed us all that an Irish band can do that – which is probably one of their greatest achievements. And what was really important to me was that they were just four, normal lads from ordinary backgrounds, like the rest of us. And they took on the world and won! They'll always be brilliant in my eyes. But what I've found is that Irish people, in the first place, don't realise what talent there is in Ireland until it breaks internationally – and then there is a lot of begrudging and bitching.

"But maybe that will all stop now, with the success of U2 and people like Jim Sheridan, Roddy Doyle and The Cranberries. People should realise we're all in this together, we're not in competition with one another. Certainly The Cranberries aren't in competition with the likes of Sinéad O'Connor and U2. But, definitely, The Cranberries have shown there is more to Ireland than just U2 and Sinéad."

Dolores laughs at what she describes as "the laziness" of those who describe her as "a younger Sinéad O'Connor" or make comparisons between The Cranberries and U2.

"People in America don't say that, only people here in Ireland," she says, smiling impishly. "So, I think I'll keep my hair short to make them look even more stupid. It's such an obvious comparison to make! But the only point of comparison I see between U2, Sinéad and us is that we all broke in America. But U2 certainly didn't influence me musically. When I was growing up, my brothers were really into their songs but I wasn't. I was more into dreamy music, whereas U2 were hard, more macho at the time."

It has been suggested that The Cranberries success story began when the originally all-male band decided that their music was "feminine" – and that they needed a female to capture this. Is that true?

"In ways, yeah. In the beginning, the bass player was 16 and the other two were 17 and 18 and the music was heavy. It was all 'We are the boys' stuff, with silly lyrics like *'I strangled my friend yesterday/ and he choked on his vomit'*. They were into that and into just having a laugh. But in time they did say that their music was softer than most, so maybe it'd be nice to have a female singer. And when I went to hear them there was a lot of space in the music where I knew I wouldn't have to compete as a vocalist. I liked that."

And so it remains, in most songs on *Everybody Else Is Doing It, So Why Can't We?* Dreamy, floating soundscapes dominate the album, which can indeed be described as highly feminine.

"That's the kind of stuff I was writing when I met the lads," Dolores recalls. "In the band the music is written by me and the guitar-player, but I do most of the music writing. I write the lyrics and structures – but most journalists in Ireland seem to get it wrong when they comment on that, so people think I write the words and the band writes the music. That's not how it is."

So what kind of 'dreamy' music, or poetry was Dolores O'Riordan into as a teenager?

"I was really into religious music, like Gregorian chants," she recalls. "One of the most amazing experiences of my life was to go into a monastery and see monks coming out at 6am and start chanting. I used to go to monasteries to get away from the whole world and all the crap that comes from teenage pressures. So that kind of raw, honest setting in a monastery was a real relief, especially listening to the music monks made.

"I also played a church organ for about a year and some of my family were in a choir. So that was the musical base. And I was really into Yeats' poetry, so much so that I wrote a song called 'Yeats' Grave' the first time I went to Sligo and saw where he is buried. I loved his passion, the dreamer he

was. And the fact that he looked beyond the material world to matters spiritual, which is really representative of the Irish people as a race. As with the native Americans and Jamaicans, I've found."

And yet the Irish can also be highly practical, as in parents telling their children to ground themselves in "a good trade, or profession" before they go pursuing their dreams. Is it true that Dolores' parents wouldn't let her join a rock band until she finished the Leaving Cert?

"They didn't want me to, but I did," she says, laughing. "But that was the best thing I could have done because, in Ireland the attitude is really small-minded when it comes to arts in schools. I'd be there and the career teacher would say, 'What do you want to do, Dolores?' And I'd say, 'I want to be a rock singer and bring out albums and get a record deal'. Then she'd say 'Yeah, but don't you think nursing would be a really nice career for you?' They'd just pick any subject off-hand, obviously believing that there is no future whatsoever in choosing a career in music. That really was small-minded of them."

UNDER A LOT OF PRESSURE
Dolores hopes that this blinkered, archaic attitude to the arts, within educational institutions, will change as a result of the influence of Michael D. Higgins as Minister for Culture. She agrees with his controversial suggestion that the work of bands like U2 and The Cranberries should be studied in schools – and not just in an artistic sense.

"If career teachers really are interested in the prospect for jobs and for making money, they should realise that the music business is one of the richest industries in the world. The amount of money that can be made is incredible, believe me. And Michael D. Higgins should hammer people in the educational system over the heads until they realise that fact. Look at it this way, there are students in my school now who will spend maybe fifteen years working to earn anything like the amount of money I've made in the past six months in the States. But then Irish schools also fail their students by not thinking enough of places outside Ireland, as in the market for music. I always realised our music had that global appeal – even financially."

As with most rock stars, Dolores is reluctant to put a figure on the amount of money she has earned over the past six months.

"All I will say is that I probably have the biggest income of all members of the band, because I do most of the writing. Three of the tracks on the first album I wrote alone. And nine of the tracks, I co-wrote the music with Noel. But we have got a great understanding about that, among the lads in the band. For example, although the bass-player and drummer don't actually write music, I don't tell them what to play so

their input means they get a share in the composing royalties. We've been very aware of all this from the outset. And the lads do accept that they can't write a full song without me, but I can write a full song without them. They know that's just the way things are."

Is anyone pushing Dolores to ditch the band and go solo?

"Loads of people, yeah," she says. "But I don't want to do that. Because the lads and I have got a great relationship going between the four of us. Nobody can come between us on that level."

Noel Hogan (guitar), Mike Hogan (bass) and Fergal Lawler (drums) also share Dolores' interest in world music, and are happy to accommodate her as she drifts off into, for example, an Arabic chant at the end of 'Dreams'.

"We're into exploring all that," she says. "Like in Santa Fe on Saturdays the Native Americans come into town and sit on the side of the road and sell their jewellery. But they also chant – and listening to them I realised the chanting was exactly like the oul' fellas out in the Aran Islands who chant intricate Irish songs and also work themselves into a kind of trance.

"That, to me, is what music is all about. In fact I believe the source was all the same to begin with. A lot of Arabic music, Egyptian, Africa — all the trilly stuff — does really link up with Irish music. And I've always been fascinated by questions of where music began."

Although The Cranberries don't necessarily present themselves as an Irish band abroad, their sound is heavily influenced by the Limerick lilt in Dolores' voice and by the Celtic longings at the soul of her songs.

"That's true," she says, "but there's a difference between us trying to push that on people and just going with that because that's how we are, or how the music is. Some people in America have asked, 'Why does she sing 'Linger' with that funny sounding R?' And when it's explained that we are from Ireland and that's the Limerick accent they go 'Oh, is Ireland in England?' And on the *John Stewart Show* on MTV one night, he introduced us as 'The Cranberries from Limerick, England'. No doubt whoever wrote that *Sunday Times* article you referred to earlier, would love that introduction. We are Irish but it's not something we ram down peoples' throats – unless we feel we have to."

On a more personal level, referring back to her last interview in *Hot Press* Dolores wishes to clarify one comment which made her appear to be sexist.

"When I said 'all men suck' I was quoting Tanya from Belly," she says. "Stuart Clark asked did I get any tips from Tanya and I said 'Yeah, the one she gave me, was that all men suck'. But that's not my point of view. I love men."

But does Dolores O'Riordan really love men? Isn't there a lot of anger, pain and betrayal in songs like 'Not Sorry' and

"I used to go to MONASTERIES to get away from the
WHOLE WORLD and all the CRAP that comes from
TEENAGE PRESSURES."

*

"As I get older, I realise there is a strong, honest, admirable side to the male race so I'd never say 'all men suck'."

'Still Can't'?

"Well, I do think that males have a problem with being open, emotionally," she explains. "Machoism I despise and there's an awful lot of it around. A lot of men, when they get together with the boys, find it difficult to even hold your hand or say things they'd normally say to you if the lads weren't around. But that doesn't make me dismiss the whole male sex. Because I believe that, underneath it all, men are just as emotional as women, and just as soft, once you strip away the crappy macho stuff.

"It's easy for a woman to hold her baby or say 'I love you' to her husband in public – but men are afraid things like that might make them 'wimp-ish' in the eyes of their mates, which is nonsense. And yet I work with men on the road and they're all 'big men' when they're together, saying 'Look at that babe over there, look at those tits'. Yet when you get them alone in a room, you find they're far more sensitive than that underneath.

"I'm going out with this guy at the moment and he's into American hard rock, Metallica and Guns N' Roses and all that – but behind it all he's a real softie. And all those guys, I've found, are like little babies, in ways. That's why I'd never be angry at all men, because I see that they're under a lot of pressure to present one image to their mates and to the world, while trying to come to terms with the fact that they are like children underneath."

Dolores believes this is particularly true of young, teenage guys.

"I often think many of them are into groups like Megadeth just to prove their masculinity to their peers," she says. "They're afraid the opposite will be read into them liking, say, more sensitive music, or 'feminine' music. Or art, or theatre. 'Real' men are not supposed to be into such things. Whereas the men I'm really interested in are those who are 'feminine' and 'masculine' in equal measures. But things are changing for the better, fortunately."

NOT ANOTHER 'ROCK CHICK'

One could suggest that the success of groups like The Cranberries also implies that this form of balancing act in rock music is exactly what's needed to prepare it for the next millennium.

"I think so," says Dolores. "Because cock-rock has ruled since the beginning. But, having said that, I wouldn't exactly go as far as the Riot Grrrl movement, because I'm not into the battle of the sexes in the way that the battle is all that seems to matter. I don't write songs for the same political reasons they do. I grew up with five brothers and I've always tried to understand men, not just put them down. That's what I wrote about for ages, though I've obviously branched off in other directions over the past while.

"When you're 18, you're just going to write about your boyfriend and your broken heart and how he betrayed you. Despite having had that experience I wasn't turned off all men, as some women are. In fact, as I get older, I realise there is a strong, honest, admirable side to the male race so I'd never say 'all men suck'."

Dolores O'Riordan believes that her own male fans respond to her on an intellectual and emotional level, rather than merely seeing her as another "rock chick".

"That's what makes it more difficult in ways, though," she says, contemplatively. "They're into your head, and want to get in further. They're not going, 'Wow, look at her arse'. But then our male fans aren't the bimbo men. Bimbo men aren't into us at all, they're into bimbo women. Our fans think about things, probe beneath the surface and respond to the band's music, and to my songs, on those levels instead. There's no doubt about that."

How would Dolores respond if she noticed a fan focusing more on her body?

"I'm really not into the female bimbo thing of letting your strap slip or teasing fans that way but if someone makes a remark along those lines I tend to become the mammy, wag my finger and say 'Now, you watch yourself, there' and they don't know what to say. There was this fella one night and I had a little skirt on, singing, and suddenly I felt this hand on my leg and I just slapped his hand and said 'Stop!'

"But that doesn't often happen, because I think our fans really do have respect for me, as a woman. I've never gone 'Here I am, lads'. All the boys that come to see us really do seem to be more into my mind. And I know the difference because I have seen fellas screaming at Tanya, or PJ Harvey, 'Get them off, get your tits out' – but nobody's ever said that to me. Maybe once or twice a little 15-year old says something like that to impress his friends. But that's easy to deal with. I just stare into their faces or point at them till they nearly die with embarrassment!"

· **Dolores O'Riordan interview by Joe Jackson, January 1994**

LIKE THE BEST OF CHRISTMAS RELISHES, The Cranberries went down a treat at Dublin's Tivoli Theatre, just a week before the big day. They've mastered the art of solo song titles with more aplomb than even Bono could muster. 'Special', 'Empty', 'Linger' betray no more and no less than the core of each song.

Being the talk of the town has done them no harm either. The voice is still unmistakably Dolores's. The pulsing guitars are still in the name of the brothers Hogan, and Fergal Lawler's percussion is as close-knit as a Walton clan gathering. Heck, this quartet sound like they've been treading the boards longer than The Grateful Dead, except the 'Berries manage to remember all their lines, all of the time.

It's a sort of a homecoming, though these children of the Treaty City did signal a touch of annoyance at the capital's distinct lack of appreciation of their worth from the early days. Looking tired and emotional, they ploughed through everything on their pristine debut – and then made us privy to a few new tunes, borrowed from the next album for the night.

'Empty', an encore, spirited Dolores behind an acoustic guitar from which she siphoned a mournful, weeping wail in the company of Fergal's unheralded but perfect kettle drums.

It's a sound that haunts, and hints at darker things beyond the water's edge. It's a feel that seeps through to the bone, with the help of the barest of strings and rhythm. It's a touch that's nowhere else to be found. The Cranberries are back in town to show us why they've been crucifying the album charts across the water.

And we may as well take note. I've heard nothing else to compare with it for a very long time. Fact is, nobody else is doing it, so why the hell shouldn't they?

Tivoli Theatre, Dublin live review by Siobhán Long, December 1993

DOLORES O'RIORDAN HAS APPARENTLY given up on trying to look 'ugly' and decided instead to go for the other worldly look that's just so hip these days. Sporting a long flowing white dress and bleached hair, O'Riordan appeared quite the pixie on stage in New York's Central Park, at times waving her arms limply as if trying to take flight.

But like Tinkerbell wielding a Strat, this other-worldly Cranberry has developed an uncanny knack for rock 'n' roll cliché.

"Hello, New York," "Thank you, New York,"

"Goodnight, New York," "Sing it with me, New York" (as if anyone else can sing those damn yodelly bits she specialises in). "Maybe you've heard this one before..." – all successful tactics for keeping the crowd riveted on this cool and vaguely drizzly evening in the Big Apple.

One of the only non-free concerts of the SummerStage season, this gig sought to raise money for next year's SummerStage and drew a sizeable twenty-something crowd. While O'Riordan's constant referral to *Everybody Else Is Doing It...* as their "first album" confused everyone ("You mean there's another one?"), several new songs went down really well. Crowd participation during 'Dreams', 'Not Sorry' and other tracks from the band's debut evidenced the strength of The Cranberries' following here.

O'Riordan's quirkiness may sometimes be cloying, but boy can that girl sing! The sound wasn't near loud enough (some kind of agreement with neighbouring apartment buildings), but on this feelgood, all 'round enjoyable evening, The Cranberries surely resonated.

Central Park, New York live review by Tara McCarthy, August 1994

"Sporting a long flowing white dress and bleached hair, O'Riordan appeared quite the pixie on stage in New York's Central Park."

Above: Dolores in 1994 by Cathal Dawson.

> "As I put on the outfit and said 'Look, Dad', he said 'Yes, that's lovely but where's the dress?'"

Above: Dolores and Don Burton's July 1994 wedding at Holycross Abbey in Co. Tipperary. Her choice of dress became a national talking point! Photos: Press 22. **Opposite:** Stills from the Samuel Bayer-directed 'Zombie' video.

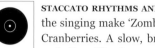 STACCATO RHYTHMS AND SUBTLE JERKS and pauses in the music and the singing make 'Zombie' more than just business-as-usual for The Cranberries. A slow, brooding Siouxsie-like buzzing guitar melody and dirge-like bass and drums counterpoint the elliptical and impassioned vocals of Dolores O'Riordan, as she works her way through the internal psychic, and external human, tragedies of The Troubles we've OD'd on, on this battered little island of ours. 'Zombie' signals a growth in confidence, as The Cranberries experiment without discarding that unique form of understatement, which distinguishes Limerick's finest from all those other practitioners of Celtic soul.

'Zombie' single review by Patrick Brennan, October 1994

IN JULY, DOLORES O'RIORDAN, sporting a new peroxide hairstyle, married Don Burton in Holy Cross Abbey, in Tipperary. Her outfit, a cream lace number, designed by hip New York designer Cynthia Rowley, caused a flurry in the tabloid press, inspiring comments along the lines of "she got married in her knickers".

The "controversy" – which she has described as "pathetic" and "typical of a Catholic country" – obviously hit Dolores hard. Mention of the incident brings forth a torrent of anger at journalists who are "about forty and are fat and insecure and have problems with themselves and are jealous of me.

"It was really pathetic," she goes on, "because every time you'd read an article that said, 'Oh, she's vulgar and she's this and she's that' you'd go: 'This has to have been written by a woman and she has to be either old or fat or ugly or in some way insecure, so much so that she has to bitch about my wedding clothes'. 'Cos I would never, ever, complain about anything another woman does. If she's happy then leave her. I don't understand that mentality, that whole bitchy thing."

You sense that she means it and that the rant is simply a reaction to a real sense of hurt. But surely she knew it was bound to happen. It was, after all, the silly season and she is a rock star.

"I didn't really think there would be that many press there," she insists. "I had an idea there would be a couple, but then the Abbey and the priests were saying that they were getting an awful lot of calls – from every newspaper in Ireland basically – and we thought, 'Shit, we'd better get some security'. But all you really want is to be an ordinary girl on your wedding day."

How did her parents react?

"They were OK about it because, well, I moved out of home when I was eighteen and it's turned out alright and I think sometimes your parents realise that you can actually make decisions about your life and they can turn out to be good decisions.

"But my dad was funny because he's a real countryman. As I put on the outfit and said 'Look, Dad', he said 'Yes, that's lovely but where's the dress?'. I said, 'Dad, I'm not wearing a dress. I don't want to be boring and predictable. I want to wear something different'. But, I mean, if you go around thinking about the peabrained Irish mentality and worrying about what people will think... I mean who gives a damn?"

Dolores O'Riordan interview by Cathy Dillon, October 1994

Zombie

"ANOTHER HEAD HANGS LOWLY
CHILD IS SLOWLY TAKEN
AND THE VIOLENCE, CAUSED
SUCH SILENCE
WHO ARE WE MISTAKEN?"

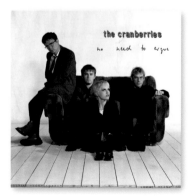

Above: It's sofa so good as The Cranberries take a Dublin time-out. Photo by Andy Earl.

 THE DOCS ARE SHINIER. The haircuts are a tad trendier. The Cranberries have been there, done that and now they're going to do it all again. The conundrum of how to follow-up an album that's sold three million is one of Confucian proportions. And Confucius says: 'If it ain't broke, don't fix it'.

Seeing your face plastered across feature pages and hearing your larynx stretched thinly over all manner of dodgy airwaves is apparently not all it's cracked up to be, if the songs on *No Need To Argue* are to be believed, (though I'm prepared to give it a shot – if anyone cares). The Cranberries have been sauce (har, har!) for every turkey and media ham on both sides of the Atlantic for the past 12 months and what their second visit to the studio says, above all else, is that they've had their spell in the fish bowl.

Dolores is coming out, guns blazing, teeth grinding and heart virtually bursting at the seams with enough melodrama to fire at least half a dozen sessions on Anthony Clare's couch. »

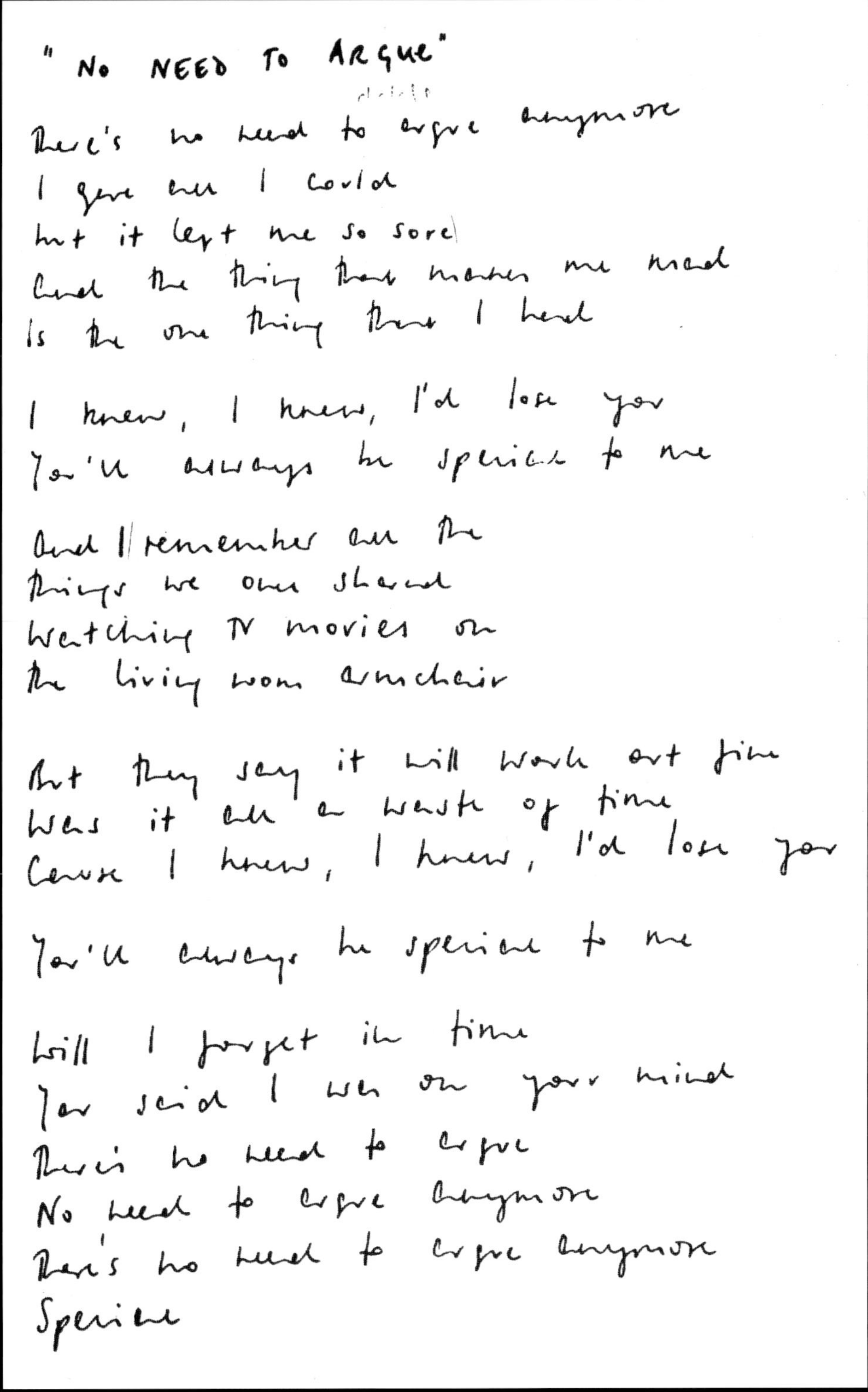
"NO NEED TO ARGUE"

There's no need to argue anymore
I gave all I could
but it left me so sore
And the thing that makes me mad
Is the one thing that I had

I knew, I knew, I'd lose you
You'll always be special to me

And I remember all the
things we once shared
Watching TV movies on
the living room armchair

But they say it will work out fine
Was it all a waste of time
Cause I knew, I knew, I'd lose you

You'll always be special to me

Will I forget in time
You said I was on your mind
There's no need to argue
No need to argue anymore
There's no need to argue anymore
Special

Dolores' handwritten lyrics to 'No Need To Argue'. © Warner Chappell Music, Inc.

O'Riordan knows trauma when she sees it.

'Disappointment', 'Ridiculous Thoughts' and 'I Can't Be With You' say it all about the tone and texture of *No Need To Argue*. When Everyone Else (was) Doing IT ... The Cranberries were too, 'cept, 'doing it' then meant (mainly) juggling with matters of the heart first time 'round, almost always a joyous discovery.

Success has many tentacles though and the 'Berries haven't been too enamoured with a few of its strands. *No Need To Argue* sets its own musical identity firmly alongside its older sibling: O'Riordan's whoops and hollers are still brittle, still stick thin, though seeming to edge an octave higher than they did before. Noel Hogan's trademark electric and acoustic guitars ply the same trade, though this time daring to linger longer past Dolores' vocals. Fact is, it's Fergal Lawler's percussion that's strayed furthest from the flock, lending a subtler scaffold than before, particularly on 'Dreaming My Dreams' and 'Daffodil Lament'.

According to O'Riordan, she's been through the mill both professionally and personally over the past two years, but the changes that've been wrought are largely inside her own head. The voice is pained and fragile, but no more than it was before. She's matured for sure: 'Ode To My Family' has a Keatslike sobriety; 'Twenty One' marks out her territory in the Big People's world; 'No Need To Argue' proclaims with religious conviction her intentions not to dwell on past debacles in the fields of love and war.

Hacks across the water may latch on to the Gregorian chant feel of 'Twenty One' to fill rain forests full of theories on her Catholic upbringing and her early choir singing. The Sinéad O'Connor comparisons could be bolstered by their joint fascination with WB Yeats (Helen of Troy may well be a worthy icon for both of them) and, well, Ph.Ds could be written on the haircuts alone.

But when the screaming and shouting's all over, *No Need To Argue* will sit quite comfortably alongside its predecessor in the family album, the likenesses clear to the eye, the differences less so. Confucius was right. And The Cranberries know it.

***No Need To Argue* album review Siobhán Long, October 1994**

And Now, Ladies & Gentlemen, For The Headline Act...

ONCE YOU GET OVER THE INITIAL AWKWARDNESS, in 'Ode To My Family', of listening to a rock and roll singer thanking her father and mother for all they've given her, you begin to appreciate what a brave thing it is to write something, which could easily be ridiculed as maudlin and self-pitying. That Dolores O'Riordan does actually carry the song off as a convincing expression of gratitude, loss and regret is evidence of just how resolute The Cranberries are.

'Ode To My Family' single review by Patrick Brennan, November 1994

PRIOR TO THEIR RETURN TO HOME TURF for a short Christmas break and their (subsequently re-scheduled) Irish dates, The Cranberries completed their first ever headline tour of America. It is some achievement for a band so young. The hectic, three-month-long US trek saw Limerick's finest musical export since Richard Harris, take their jangly Celtic strains across the length and breadth of the country that gave them their initial breakthrough.

Noel Hogan, guitar player and co-songwriter with the band, spoke to *Hot Press* about their seemingly unstoppable ascent to the premier division of the US rock circuit as well as more important matters, like the creature-comforts success can bring to the drudgery of touring.

"The main difference now is that we have a bigger crew and we stay in much

Reel gone kids: The Samuel Beyer-directed 'Ode To My Family' video shoot.

nicer hotels," he laughs. "It's also great being able to play in decent venues for a change, rather than some of the dodgy clubs we had to do on our first tour over there. We play in theatres mainly now and every venue on the tour was completely sold out – which was great for our first ever headliner. We've been supported by two American bands – Gigolo Aunts and MC 900.

"Apart from that it's been pretty much all go," he adds. "There wasn't much spare time on the tour – when we weren't playing, we were travelling so it's nice to get home for a bit of a break, however short."

Their current unscheduled lay-off notwithstanding, The Cranberries have certainly been busy over the past six months. After a couple of summer festival dates in the US, including an appearance at Woodstock '94, the band toured Europe in the Autumn and kicked off the US tour proper, at the beginning of October. Their second album, *No Need To Argue*, already a multi-million seller, happily made an impact almost immediately – in stark contrast to the prolonged and anxious simmering period they experienced with *Everybody Else Is Doing It, So Why Can't We?*

"It was a lot better the second time around," says Hogan. "It meant that we didn't have to tour for two years just to get the songs heard. Everybody knew who we were already, so it was just a matter of getting the songs out there. After we'd finished recording the first album, we had started writing songs straight away, so we had over two years to get them together and to try them out live."

The American market, being notoriously regional, often means that a band can be huge in one city and almost unknown in another, but according to Hogan there aren't too many parts of the USA which The Cranberries have yet to crack.

"We seem to be equally popular almost everywhere," he says. "Although the big cities like Chicago and San Francisco are particularly mad when we play there and Atlanta is always good for us. We even got to do a gig in Mexico City, which was pretty amazing – they have a population of about 25 million, so it puts it all in context."

CRUCIAL TURNING POINT

Another recent development in The Cranberries camp concerned the band's business affairs and their change of management from Metropolitan to Left Bank – a move which was seen by many as a sign of their increasing influence and muscle within the business. Hogan sees it more as a natural progression, consistent with their higher profile.

"We were moving on a bit from where we started and the truth was, we weren't really happy with the way things were with Metropolitan. We didn't have a binding contract or anything like that, so it was a straightforward move to change over to Left Bank. It really only affects our management in the States anyway, so it won't make much difference to our European operation."

Right now, it seems the band can't do anything wrong commercially. The most successful Irish rock band since U2 – certainly in terms of initial record sales – The Cranberries' enormous success still perplexes many observers in the business because of its sheer scale. There've been dozens of Irish bands over the past ten years with impeccable credentials, huge reputations and major record deals – yet none has hit pay-dirt in the way The Cranberries have. Even Hogan himself is at a loss to explain what his band have that makes them stand so far above the competition.

"No one in America has been able to pinpoint exactly why we're so popular over there," he admits. "We seem to appeal to quite a wide audience which might

> "No one in America has been able to pinpoint exactly why we're so popular over there."

Kids in America: an All Access pass for the US leg of the *No Need To Argue* tour. Photo by Sören Szameitat

surprise people who think of us as an indie-type guitar band. The age-range at concerts is from fifteen to fifty and you see whole families coming to the gigs together... it's very strange!

"Luck definitely played a big part in it," he adds cautiously. "With us, it was a combination of things. Luck, the music, being in the right place at the right time. We just write songs that we like ourselves and if other people like them, fine. But if nobody had bought the album we'd still think they were good songs."

Ironically, the crucial turning point in the band's fortunes came at a time when the future looked decidedly uncertain.

"We were on a tour of Europe with The Hothouse Flowers and we took a week off to do some gigs of our own in England. The album had been out for a while and there seemed to be no interest in it. We were getting really pissed off with our lack of progress. Then, out of the blue, we started getting these phone calls from the States telling us that the album was getting airplay and looked like taking off and asking us to go over there straight away.

"So we did and that was the start of it. We were playing small clubs at the start but they were sold-out and it just grew from that point onwards."

START A FAMILY
Whatever about their popularity across the Atlantic, there is still a sense that The Cranberries have yet to prove themselves on the live front at home. Last year's Féile appearance by the band received a mixed reception from the critics, with many feeling that they lacked somewhat in the energy department. On reflection, Noel Hogan feels that the band probably weren't firing on all cylinders at the time.

"It was just OK," he says. "It probably could have been a lot better. Féile was our first gig in about seven months – we hadn't played since the previous Christmas and we were a bit out of practice. But we're a lot tighter now and we're looking forward to playing in Ireland again."

On the question of the band's immediate future, Dolores O'Riordan is on record as saying that she would like to take some time off to start a family, sooner rather than later. According to Noel Hogan, the band's diary is full for most of 1995 and it will be late next year before they get a break.

"The way things are going, we'll be touring for a long time to come," he concludes. "After the Dublin shows we have the Royal Albert Hall in London, then it's off to Europe, Japan and Australia. In the summer we'll probably be doing the R.E.M. shows and there's talk of doing some Rolling Stones dates in Europe, as well as a few of the big festivals."

It's a dirty job - but somebody's gotta do it.

· Noel Hogan interview by Colm O'Hare, January 1995

"DOLORES *is coming out*, GUNS BLAZING, TEETH GRINDING *and* HEART VIRTUALLY BURSTING *at the seams* WITH ENOUGH MELODRAMA to fire at least half a dozen sessions on Anthony Clare's couch."

View To A Thrill

Beguiled by 'Linger', Simon Le Bon was instrumental in The Cranberries heading out on tour with Duran Duran just as *Everybody Else Is Doing It, So Why Can't We?* was breaking in the States. He talks to Stuart Clark about the Dolores O'Riordan he knew, and introducing her to Princess Diana.

PORTRAIT: STEPHANIE PISTEL

The Cranberries got their first taste of arena rock on October 15, 1993 when they hit the stage in Dayton, Ohio's Ervin J. Nutter Center as tour support to Duran Duran.

By the time they'd said their final "Thank you, goodnight!" just before Christmas in Vancouver, it was clear that when they returned to North America it would be as chart-conquering headliners.

"That was an amazing tour," Simon Le Bon reminisces fondly from his hotel room in Manhattan. "We had a great record, *The Wedding Album*, out and played to a lot of people. We love giving up-and-coming bands an audience to play to, and The Cranberries did an incredible job. They really entertained the Duran Duran fans and won them over."

Shortly before heading out with the Duran Duran (wild) boys, Dolores had told us about how as a teenager her bedroom walls had been decorated with posters of Morten Harket, Nik Kershaw and, yep, Simon Le Bon.

"Ha!" he laughs "As a band they were still in the kid in a sweetshop phase. When I was having a chat with Dolores she told me, 'I go and stand underneath the stage when you're playing 'Ordinary World' and just enter into a dream state.'" Did she seem star-struck?

"Um, no. Dolores held herself in reserve and wasn't a gushing sort of person ever. She was cool. I think the phrase 'still waters run deep' comes to mind when I think of her. She might have been incredibly excited about something, but you could never see it."

There was a bit of a disconnect between the offstage Dolores who liked to keep things low-key and the supremely confident frontwoman who stalked the boards every night making sure that rows A through ZZZ got their money's worth.

"The starting place for an artist's confidence is knowing you've got great songs, which even then The Cranberries had in abundance," Simon reflects. "When we go on stage I always say to the guys, 'Let the songs do the work. All we've got to do is serve them.' When you've got a really great piece of music, it makes standing in front of however big an audience much, much easier. You get the same thrill from it as they do, and once that happens you lose your self-consciousness and just become a conduit for the song. I'd watch The Cranberries from side-of-stage and, once, at the mixing-desk and see that in Dolores, totally."

Simon and Dolores struck up a firm friendship and, invited in 1995 to be part of Pavarotti's Children of Bosnia concert in Italy, decided to perform 'Linger' together.

"Bono, The Edge, Meat Loaf and Michael Bolton also performed so it was an incredible line-up," he resumes. "It was one of those 'leave your egos at the stage-door' nights. Everyone was focused on the reasons for being there and some lasting friendships were made.

"As an artist your first songs – which are the purest, the most innocent, the most naïve – are often your best. 'Linger', which is what turned me onto Dolores and The Cranberries, has all those qualities. I'm still a huge fan of that song. I asked her if she'd be up for doing it, she said she was, we rehearsed and it sounded bloody brilliant, it really did."

Accompanied by Michael Kamen and L'Orchestra

The Italian job: (l-r) Brian Eno, Bono, Zucchero, Dolores, The Edge and Simon Le Bon at the 1995 Pavarotti & Friends concert. **Opposite**: Dolores rocking Atlanta in 1994 by Jim Leatherman.

Filarmonica di Torino, their Parco Novi Sad, Modena duet made it onto the *Pavarotti & Friends Together For The Children Of Bosnia* highlights album.

"I picked up on not only the melody and the words, but also the intonation – the way Dolores kind of swung around a note like how you swing around a lamppost. I could feel how it plucked at the heartstrings. I tried not to impersonate Dolores and still be me up there whilst honouring the emotional impact of the song. It's a proper duet in that it really was the sum of our two voices."

If ever there was a time to be scared witless about performing it was that balmy evening in Modena.

"She never said to me 'I'm frightened'," Simon states. "There were nerves but you accept them when you're a performer. It's what stokes you up. It's not fear; it's adrenaline. It's your mind and your body ramping up to make you do something extraordinary. Dolores accepted that.

"We helped each other on stage," he continues. "When I needed support I looked at Dolores and when she needed support she looked at me. We were a good team."

No matter how far or for how long The Cranberries strayed from home, Dolores' accent always remained proudly, defiantly Limerick.

"That line: *'I'm just a fool for you...'* The way she sings it makes your ears prick and gets through any armour," Simon reflects. You know *exactly* what Dolores meant when she sang that and the accent is a really important part of what makes it work."

Dolores' night in northern Italy became even more surreal as she also performed a haunting 'Ave Maria' with Pavarotti and got to shoot the backstage breeze with one of Simon's old pals, Princess Diana.

"I think I took Dolores to meet her that night. Diana knew me from years back – we played the Prince's Trust in front of her and Charles in 1983. Dolores loved the whole buzz of that night."

It was clear talking to her that Dolores regarded Simon as both an elder brother and, in terms of the work/family balance he'd managed to strike, a role model.

"Yeah, I think you're right," he agrees. "I felt that there was a good bond. We talked about family, relationships, love affairs, partners. Dolores really helped me with something, so it went both ways."

Dolores was also very impressed with how Yasmin Le Bon managed to be a total hands-on mum to three kids whilst maintaining her modelling career.

"That would make sense, yeah," Simon nods. "Fame was just part of the job for her and I think she was very, very well adjusted to that job. She was equipped to deal with it. I personally wonder if she fell in love with the right person, but I don't know and I'm not passing judgment on that. The only question I'd have is, 'Did she have the support she needed all the time?'"

Simon's face breaks into a big smile when I mention Dolores' bawdy sense of humour and a willful streak as long as the Shannon.

"Absolutely, that comes from being part of a big family," he concludes. "She had a composure and confidence in her own inner strength, 100%. Dolores wouldn't take shit from anybody and she didn't have to make a big noise about it. She was very capable of saying 'no' – or rather, 'no, thank you.' Dolores was always impeccably mannered and just a really, really nice person."

· Simon Le Bon in conversation with Stuart Clark, July 2021

"The way DOLORES KIND OF SWUNG AROUND A NOTE like how you SWING AROUND A LAMPPOST. I could feel how it PLUCKED AT THE HEARTSTRINGS."

When We Were Young

Given the scale of the success of their first two albums, by 1996 The Cranberries seemed to have the potential to eclipse even U2 in the Irish megastar stakes. However, the backlash that greeted their third album, *To The Faithful Departed*, was an eye-opener, putting the band under a different kind of pressure than anything they'd experienced to date. In *Hot Press*, we felt it was a good time to look back to the early days in Limerick, as well as capturing the spirit of what was a difficult moment for the quartet.

Opposite photo courtesy of Melodie McDaniel

DON'T LOOK BACK IN ANGER

These have been turbulent times for The Cranberries. In a powerful and revealing feature, Stuart Clark talks about early stirrings and present controversies to Dolores O'Riordan and Fergal Lawler as well as friends and supporters from those vital early days in the Treaty City.

The first time I had an in-depth chat with Dolores O'Riordan was in 1990 at Limerick's Glentworth Bar. Just 18 and celebrating passing her Leaving Cert exams, she was making serious in-roads into a pint of Guinness and wondering whether or not she should put college on hold, to hook up with the scruffy-looking individuals calling themselves The Cranberry Saw Us. I doubt whether me telling her that they were a nice bunch of lads and she should give it a whirl had much bearing on Dolores' decision to go for the rock 'n' roll option, but at least it demonstrates that for once in my journalistic life I was in the right place at the right time — witnessing the band as they went from the humblest of support band origins to selling upwards of 15 million albums.

Naturally, success has its price and in The Cranberries' case that's involved having to do much of their growing up under the watchful – and often spiteful – eye of the media. Like Sinéad O'Connor before her, O'Riordan discovered pretty early on in her superstar odyssey that the tabloids reserve their worst abuse for women. Within weeks of *Everybody Else Is Doing It, So Why Can't We?* crashing into the American charts, our super, soaraway chums had embarked on a crusade to expose the real Dolores.

These penetrating and, naturally, painstakingly researched psychological profiles soon revealed the poor girl to be a victim of multi-personality disorder. In one piece she'd be depicted as a naive little airhead having her strings pulled by record company puppetmasters, and in the next a calculating minx who'd hand over her pet puppy for vivisection if it meant advancing her career. Add to that 'reports' of temper tantrums, manic depression and a spot of anorexia and, wow, hold the front page.

There was, however, a minor problem with these stories. Most of them were complete bollocks.

"I used to think, 'Oh, their sources are wrong', but now I honestly reckon they make it up hoping you won't sue, which normally you don't because it's too much hassle," reflects reformed scruff Fergal Lawler. "I've read stuff about Dolores supposedly having a nervous breakdown on tour and know it's not true because she's sitting beside me with a big smile on her face, looking forward to the next gig.

"Journalists are always saying, 'You must resent the attention she gets', but no way would I want my life to be examined in the same minute detail hers is. Really, she's in a no-win situation. If she puts up with it she's made out to be a brainless bimbo, and if she argues the toss she's a bitch."

Speaking on The Cranberries' first day back at work after the Christmas holidays, Fergal Lawler probably didn't realise just how prophetic his words were to become. Unless you've been residing in a sensory-deprivation tank, you can't fail to have noticed that Dolores has been making the headlines for all the wrong reasons over the past month.

First there was the ex-boyfriend threatening to sue over allegations that he used to beat her up; then a £5,000 cheque and public apology from *The Daily Sport*, who'd falsely accused her of going on stage in Germany *sans* underwear; and now a High Court writ taken out in London, which prevents the publication of an article apparently written about her by an American journalist.

That her demonisation by the press has affected Dolores is clearly underlined in 'The Picture I View', the B-side of their next single, which includes the lines, *"I haven't changed, but my life has/ People are strange when it's like as/ I did something wrong to them/ And I don't even know your name."*

Is the song autobiographical?

"I guess you could say it's speculative," Dolores proffers cryptically. "There's also another bit that goes, *'I swear that he looks out for me/ And I swear that he's good'*, which is a sort of reply to those people who thought, 'She's only marrying this Canadian guy because she's insecure and wants someone to look after her'. That and, 'Oh, she must be pregnant'. The way it happened is that we fell in lust, then we fell in love and decided we wanted to spend the rest of our lives together. I suppose I knew after the first week that it was more than a fling and, sitting here now, I can hand on heart say I've never felt happier. I know the 'poor little rich girl' theory is far more intriguing but, sorry, it's not true."

Judging by the look that comes over her face every time her husband's name is mentioned, things on the marital front are progressing A-OK. Having spent the festive season playing surrogate mum to Don's four year-old in Canada, Mr and Mrs Burton are now looking forward to the completion of the house they're having built for them in Kerry, which should be ready by June. The trouble with domestic bliss, though, is that it doesn't sell newspapers.

"I'm sure they're looking forward to the trial separation and the divorce battle — and maybe even the custody wrangle — but I'm afraid they're going to have to wait for a while," she laughs mischievously. "Unless, of course, there's something Don hasn't told me."

When she laughs, all traces of wariness someone in her position inevitably feels when talking to the press slip away. Six years of constant hard slog and a bank balance that would impress even the likes of Michael Smurfit are bound to have some effect on a person's character, but in Dolores' case it's still easy to recognise the precocious teenager I went drinking with at the Glentworth.

"The key to all of this," she confides, "is learning how to cope with it. There are a lot of very fucked-up rich people around. In fact, I was halfway to becoming one myself before I got married.

"The worst period was when the first album charted in America and I started getting these letters saying, 'We decided

VOL 20 NO 8 • 1 May 1996
PRICE £1.95 (INCLUDING TAXES)

TREADING ON TOES
THE MICHAEL FLATLEY INTERVIEW
by Joe Jackson

HOT PRESS

The Secret History of The Cranberries

Interview and report: Stuart Clark

Exclusive: **A Sneak Preview of Neil Jordan's Michael Collins!**

The Divine Comedy · Joe Ely · Paul Westerberg · Carl Cox
And introducing: **The A to Z of Weird Sex!**

"The key to all of this, is learning how to cope with it. There are a lot of very fucked-up rich people around."

to get married because of this song you wrote and you've made us so happy', and I'm thinking, 'Why can't I have some of that?'. There I was, supposedly providing the answers, and I was even more confused and vulnerable than them. At the time, I thought I was heading for the loony-bin, but now I realise it as the transitionary period that anyone my age – and faced with those pressures – goes through."

The flagship single from their *To The Faithful Departed* album, 'Salvation', makes no bones about where The Cranberries stand on the drugs issue, but was Dolores ever tempted at her greatest times of stress to indulge in the old showbiz sherbet?

"No, never," she insists with a shake of her freshly number-twoed head. "When you've seen people, like I have, face-down

You can't argue with that: The Cranberries' RIAA Award for selling five million copies of their second album in the States. Photo by Sören Szameitat. **Opposite:** The band shot in 1996 by *Rolling Stone*'s Mark Seliger.

in pools of their own vomit, you soon realise that drugs are the last thing that are going to solve your problems. I'm not going to mention names because, at the end of the day, it's their business, not mine, but I've seen a lot of perfectly good careers fucked up by cocaine and heroin.

"I suppose where I was a bit naive was when we first went on the road and there'd be these dodgy looking characters hanging around backstage who knew the promoter, or knew the crew, but didn't actually do anything. When you're starting out you have to accept it because you need the gig more than the gig needs you, but now if they're not gotten rid of, we don't play. Simple."

O'Riordan admits that her new-found militancy has been inspired, in part, by renowned take-no-shit merchants like Bono and Simon Le Bon, who are both on the other end of the phone if she ever needs a bit of a gee-up.

"What I admire about Simon and Bono – apart from their success, which has been pretty spectacular – is the fact that despite all the madness, they've managed to remain happily married and raise a family. Yasmin's brilliant as well, because while the normal thing in the supermodel world is once you have a child your career's over, she's had four kids and, when she was ready, just strolled back to the top of her profession."

Which prompts the question of whether or not Dolores will be seeking record company permission before starting her own brood?

"I will, me bollix," is the swift and unequivocal answer.

"Obviously, with me being married and Mike and Ferg engaged, it was necessary for us to sit down before the tour for this album was planned and discuss how we were going to offset our private lives against our professional ones. We're going to be on the road for at least 18 months, so, as of this precise moment, there are no plans for any of us to either get or make somebody else pregnant. I don't know, maybe that'll change. And if it does, it'll be down to us to decide how we deal with it – not management, not Billy up the road and certainly not the record company."

With all the other baggage surrounding them, it's easy to forget that The Cranberries have, on occasions, been known to make the odd record.

No Need To Argue – 10 million copies sold and counting – may be a hard act to follow but in *To The Faithful Departed*, the band have produced what is without doubt their most musically ambitious collection of songs yet.

"The best thing about *Everyone Else Is Doing It, So Why Can't We?* being such a big hit was when it came to making *No Need To Argue* and this album, no one from Island came near us until the final week," resumes Fergal. "We were a bit worried that they'd object to us changing producers – if it's not broken etc., etc. – but when we said we wanted to bring in Bruce Fairbairn, their attitude was, 'OK, it's your record.'

"We'll always be grateful to Stephen (Street) for what he did for us, but towards the end of *No Need To Argue*, there were things we were trying to explain to him that he couldn't get."

Such as?

"The rhythm section. We wanted the drums and the bass to have a rougher feel, but the way Stephen put 'em down, they were too light and soft. It really hit home when we went out on tour and people said we sounded much better live. So, this time, we put down the rough tracks in three or four takes, and had the whole album completed in less than a month."

Having been aware of The Cranberries in their infancy –

It's not really a black and white issue, is it? Photo by Andy Earl.

"The Pixies wouldn't have shifted nearly as many albums as us, but I still wouldn't consider myself fit to lick Black Francis' boots."

indeed I was rewarded with a bottle of Mr. Daniel's finest for helping mail out their first demo – I feel well qualified to shatter the myth that O'Riordan would have made it with or without the lads.

To begin with, it was their band she joined, not vice versa – something which Dolores herself hasn't forgotten. There's also the small matter of Noel writing the key songs that broke them and Ferg and Mike possessing the musical world-view that O'Riordan certainly lacked when she first hopped up on stage.

"It's a case, really, of us coming at it from different angles," Lawler continues, "Dolores started singing in church and at school, whereas we were your typical indie kids into the Pixies and The Breeders, who wanted to be in a band and get signed to 4AD. That's why, to this day, I want The Cranberries to be credible, as well as selling shit-loads of records. And I honestly think that if *To The Faithful Departed* was coming out on 4AD or Sub Pop, we'd get far better reviews in the indie press than we do now."

"Yeah," Noel Hogan concurs, "I don't see why we should have to apologise for being successful, particularly as we're not the type of group who says, 'We're better than them because we sell more records'. The Pixies wouldn't have shifted nearly as many albums as us, but I still wouldn't consider myself fit to lick Black Francis' boots."

While Hogan and Lawler both baulk at the prospect, there's a very real danger that, ready or not, *To The Faithful Departed* will catapult them into the stadium league. Besides 'Salvation', there are at least half a dozen other songs that could make it to the outerextremities of the bleachers. Where's their precious credibility going to be then, eh?

"It's not so much being frightened by the idea, as wondering whether we're ready for it yet," Fergal resumes. "I think to play a stadium you need a catalogue of six or seven albums to choose from, otherwise you're going to have to include songs that don't work in that kind of setting. That's why in places like Boston and Chicago, we're going to try and do two or three amphitheatre shows, rather than one huge one, where the crowd are dots on the horizon."

On *To The Faithful Departed*, nine of the 13 cuts deal with loss, death and loneliness in all its myriad forms. Not exactly

nun to

there
these
people
e. Her
blame
him.
g and
I was
rd the
epted,
ith."
eople
ng in
that I
with
They
ower
Cert
n six

efore
knees
big

ping
bably
and
se?'"
ut of
case.

and
ding
itled
if I
ause

only
alue,
got

n the
kets
tter
ame
se it

ting
ones

for Th
gig at
just n

"I w
origi
Cran
Dolo
who'
three
The t
playe
own
man

"Ar
own
front
until
from
whit
for i
pare
Sept

Lo
of tl
have
and
O'D

De
colo
dow
Cru
rec

"B
mus
The
was
reh
in e

"T
bet
pro
alw

"F
mo
Dov

106

Above: The Cranberries arriving home at Shannon Airport
in December 1993 by Dermot Lynch/*Limerick Leader*

"So, after duly trotting out our stuff which she thought, yeah, she could do something with, she plugged in her keyboard and announced she was going to do a Sinéad O'Connor cover. Before she'd got halfway through the first verse, everyone's jaw was hanging down.

"Even afterwards, though, Mike still had his doubts. He agreed she had a great voice but kept going 'look at the fucking state of her, you can't put that on stage.' But they stuck with it and the rest, as they say, is history."

Dolores is adamant that even if the shiny pink tracksuit had cost her the audition, she'd still be making a living out of music.

"If the lads hadn't given me the gig, I'd probably have done my Leaving Cert and gone off to find a band in Dublin or London," she muses. "At first my parents were like, 'Umm, who are these guys?', but then they came round the house one afternoon and they realised they were relatively harmless."

Within a month of her joining, Dolores had co-conspired with Noel Hogan to write the two songs which eventually led to The Cranberries cracking America — 'Dreams' and 'Linger'.

"Before Dolores arrived on the scene, The Cranberries were very much the junior band in Limerick," recalls former They Do It With Mirrors drummer Damian Clifford. "The scene back then was actually very healthy. We'd just about done a deal with Setanta to go over to England, A Touch Of Oliver were in a similar position with Bar None in the States and The Hitchers were regularly getting 300 or 400 people at their gigs.

"To be honest, when Niall left we all thought they'd fold, but then they found Dolores and recorded a demo which was far, far better than it had a right to be. The bastards had only been together a matter of weeks and they'd come up with two hit singles!"

As adept as they were in the studio, The»

Back To School

No matter how much a fan loves the music, no matter how many gigs they go to, they can never get beyond the surface of the performer. But if we're talking character analysis, it helps to rewind to the late '80s, when Dolores O'Riordan was a pupil at Laurel Hill school.

The observation in one of *To The Faithful Departed*'s stand-out tracks, 'The Rebels', that *"We wear Doc Martens in the sun/ Drinking vintage cider, having fun"*, certainly strikes a chord with fellow ex-pupil, Nicole Dunphy.

"Everyone at Laurel Hill — and there was near enough a thousand of us — knew Dolores," she laughs. "This thing about her being shy and timid is absolute rubbish. I'll always remember being new in First Year and Dolores, who was 13 or 14 and in Third Year, bursting into the classroom to introduce herself. There was no reason why she should have done it, other than that we were sort of her babies.

"There was another time she ran in wanting to borrow a tie because she was late and had been told by whoever was on the gate to report to Sister Catherine. The school had a strict dress code and she was always getting into trouble for having too many earrings and Docs. Docs were the big thing back then, partly because the teachers hated them.

"I don't know what her grades were like, but Laurel Hill was generally regarded as having the highest academic standards in Limerick, and to get into the Irish 'A' School, you had to be pretty bright."

O'Riordan's first chance to wow all and sundry with her vocal prowess was as Sister Eileen's star pupil in the Laurel Hill choir.

"She got a solo spot most times there was a school service," Dunphy continues. "Two songs I remember her doing absolutely

School daze: Dolores in her Laurel Hill year photo.

brilliantly were 'A íosa' and 'Canagaí Amhrán' ."

Dolores' own memories of those far-off, convent school days are fairly similar.

"I was a prefect in First Year but then I was caught dossing and they never asked me again," she chuckles. "The school was in the city and I was from the country, so I was a bit different to some of the other girls, but nobody was too snobby. With us knowing Simon Le Bon so well, I had to confess to Don recently that my big pin-ups then were Duran Duran. He took it quite well. Nik Kershaw was another and that guy out of A-Ha, Morten Harket, he was cute too."

In those days, O'Riordan's nocturnal activities were confined to the very occasional youth club disco, with her elder brothers on hand to guard against any over-enthusiastic male attention.

"They were very, very protective. But in a nice way. Looking out for me."

By the time she graduated to hanging out in bars with journalists — albeit local ones whose influence barely stretched down the road — Dolores was well able to hold her own in company. My first impressions were of a bright, bubbly girl, whose ability to take a slag was matched by the gusto with which she dispensed them. Flirty in a mischievous rather than a sexual sort of way, she was no less clued-up than any other girl of her age, except maybe in one area. Music.

"I remember mentioning all these different bands to her," recalls Eugene Larkin, "and getting some extremely blank looks in return. A lot of people back then thought she sounded like that woman in The Sundays, Harriet Wheeler, but Dolores

had no idea who they were." (Hopefully that will lay rest the old canard about Dolores being influenced by The Sundays! - Ed.)

As the local roadie-about-town, Larkin was called in to organise the crew for the revamped Cranberries' first gig in Ruby's, the dingy basement nightclub in Cruise's Hotel, which made for a somewhat incongruous rock venue.

"I've never, my whole time in the business, seen anyone even remotely that nervous," he recalls. "Dolores spent the entire set looking at her feet, the ceiling, the drumkit — in fact, anything apart from the crowd. She'd sound brilliant for half a song and then have another panic attack and go completely out of tune.

"Fair play to her, though, she got through it and the next time I saw her in town, she wouldn't shut up about this now being all she wanted to do. You don't really see her in Limerick anymore, so I don't know if she's changed, but back then she was a nice lass."

That affability may have been tempered by one journalistic hatchet-job too many but otherwise, judging by today's encounter, she still is. The barriers are up when the interview starts but mention of the fact that my girlfriend is another Laurel Hill past pupil and 11 years my junior, brings them crashing down.

"You dirty old man," she shrieks with delight. "You're as bad as Don. He's nine years older than me and keeps saying he's going to trade me in for a newer model. Jeez, Stuart, go for it!"

Same as ever it was.

Cranberries initially had serious problems doing the business live. Their first Dolores-fied gig was downstairs at Cruise's Hotel and as promoter Bob O'Connell recalls, it proved to be very much a qualified success.

"From the point of view of getting up on stage and completing their set, they did well because Dolores was sick beforehand with nerves. It was a Leaving Cert results night with The Cranberries playing support to They Do It With Mirrors and I guess there were 60 or 70 people there which, as the venue was so small, meant it was stuffed. I didn't actually see them myself because I was too busy running around organising things, but I'm told Dolores basically spent the whole gig devising ways of not having to look at the crowd. Musically, though, the comments were virtually all favourable."

"It wasn't just Dolores who was shitting herself," reveals the stage manager that night, Eugene Larkin. "Noel, for example, had to be convinced that it really would be better if he didn't play behind the drumkit and apart from Ferg, who was a bit of a lad, I can't remember any of them grunting more than the odd word.

"What I do remember, however, is that they played an absolutely wonderful version of 'Linger' which, so legend has it, was about a former boyfriend of Dolores', Woggie, who was this mad Jesus & The Mary Chain fan from Glasgow."

"She may have gone through agonies up there," Bob O'Connell resumes, "but I remember meeting Dolores the next day outside Supermac's and her saying, 'I'm doing nothing else for the rest of my life. 'Tis a great job!'"

Having survived their baptism of fire at Cruise's, The Cranberries became almost omnipresent on the Limerick live circuit, using these gigs and a constant stream of demo tapes to seduce, among others, freelance journalist and talent scout Jim Carroll.

"I first came into the picture at the tail end of 1990," he explains. "I was doing A&R at the time for the English indie label, Dedicated, and started hearing rumours about this amazing band from Limerick called The Cranberries.

"Word had it they were meant to be signing to Rough Trade but knowing how these things can fall through, I decided I might as well go down and check 'em out. That would have been in the middle of January 1991 when they played at the University of Limerick Stables Club. It's a big L-shaped venue and I'd say of the 200 or 300 people who were there a maximum of 40 were watching the band.

"How did they sound? Dead cool. Really fresh and exciting and unlike anything that was going on at the time in Dublin. It was obvious that they knew fuck all about stage projection, but the fact that it wasn't contrived only added to the charm.

"Apart from myself," Carroll continues, "the only other industry people there were Olan MacGowan from Sony and RTÉ's Colm O'Callaghan who wrote a review of the gig for *Hot Press*."

That he did, wrapping up a suitably glowing testimonial to the band's youthful talents with the assertion that, "The Cranberries are twenty of your sweetest dreams and an unending walk down Paradise Way." Mills & Boon, eat your heart out!

"Colm, I know, loved 'em," Carroll concurs, "and Olan was relieved that, finally, here was a young Irish pop group that had absolutely no interest in being the new U2. In that respect, they fell into the same 'culchies with attitude' bracket as the Franks and Sultans who were both starting to take off big time in Cork and had a similar lack of respect for the stadium rock brigade."

The value of The Cranberries' stock increased sharply with the release of *Nothing Left At All,* a Gilmore-financed five-track cassette EP which was the cause of much salivating in British A&R circles.

As someone who had numerous encounters with the band in their infancy, would Jim Carroll say that The Cranberries were just a little too wide-eyed and innocent when they started out?

"Yes, they were in some ways incredibly naive, but no more so than any other bunch of 19-year olds removed from the so-called 'music centres' of the world, who suddenly find themselves being courted by the international A&R community. But – and this is an important but – they were bright kids who only had to be told things once to understand how they worked."

The band may have been too busy working on the songs that later made up their *Everybody Else Is Doing It, So Why Can't We?* album to realise, but beyond the confines of the studio the battle for their signatures was reaching fever pitch.

"Pearse copped that if Dedicated and Imago were that interested in the band," Carroll proffers, "there was a fair chance the majors would be too, and he was proved right in April when The Cranberries played a University of Limerick Rag Week gig in this huge barn-like venue called the Jetland.

"I'd never encountered anything like it – well, not since An Emotional Fish. Sitting in Jury's beforehand, I counted twenty-five A&R people and those are just the ones I recognised. I'd heard through the grapevine that Island were favourites to get 'em and, sure enough, Denny Cordell was at the Jetland and the Cork Rocks gig they did at Sir Henry's two or three weeks later. Geoff Travis – who, of course, ended up becoming their manager when Pearse Gilmore left the fold – was also in Cork making a last ditch attempt to sign them to Blanco Y Negro, but by then Denny had pretty much sewn up the deal."

Back in 1996, Dolores O'Riordan is in almost indecently good form, looking forward to going out on the road and *giving it some* after an eight-month break from gigging.

"At first it was a relief to stop," she acknowledges, "but then

"At first it was a relief to stop, but then you start missing the buzz of travelling to different places and the sense of family you get from hanging out with the same close-knit group of people, day after day."

you start missing the buzz of travelling to different places and the sense of family you get from hanging out with the same close-knit group of people, day after day. It's not just the lads I miss but Sett, our tour manager, and Dekko, our roadie, who are both from Limerick and as much a part of The Cranberries as we are.

"There was a time on the last tour when I thought, 'Jeez, I can't keep this up', but one of the luxuries of being successful is that you can say, 'Right, we'll do the year-and-a-half long world tour but for every three months on the road, we want two weeks off to chill out."

Kicking off last week in that notorious rock'n'roll hotspot, Bangkok, The Cranberries' latest circumnavigation of the globe will take them well into 1997 with Irish dates provisionally pencilled in for next January. Contrary to popular tabloid opinion, certain members of the entourage won't be travelling first-class while the others go economy.

"If I'm feeling tired," Dolores explains, "I'll sometimes travel to a gig by plane while they take the tour bus, but that's as much their decision as it is mine. The lads were friends long before The Cranberries started, so it's understandable that they're going to hang out together while I spend more of my time with Don who, after all, is my husband.

"Some journalist made a big deal of us having separate dressing-rooms which is so fucking stupid. Does he really expect me to get undressed every night in front of three blokes and their mates? Maybe he hasn't noticed, but I'm a woman."

An anorexic one, as some gossip has it?

"No," she replies, a tad wearily. "When The Cranberries started I was 18 and still had my puppy fat but as soon as I hit 20, boom, it all dropped off and everyone started saying 'Oh, she's fucked up, she's not eating properly'. This was when we were halfway through a six-month tour and jumping around on stage every night for an hour. You have to be reasonably fit to do that."

OK, your sympathy for anyone who's got – last estimate – £10 million stashed away in the bank may on occasion be measured, but there are times listening to O'Riordan on the defensive, that you have to feel sorry for her.

"If it was the music they were slagging off, fine," asserts Fergal Lawler, "but some of the personal stuff – particularly here and in the UK – has been totally over the top. When she got married, there were these whispers about Don but he's great, thumbs up all the way.

"We definitely have an easier time of things than she does. For instance, we can walk down the street, pretty much anywhere in the world, and no one knows who the fuck we are. And if you do get recognised, it's usually, 'Hi, can we have your autograph?', rather than, 'My boyfriend's left me and I know you understand because you wrote *blah, blah, blah* in one of your songs'. That sort of thing can get pretty heavy."

Our colonial cousins have been a little kinder, but on this side of the Atlantic, the band's latest offering has been ripped apart with the sort of frenzy normally reserved for the Dublin Zoo lion's enclosure at feeding time.

The main target of this journalistic vitriol has been O'Riordan's lyrics which, well intentioned or not, aren't always of Shakesperean depth.

Examples? How about, *"With a Smith & Wesson/ John Lennon's life was no longer a debate"*, from 'I Just Shot John Lennon; or, *"Bosnia was so unkind, Sarajevo changed my mind/ And we all call out in despair, all the love we need isn't there/ And as we all sing songs in our room, Sarajevo erects another tomb"*, from, you've guessed it, 'Bosnia'.

Hasn't Ferg ever been tempted to tap Dolores on the shoulder and say, "Hang on a sec"?

"To tell you the truth, I've never come across anything I've objected to," he insists. "The lyrics are very special to her, they're what's on her mind and that's the way it should be because she's the one who has to sing them. If there was something I really disagreed with, I'd tell her but it hasn't come up."

Honestly?

"Yeah. The lyrics — whatever context they're in — are basically just Dolores' perception of what she sees or what she reads in the paper. She doesn't have to be a politician and get all the facts right. It's her gut reaction and people are free to agree or disagree with what she says."

In the end, it'll be the fans who vote with their wallets, and here's one punter willing to stake his shirt on *To The Faithful Departed* continuing The Cranberries' multi-platinum exploits.

As many a wise philosopher has said down through the centuries, fuck the begrudgers!

· Dolores O'Riordan and Fergal Lawler interview and Cranberries history by Stuart Clark, May 1996

KEVIN BARRY *On The Cranberries*

HEART OF THE CITY

Before becoming a multi-award winning author, Kevin Barry was a frequenter of biker
bars, sticky carpeted nightclubs and grotty bedsits. He paints a vivid picture of the
'80s Limerick that produced The Cranberries.

PHOTO: LOUISE MANIFOLD

Fergal, Mike and Noel would have been a year behind me at CBS Sexton Street, which is one of the Limerick secondary schools.

Sixth years would never have deigned to talk to fifth years, but we'd have nodded at each other because we had music and tragic indie haircuts in common.

The demographic make-up of CBS in the '80s was two-thirds working-class background from around the inner city – sort of Hyde Road out towards Ballinacurra where I was from. The rest were lads from the country who were good hurlers.

My most vivid memory of the place is robbing flowers from the school chapel to throw at Morrissey's feet when The Smiths played The Savoy in November 1984. 'What Difference Did It Make?' was just out as a single, so it was fairly early on in The Smiths' rise and at best there were two hundred people there. James were the support and, at the time, a much hipper band than The Smiths with a travelling following of two dozen of the coolest Mancunian kids you'd ever seen. We were in awe watching and learning the dance moves. My synapses haven't snapped back in enough to recall if any of the Cranberries lads were there, Dolores definitely wasn't, but it was a seminal moment in Limerick rock history. I've talked to so many people who saw The Smiths on that tour – they also played in Dublin, Galway, Cork, Letterkenny, Coleraine and Belfast – and the next week went and started their own bands because of it. It's

what us older cats would have called the 'punk DIY ethos'. You don't need to be a big rock band signed to a huge label to make great music. You can do it at a more local level, print your flyers and then play in the Flag Café, which is where the first Cranberry Saw Us gig was. The Flag was this cooperative place down around the art college, which was rammed with forty people in it.

Limerick back then had the reputation of being a tough city and it was thoroughly deserved. There was absolutely an atmosphere on the streets, which isn't there now. It reminded me of Liverpool where I lived for three years in the noughties – no-nonsense port towns and, outside fried chicken joints in the small hours of the morning, not always fluffy. It had this dark side, especially down by the docks, which made it absolutely apt to have Joy Division on your Walkman walking around the place.

The battering I received near one of those chicken joints was entirely of my own making. Myself and my pal Dave thought we were being hilarious shouting abuse from across the road at these two rugby types who were coming out of Ted's, a nightclub that none of us scruffy urchins would have wanted to go or indeed been let into. They came over and thumped the shit out of us. It took about thirty seconds for it to register, but then it stopped in any way being funny.

My preferred alternatives to fried chicken joints were Friar Tuck's, which was for connoisseurs of the curry chip and Papa Gino's, a tiny pizza joint opposite the Vintage Club. I can still taste the tuna!

"That's the SIGNATURE SENSUAL FEELING of
THE 1980's – FAG INTO THE GAS FIRE!"

*

"Like many others my first pint was in Costello's Tavern, where you demanded your money back if by the end of the night The Smiths hadn't been played five times."

Above: Noel, Mike and Ferg were Costello's Tavern regulars. **Right:** The Cranberries with Mayor of Limerick, Jan O'Sullivan, at their 1993 Civic Reception. Photo: *Limerick Leader*.

Like many others my first pint was in Costello's Tavern, where you demanded your money back if by the end of the night The Smiths hadn't been played five times. It was impossible to fall over in there because the floor was so sticky and there was never toilet roll in the loos because they were constantly being nicked by people before going back to their grotty bedsit flats.

I was trying to get a sense of those '80s bedsits for a story I was writing, and came up with "You weren't there unless you remember trying to light a fag off a Calor Kosangas Superser heater at five in the morning and singeing your eyebrows!" That's the signature sensual feeling of the 1980s – fag into the gas fire!

The pub you went to in Limerick said more about you than words ever could. Mine was Buddie's, this motorcycle outlaw bar on Fox's Bow in the middle of town. If you were an impressionable twenty-year-old with chemical inclinations, walking down the lane to Buddie's felt like you were in Oakland, California. The hogs arrayed outside in the evening sun, sky-high psychedelic murals on the wall and people only too eager to sell you five old Irish pounds worth of cannabis resin, often from the Lebanon.

The jukebox blasting out of Fox's Bow was spectacular and pretty open-minded – while into their Black Sabbath and other classic '70s rock and metal, the lads with the Harleys weren't adverse to some hip-hop or indie stuff.

You'd hear of the occasional difficulties with rival motorcycle clubs, but I never saw any violence there.

In fact, I'd go as far to say that most of the time the mood was mellow.

Every Friday after working in the *Limerick Tribune* and then the *Limerick Post* it was straight down to Buddie's for a bottle of Newcastle Brown Ale and a five-spot, which eventually went up to a ten-spot but, hey, that's inflation for you.

Town back then had a very sort of analogue flavour. There were no mobile phones so you'd duck into a bar to see if there was anyone in there you knew and duck out again if there wasn't. The White House was good if you were planning on getting trashed – many a lunchtime sharpener was had in there – and The Vintage Club on Ellen Street was a big music heads pub. You had a good chance of spotting the Cranberries lads there before going round the corner to gig in Cruise's, which is another place they played a few times.

There were some quite big shows like Ned's Atomic Dustbin and The Wedding Present out in the Parkway, and smaller ones in The Stables, which was the University of Limerick campus bar.

I started a European Studies course at UL – the diplomatic career alas never materialised – but left after a week-and-a-half when the *Tribune* offered me a job, which were like hen's teeth back then. I remember going to my college advisor and him saying: "Run, don't walk!" I was told at the time that I was the quickest ever dropout and I'm clinging to that.

I don't remember a whole lot about my first Cranberries gig – doubtless I'd been to Buddie's beforehand – other

than that as soon as Dolores opened her mouth and started singing I thought, "Superstar!" A lot of young artists can write and play really well but they don't have the 'wow' factor she did. Dolores was extremely charismatic on stage.

There'd been a tendency in Limerick towards stadium rock, but The Cranberries would have been influenced by the likes of the Pixies who were the band you played while lighting your fags off the gas fire.

As I was saying earlier, I'm fetishistic about bands playing in grotty hotel basements to their mates, getting really good and suddenly against all the odds taking on the world, which is what Dolores and the guys did.

Another of my dubious claims to fame is that I recorded in the same studio, Xeric on Lord Edward Street, as The Cranberries did. I'd go into the booth once a week quaking with fear and say, "This Thursday in the *Limerick Tribune* read my *City Limits* column…" I probably used the same microphone as Dolores did!

An early gig I have far clearer memories of is The Cranberries in Cork. I was down for the *Thursday Night Sweat* rave gig in Sir Henry's and they were playing in The Village next-door. One of the local music heads, Shane Fitzsimons, said, "G'wan, let's sneak in for ten minutes" so we did and found a roomful of people with their jaws hanging thinking, "Fuck, this is the real deal!"

Unlike Liverpool, what Limerick had in the '80s/early '90s was a sense of cultural inferiority. If you were in any way creative the first thing you'd have thought when you left school was "How do I get my arse out of here?" Galway up and Cork down the road seemed like far more Bohemian places. I used to go to Galway a lot at the weekends and eat packets of Cheese & Onion Tayto on the bus as a defence mechanism against nuns sitting next to me. On a humid sort of June day they'd ward anybody off.

That complex has completely disappeared now thanks in no small part to The Cranberries and the city's present day hip-hop scene, which has given Limerick another injection of pride and confidence. Musically they're very different, but Denise Chaila reminds me confidence, charisma and spirit-wise of Dolores.

An unlikely early fan of The Cranberries was Jim Kemmy, a local councillor and TD who was a proper old socialist and local historian. He was a great man for the vodka-tonics and gave me the first line of my novel, *City Of Bohane*. I met him down on Poor Man's Kilkee by the Shannon at a troublesome time when there'd been quite a lot of stabbings and stuff in Limerick. I said, "Jim, what's wrong with us?" and he replied, "I don't know, but it's coming off that river." I saved that for years. Nothing gets wasted!

After canvassing for him one night – I was supposed to be reporting on his campaign but my revolutionary zeal got the better of me – we went drinking in Costello's and he said, "We have this amazing river going through Limerick, but the city's turned its back on it and it's ridiculous. There should be cafés all along there and people walking up and down."

Other councillors would be like, "Have we got to be sitting down in our overcoats?" but Jim had the vision which Jack Higgins, a great City Manager from Cork, turned into a reality. It's great to go back now and walk down from the Clarion hotel to King John's Castle which is close to the brilliant Dolores O'Riordan mural.

It's a city that Dolores and The Cranberries helped transform and for that they should be eternally celebrated.

· **Kevin Barry in conversation with Stuart Clark, July 2021**

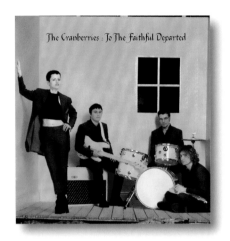

The Cranberries : To The Faithful Departed

"'Hollywood' becomes a metaphor for O'Riordan's publicly declared disenchantment with the rewards of rock superstardom."

MINDFUL OF THE FACT that it has already received something of a slating in some of the UK inkies, it's probably worth reminding ourselves that spirituality and mortality – the dominant, though not overriding themes on this album – are hardly seen as the hippest of concerns in the current climate. In part, that may explain the hammering The Cranberries have been getting. As for the rest, clearly an antipathy to Dolores O'Riordan has been nursed by certain writers and their bile has to be considered against that background.

It's curious. The single, 'Salvation', has been attacked for the preachy directness of its sermonising: *"To all those people doing lines – don't do it/ To all the kids with heroin eyes, don't do it."* Now, whatever about its ultimate execution, this is clearly how O'Riordan feels about drug-taking. So why shouldn't she express those feelings openly? Or is it that contemporary rock culture remains more comfortable romanticising and eulogising drug taking, and is unable to cope with such bluntness from a woman, and a white woman at that? There've been dozens of anti-drug songs which haven't been dismissed in the same manner, from Neil Young's 'The Needle And The Damage Done' to U2's 'Bad'. But the most relevant comparison is with Grandmaster Flash and Melle Mel, who expounded virtually the same message 13 years ago on the classic 'White Lines (Don't Do It)'. Whether 'Salvation' is a great tune or not is the real issue and it certainly isn't one of the strongest on *To The Faithful Departed*. But neither is it the turkey that the detractors would have you believe. And that is true of the whole album.

The album's opener 'Hollywood' takes up, both sonically and structurally, where 'Zombie' left off. With a dense, crashing power-riff and O'Riordan's habitual wailing chant/mantra being introduced gradually into the mix, it kicks into life. In this context, 'Hollywood' becomes a metaphor for O'Riordan's publicly declared disenchantment with the rewards of rock superstardom. *"This is not Hollywood like I understood,"* she sings, almost despairingly, before concluding that, *"The greatest irony of all, it's not so glamorous at all."*

'When You're Gone' could've been titled 'Ode To My Husband', alluding as it does to O'Riordan's post-nuptial state of domestic bliss, while at the same time exposing her own insecurity and vulnerability. *"And in the night, I could be helpless/ I could be lonely, sleeping without you,"* she confesses. *"In the day, everything's complex, there's nothing simple/ When I'm not around you."* An obvious future single, it boasts a classic '50s doo-wop vocal arrangement, reminiscent of The Skyliners' 'If I Don't Have You'.

A similar, if even more soul-baring mood permeates 'I'm Still Remembering', with O'Riordan acknowledging her elation when Mr. Don Burton first popped the question: *"I'm still remembering the line/ You said you would be mine/ Yesterday was cold and bare/ Because you were not there."*

'Free To Decide' is a scathing attack on the media's intrusion into her private life, with O'Riordan angrily declaring, *"I'll live as I choose/ Or I will not live at all."* But even here, she retains a sense of humour remarking that she's *"not so suicidal after all."*

The critical point musically is that The Cranberries' penchant for penning hook-laden, dreamy melodies is still well in evidence on *To The Faithful Departed*, and to that extent the record works well. To judge the album on its lyrics alone, as many reviewers seem to have done, is clearly absurd. The point is that you can never separate what's being said from how it's being said in rock'n'roll.

Or to put it another way, the polemical lyrics alone certainly cannot rescue songs like 'War Child' – *"... victim of political*

pride, plant the seed, territorial greed" — when the musical muscle isn't there to back them up. Despite the intensity of the singing and the addition of string and horn embellishments, it simply doesn't work on an emotional level.

And whatever the intent, 'I Just Shot John Lennon' also comes across as a poorly realised exercise, smothered by a decided absence of lyrical dexterity – *"He had perceptively known that it wouldn't be nice/ Because in 1980 he paid the price"* – and a matching lack of musical focus.

There are interesting departures elsewhere, however. The hymn-like 'Electric Blue' is rooted in church music; 'Joe' is a genuinely poignant elegy, dedicated to her grandfather; while the unashamedly nostalgic 'The Rebels' chronicles the band's aimless, teenage years in Limerick to considerable effect.

Despite its occasional lack of cohesiveness, *To The Faithful Departed* has enough exemplary moments to make it worthy of attention and – the often gratuitous attacks it's been subjected to notwithstanding – it should see The Cranberries maintain their position as one of the biggest bands in the world. Because Dolores O'Riordan still has the most distinctive, unique female voice in rock right now, and that counts for a lot. No argument!

To The Faithful Departed album review by Colm O'Hare, March 1996

The Rise And Fall (And Rise) Of The Cranberries

Three albums in. Millions of records sold. Fan adulation at its peak. All might have seemed thoroughly fab in the world of The Cranberries. And yet trouble had been brewing for some time, before finally spilling over. The band's third album, *To The Faithful Departed*, had been dedicated to the man who'd signed The Cranberries to Island Records, Denny Cordell and to Dolores' grandfather Joe O'Riordan, both of whom had died that year. The psychological impact of the sudden loss was immense. The intense swirl of emotions resulted in burn-out, disillusionment, tour cancellations and an inescapable feeling that this might indeed be the end of the line for them. The good news, as the new Millennium hoved into view, was that the band had regrouped successfully – and that they were now ready to rock again...

Opposite photos: Liza Caldwell

FINDING THE BALANCE

Trailing a new album and a new contentment, Dolores O'Riordan tells Stuart Clark about
how she got rid of her hang-ups and learned to love being a pop star.

"**G**O ON, have a feel."
I've been in some odd situations, but this is the first time a millionaire rock star has invited me to inspect her stomach. One reason I can think of for not acceding to the request is that the midriff-owner's big, burly husband is shooting daggers at me from the doorway.

Dolores O'Riordan wants her tummy prodded, though, and I'd be failing in my journalistic duties if I were to refuse.

"Not bad for someone who's had a kid," laughs the 28-year-old, who's only a couple of bottles short of a six-pack. To indulge in a bit of *HELLO!*-speak, O'Riordan is a woman who's finally learned how to enjoy her celebrity. While never in my experience the *"I'll schweem and I'll schweem and I'll schweem"* prima donna the tabloids made her out to be, it was obvious meeting her three years ago that she was underweight and over-stressed. Our familiarity doesn't extend to me sticking her on the weighing scales, but since then she's put on at least 8 or 9 lbs and is postively exuding good health. She's also swapped her severe crop for a glam blonde bob which makes her look decidedly more feminine. If that's not a politically incorrect thing to say...

"It probably is," she laughs, "but, yeah, I do feel more feminine and like my old self again. When I came off the *To The Faithful Departed* tour, I thought I'd never sing again. I really hated singing and I really hated what had become of the band because it was just a work machine. Every day, every hour, there was something scheduled. It was just so

crazy, I couldn't sleep.

"So I kind of got consumed by things on the third album, and we just over-toured and overworked and I got burned out. We were thinking of splitting up and not making any more records because I, *we*, were all so sick of it."

Echoing those sentiments later on, guitarist Noel Hogan talks of being "totally disillusioned with the whole thing. It reached the point where we didn't care about selling another million records, we just wanted some time off to enjoy ourselves. I'd be sat there in a 5-star hotel romanticising about when I was on the dole, because at least then I got to go on the piss with my mates. The buzz we'd always got from playing live was gone and we were hardly talking to each other."

Realising that they were about to implode, The Cranberries pulled a major North American tour and headed back to Limerick for copious amounts of pint-quaffing, and spending the whole of the next day in bed recovering. The record company were distinctly unimpressed, but as Dolores stresses, "It was really important to take a break. It made me realise that I don't have to kill myself working any more. Maybe I'm allowed to have fun. Maybe I can have a life outside of the band. Maybe I don't just have to be a singer and spend the rest of my life being judged and criticised, because at that stage the media were doing my head in. If they see a weakness they kind of pounce and I was weak at the time, so there were all of these malicious rumours going around."

These included talk of temper tantrums, rows with husband

VOL 23 NO 7 • 28th April 1999
PRICE £1.95 (INCLUDING TAXES)

HOT PRESS

The MICK McCARTHY Interview
by Stuart Clark

UNSAFE EUROPEAN HOME
Eamonn McCann on Kosovo

Dolores O'Riordan

THE CRANBERRIES: The Sweet & Sour Taste Of Success

Marc Almond • Gene • DANGEROUS VISIONS - Peter Murphy on Music Videos

TAKING ON THE GM GIANTS: Adrienne Murphy's Story

The Great Record of Irish Music | Goes To Galway

On the button: Dolores indulges in some navel-gazing with Stuart Clark. Photo by Liza Caldwell.

Don Burton and going on stage in Germany *sans* underwear. *The Daily Sport* had to cough up £5,000 for that particular work of fiction, but still the tele-photo lenses remained outside her Dingle home. Meanwhile, there was no respite on the artistic front with virtually every UK and Irish reviewer panning *To The Faithful Departed*. The most vicious asides were reserved for tracks like 'Bosnia' and 'I Just Shot John Lennon' which will be remembered for the immortal couplet, *"With a Smith & Wesson .38/ John Lennon's life was no longer a debate."*

Looking back now, Dolores acknowledges that she rather lost the lyrical plot.

"You can't write about normal things because you don't have a normal life," she pleads in mitigation. "When you want to go from A to B you have to have security around and there are people screaming at you all the time, so basically you become a little bit weird and isolated and feel like you're in a cage. Your only form of escape is the TV. You watch CNN and go, 'Oh my God, that's awful, I'm going to write a song about this.' So you do become the sad old rock star, viewing the world from a hotel room."

Dolores is guarded when it comes to talking about her marriage, but admits that without Don there are times she might have gone under.

"You get to a point in your life where you've done the dating and all that stuff, and just want the one big love thing. It really helps if you have a partner behind you that loves you unconditionally, and no matter what shit you go through, they're always there and take your side. You go through your ups and downs, but that person is still there, loving you, no matter what."

Tired of suffering from what she calls 'Poor Little Rich Girl Syndrome', O'Riordan set about reclaiming her life. First on the agenda was a move to a stud farm just outside of Kilmallock in County Limerick, which can only be described as palatial. The umpteen-acre spread includes her own studio and rehearsal stage, which means she can put in a full day's work with The Cranberries, and still be there to kiss her son, Taylor, goodnight.

"Where I live now is nice because it's not in a tourist area," she enthuses. "The house in Kerry was beautiful, but every single day the Dingle tour buses were pulling up and all the people were looking out, going, 'Is that where she lives?' I remember being three months pregnant and I was coming

"I'm glad I joined the band when I did because I don't think I'd have accomplished so much otherwise."

down my path one day and this guy stopped in a car. I said, 'Look, this is a private residence', and he blew a gasket on me. He goes, 'I wouldn't say that to you if you came to my house', and I'm like, 'I'm pregnant. I'm not on a showcase here. I'm just a woman having a baby, please leave me alone.' So I guess I had to get a house somewhere quieter with less access. Here's perfect because it's generally farmers and there's no tourists."

The plethora of gold discs on the wall and crate of vintage champagne in the corner are a reminder that there's an upside to this rock star lark. O'Riordan could retire tomorrow and never have to worry about where her next bottle of Dom Perignon's coming from.

"I'm glad I joined the band when I did because I don't think I'd have accomplished so much otherwise," she acknowledges. "It was nice to be able to have a baby – I'm 27 and my son is one-and-a-half. The band have sold 28 million albums worldwide; it's our fourth album and we're doing it purely for the music. We've done the fame thing and it's not for the money. We don't have to worry about that. It's really nice that after everything that's happened, songwriting and being in a band is still really fun. And I mean being in a rock band where you're in control of everything – the videos, the clothes, the songs, *everything*."

While the O'Riordan family flitted off to their other home in Toronto, Noel Hogan indulged in a six-month orgy of watching daytime TV and strolling into town to get bladdered with his mates.

"I just sat there with the remote control going, 'Great, *Emmerdale*!'" he laughs. "I didn't do anything for months and months, but then I found myself picking up an acoustic and wanting to write songs. It didn't register at the time but what I was doing was going back to how we used to work in the beginning. *Everybody Else Is Doing It, So Why Can't We?* came about as a result of me sticking a tape recorder in front of my guitar at home, and giving the tapes to Dolores. The only difference with *Bury The Hatchet* is that I had to get them couriered over to her in Canada."

A couple of Fed-Ex deliveries later and The Cranberries were back in business.

"Dolores had also been writing, so with her pregnant and unable to travel, we couriered ourselves over to Toronto to do some demos," Hogan continues. "As soon as we heard the playbacks it was, 'Right, we have to do another album.'"

Out this week, *Bury The Hatchet* is probably the record the band would've made if *Everybody Else Is Doing It...* had flopped and they'd been given a clear run at the follow-up. Having been rather over-gymnastic with her vocals on *To The Faithful Departed*, Dolores keeps things nice and simple and demonstrates on 'Just My Imagination' that she's still capable of sending whole cold fronts down spines. The same goes for the subject matter, which is mainly straightforward relationship stuff. The notable exception is 'Fee Fi Fo' which – with lines like *"How can you get your satisfaction from the body of a child?/ You're vile, you're sick"* – is a scathing attack on child abuse.

"It's the worst crime," she says unequivocally. "They should be castrated. People who sexually abuse children get off too easy. They get back out after a couple of weeks because, 'Oh, he's psychologically ill.' Which I can understand, but then people get thrown in the can for eight years for smoking dope or something. The system is weird that way. It hammers people who are doing harmless things while these perverts, these paedophiles, are shown leniency."

You don't have to agree with Dolores' opinions to find it refreshing that she has them. Ever since Sinéad O'Connor was crucified for tearing The Pope up on the telly, there's been a reluctance among Irish artists to say anything that may impact on their record sales. That includes going against the liberal grain, as O'Riordan did when she discussed abortion.

"I think Sinéad's pretty cool," she says. "She's Irish and outspoken – sometimes to a point where it's her own undoing – but at least she's original and does her own thing. She's not a safe Mary O'Shea kind of head. She's a little bit crazy sometimes, I guess, but I think we all are.

"*(As for what I said)* I can understand people having to have abortions when they get raped or whatever. In certain situations, grand, but still I don't like the idea of a baby being sucked out and thrown into a bucket squealing and crying. It's sick. I think, as well, that they shouldn't abort fetuses after a certain amount of time because they do start moving. I had a baby so I know. It's one of those things where I've always said what I thought. I could never not give a toss, y'know?"

Does she agree with what Sinéad says about women having

"You catch more flies with honey than you do with shite."

a tougher time of things in the business than men?

"I was never a man so I don't really know! It's debatable. Maybe from her shoes it's harder, but from mine it's kind of handy because if you know how to play it properly you can use it to your advantage. You can always sit back and say to your husband, 'Honey, everything's falling apart out here, can you fix it?' Because you're the woman you can sit inside. So I like to sit back and play the lady thing. I enjoy being a woman."

A further insight into her sexual politics comes later on when she observes that, "You're always best to play the sweet Colleen, if you can. You catch more flies with honey than you do with shite."

While not much gone on role models, Dolores admits to being taught the prime women-in-rock directive by Tanya Donnelly and the rest of Belly.

"Tanya was the first time I'd met a female on the road," she enthuses, "and it was just so nice having girls around because up till then it had always been boys. The bass-player, who used to play with that punk band L7, was a crazy rock 'n' roll babe, and it was great seeing her and thinking, 'Hey she's worse than the guys. Cool!' They were really well able to deal with whatever happens when you're on stage and you're a female."

As possibly the only Irish woman that every American teenager could name, does Dolores have any sense of representing her country or her gender?

"I guess I feel more like an ambassador for myself, but as far as Irish women go, I represent them pretty well because I'm not totally crazy and I'm not too conservative. I'm kind of in the middle of the road. I'm pretty normal, really."

Well, as normal as someone who's sold 28 million records can be. O'Riordan's face doesn't so much cloud as storm over when, as a throwaway aside, I suggest that The Cranberries have paved the way for The Corrs.

"I don't like their music. I don't like people who put skid-li-ay into rock or pop. To me, it has to be either trad or rock. Mixing things is like, 'Uuuuuurgh!' I hate it.

"I went to see *Riverdance* in England and was pretty impressed," she continues. "I thought it would be kind of tacky, but it's well done. It's very, very traditional which I can handle much better than something like The Corrs. It's easier to do skid-li-ay because you grew up with it. It's an easy trade off, and foreign people like it because it's different

for them. For me, it's a bit cheesy to do that. Trad is trad and that's it. It's way more challenging to do presentable global rock which appeals to people everywhere."

What about the pre-*Riverdance* bouts of Irish dancing that Dolores used to treat American audiences to?

"It was something that I grew up with and thought, 'Hey, maybe I'll do a bit of skipping round the stage here for two seconds to make the show more interesting.' I was never a genius, though, when it came to Irish dancing."

Four years is a long time to be out of action, but with kindred spirits like Alanis, Jewel and Ani Di Franco dominating the American charts, The Cranberries should be able to pick up where they left off in the States. They may have a tougher time of things in Europe – a guest appearance at the MTV Awards in Milan demonstrated to Dolores just how much the musical landscape has changed.

"When we took the career-break, there were a lot more rock 'n' roll bands on the scene, and now it's weird because it's like a different world. It's full of polished boys and girls with not a lot of talent. Just three years beforehand, I remember doing the MTV Awards in New York, and Metallica were there and Alanis Morissette was there. Maybe the scene is just really different in Europe.

"There was one band *(in Milan)* that kept screaming, *'Cleopatra, comin' atchya'*, and it was like, 'Okay, you've said it, now stop!'. Actually, I found Rammstein the best performers. They were interesting."

There was a far more civilised atmosphere in November when The Cranberries journeyed to Oslo for the presentation of the 1998 Nobel Peace Prize.

While not quite in the Marilyn Manson league, the band caused consternation among the suits and twin-sets when they launched into *Bury The Hatchet*'s flagship single, 'Promises'. Whatever about Gerry Adams' mob, here were The Cranberries steadfastly refusing to decommission their guitars.

"I thought it was really nice because I've always had respect for it, and associated it with Ghandi and things like that. When we got to the venue A-ha were on stage, and that was pretty weird because I used to be a fan of theirs. It was like being a kid, except I'd gotten older now and was in a band. Phil Collins was there and said we rocked because we did 'Promises'. I tell you, 'Promises' live is so loud. There were all these people with dickie-bows and stuff, and it was like 'woooooagh!'"

"It's so different to walk into my hotel room and have my son and my mum and my husband there. It's like, 'This is nice. I feel human. I have a family.'"

Forget Montessori, Dolores O'Riordan is very much from the rock 'n' roll school of parenting. Young Taylor can plead as much as he wants, but there's no way he's going to be bought one of those boy or girl band records.

"Absolutely no way," his mother shrieks in horror. "They're barred. If he wants to listen to Boyzone and the Spice Girls, he has to do it in his room. He's not allowed to listen to it in front of me. I'm sure they're lovely people but I can't handle that kind of music. It hurts my ears in a big way."

There's no need to sit on the fence.

"That Ronan Keating guy – eeeeeurgh, he's just so bland. Why does someone who's 22 want to sound like they're 102? I know I'm going to have lots of girls shouting 'bitch' at me, but it's product not music."

Mindful of just how fucked up the last Cranberries world tour left her, Dolores is insisting on promoting *Bury The Hatchet* in handy bite-size chunks. No trip away from home will last for more than a month, and there'll be a couple of extra O'Riordans on the bus.

"The nipper's coming everywhere with Mamma," she confides. "I've already done publicity in LA and New York, and it's so different to walk into my hotel room and have my son and my mum and my husband there. It's like, 'This is nice. I feel human. I have a family.' It's so much better than being on stage and having this kind of fake love, and then going into a hotel room and getting really depressed because it's so quiet and dead and you can't go out because the fans are in the lobby and you're stuck in a kind of prison or something."

Asked about his bandmate's more relaxed approach to life, Noel Hogan smiles and says, "Motherhood agrees with her. When things started going wrong three years ago, all any of us had to focus on was the band. Getting married to Don and having Taylor has made her realise that there's life outside of music. I've known her 10 years and she's never been happier."

Dolores is certainly at her most animated when talking about Taylor who, celebrity mum or not, is going to go to the local national school and muddy his knees playing GAA.

Shouldering the responsibility: Noel was to blame for Dolores getting carried away.

"I'll raise my son in Ireland, yeah. I think it's a great place for kids to grow up. As countries go, it doesn't have a very high crime rate and it doesn't have a lot of violence. My mum takes him to church all the time, so she's doing the religious stuff. I like the idea of him getting first communion and confirmation because I got it. It's nice to give your kids something to believe in, spiritually."

The spirit concerning her now is the one she was imbibing far too freely last night at Limerick's swankiest drinkerie, The Globe.

"I've got two inches of make-up on and I still look like shit," she growls in very un-mumsy fashion. "That's what life's about, though, isn't it? Going out with your friends and getting pissed."

We'll drink to that!

• Dolores O'Riordan interview by Stuart Clark, April 1999

"This is music for grown-ups. Or at least for people who like their music to last beyond the current Warholian 15 minute dictat."

THEY'RE BACK. WITH A BANG. Never ones to do it colour by numbers, The Cranberries waited 'til their third trip to the studio before encountering the difficult album syndrome. And now that *To The Faithful Departed* has finally well, departed, Dolores & Co. can get back to doing what they do best: writing divine melody lines and conjuring vocals that sometimes sound like they've come from some Elysian field and at other times, are nothing less than demonically possessed.

The Cranberries took a three-year leave of absence from the business, an act of bravery that most outfits wouldn't dare dream of, and while they mightn't merit a purple heart for it, the gamble has paid off handsomely. *Bury The Hatchet* sees them back at the ranch, guns blazing, horses chomping at the bit, and best of all, bellies hungry for a chunk of cow pie.

'Promises', the first single release, is more than a tad misleading, if it's a thermometer reading of the album you're looking for. Strident, stubborn, and bland, it tries too hard and stands out alright, but only as a weak track in the line-up. Elsewhere, there are far more challenging and adventurous seams worth mining, and most of them lead back to the core of *Bury The Hatchet*, which is a far more mature attitude than The 'Berries have demonstrated to date.

Now, it seems that they're not trying to prove anything anymore. Like so many of their predecessors who felt themselves under siege (everyone from Brian Wilson to Damon Albarn) they reacted by thrashing and flailing aimlessly. Now though, real life has re-entered the arena, they've had time to smell the roses, and the conclusion seems to be that even the coffee smells OK these days.

'Animal Instinct' is a gorgeous opener; an acoustic guitar-driven commentary on domestic relationships, it's a pitch perfect marriage of Dolores' trademark razor-sharp vocals with the rest of the band's penchant for catchy basslines and straightforward percussion – a fine calling card.

Shifting landscapes are remarkably captured on 'Copycat', a wry telephoto lens take on the candyfloss world of pop that rules today. With lyrics that tell it like it is (*"Everyone wears the same clothes now/ And everyone plays the game"*), and driving, muted guitars punctured by cocky percussion, this is Cranberries with attitude – but one that's more considered and worldweary than vehement.

Real life impinges everywhere else too, with lyrical preoccupations ranging from child abuse ('Fee Fi Fo') to, unsurprisingly, motherhood ('You And Me'), the perils of peer pressure ('Shattered') and the comforts of emotional security ('Dying In The Sun'). But while the lyrics reflect a far more relaxed mood, it's the cool-headed arrangements that leave their mark. Take 'You And Me', with its classy ice-cool brass lines and veiled sequencers underscoring one of the catchiest melodies on the album.

Maybe one of the keys to The Cranberries' triumphant return is the decision they've taken to sit at the production desk, alongside Benedict Fenner who's played knob-twiddler for the likes of Brian Eno and Laurie Anderson. This way, the personal moods and nuances of the original songs are far less likely to get lost in the mix.

Fourth time round, The Cranberries are best listened to with the shutters wide open and the headphones cast aside. Because this is music for grown-ups. Or at least for people who like their music to last beyond the current Warholian 15 minute dictat.

Welcome back lady and gentlemen. Reunions can be such sweet things.

***Bury The Hatchet* album review by Siobhán Long, April 1999**

Right: The Cranberries feel the heat in this Andy Earl promo shot.

Older And Wiser

Mojo comprehensively rediscovered it was a happier, wiser, less embattled Cranberries who went into the studio to make their fifth album, *Wake Up And Smell The Coffee*, with a back-in-the-fold Stephen Street. One of the record's standouts, 'Never Grow Old', would go on to earn a particularly poignant place in fans' hearts. When not in the studio, on the road or modelling for Calvin Klein – nice work if you can get it! – Dolores was enjoying family life on the palatial County Limerick stud farm the O'Riordan-Burtons now called home.

Opposite photo: Mick Quinn

UP CLOSE AND PERSONAL

After years when her triumphs were in danger of being masked by her tribulations, Dolores O'Riordan is back in defiantly upbeat form. She talks to Stuart Clark about confidence, critics, Calvin Klein and her "confirmation-size breasts"!

PHOTOS: MICK QUINN

"**Y**ou think I'm going to talk to you now, you bastard? You were supposed to be here at 12 o'clock. TWELVE-O-FUCKING-CLOCK! Now sod off or I'll set the dogs on you!"

Dolores O'Riordan says none of these things as myself and *H.P.* sharpshooter Mick Quinn arrive 45 minutes late for our *tête-á-tête* with The Cranberries frontperson. The one thing they neglect to teach you at journalism college is how to overtake tractors – the Clarkmobile's arrival in Kilmallock was delayed by a particularly slothful Massey Ferguson.

Obviously confusing *Hot Press* with *Hello!*, Dolores has invited us into her beautiful County Limerick home, a palatial abode which befits her status as one of Ireland's richest women. There's no sign of her full-time security team, although it's possible that the three old fellas tending her herbaceous border have Special Services training.

Not being a fan of the new rock Puritanism – I'm talking about you, Thom Yorke – I'm pleased to report that chez O'Riordan is a shrine to *loadsamoney* self-indulgence. After pausing to admire the stained-glass window, which has the lyrics to 'Zombie' inscribed on it, we're ushered into the gaff's very own Jungle Room.

I'm not sure what I'm most impressed with – the full-size Wild West bar or the saddle-stools lined-up in front of it. To the right of that are a giant sofa, a snoozing bearskin and the biggest fuck off telly you've ever seen.

As for Dolly herself, there's no sign of the edginess which

a few years ago made interviewing her such a minefield. Having ditched the peroxide in favour of a more natural reddy-brown do, she doesn't look a whole lot different to the girl I first met a decade ago in a Shannonside hostelry of ill-repute. Except for her T-shirt, that is. The teenage O'Riordan would never have worn a top with the legend "psychobitch" emblazoned across it.

Taking care of bartending duties is her Canadian husband, Don. Looking slightly offended when we decline a snorter of the bourbon he's imported from back home, he does the honours with the Diet Cokes and talks enthusiastically about the Japanese steak house that him and the missus are opening in D4. Further evidence of the O'Riordan Burtons' penchant for good grub is provided by the Italian pizza oven plonked in the yard.

Asked later if Don is The Cranberries' Yoko Ono, drummer Fergal Lawler laughs so hard he almost falls off his saddle.

"It might seem like that from the outside but, nah, he's never got in the way of our relationship," he says, once he's regained his composure. "In fact, he's really helped with the business side of things."

Which, contrary to what you might have read elsewhere, is booming. Despite a relatively poor showing in the States, the band's current album, *Bury The Hatchet*, has just sold its five millionth copy.

Gigs in Europe and South America are still deemed intimate if there's less than 20,000 people there, and it didn't take long for Calvin Klein to come knocking when he needed an instantly recognisable face for his ad campaign.

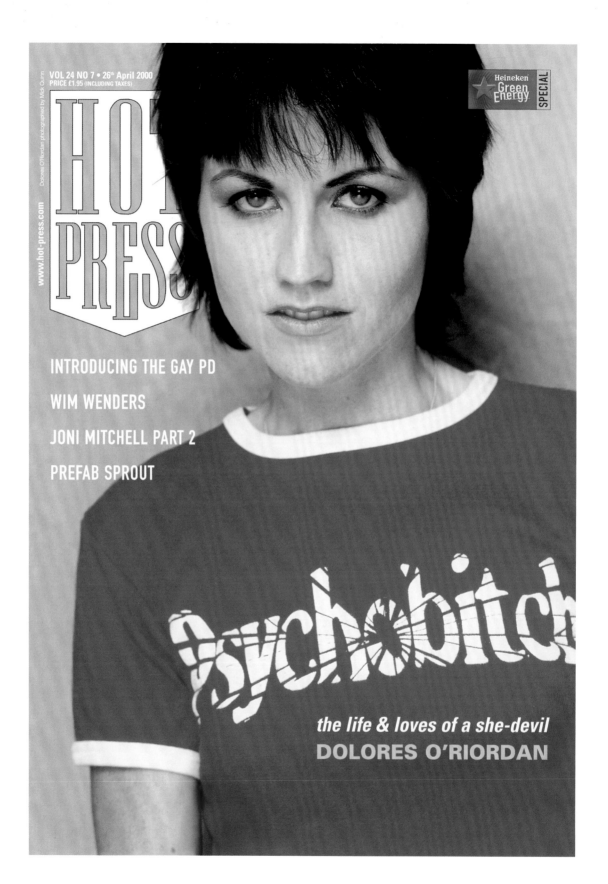

VOL 24 NO 7 • 26th April 2000
PRICE £1.95 (INCLUDING TAXES)

www.hot-press.com

Dolores O'Riordan photographed by Mick Quinn

HOT PRESS

Heineken Green Energy SPECIAL

INTRODUCING THE GAY PD

WIM WENDERS

JONI MITCHELL PART 2

PREFAB SPROUT

the life & loves of a she-devil
DOLORES O'RIORDAN

"If it ever got to the stage where I couldn't go out and do what I wanted, I'd knock it on the head. Band over."

Stuart Clark: Did you enjoy your first taste of being a fashion model?
Dolores O'Riordan: I got loads of free jeans and some cash as well, so it was great. If it had been for something more girlie I'd probably have said "no", but that denim and black eye look is what I'm into myself. The fact that Moby and Macy Gray were the other people doing it shows that, in the States anyway, we're still thought of as being "alternative". To be honest, I wouldn't have got the gig if they were looking for a mainstream babe. I haven't got the legs or the boobs.

Were there big bucks involved?
I'd say it's pretty big for models, but most of the artists get about £20,000 to do it.

After that, I was expecting you to be the first to volunteer for catwalk duties at the recent charity fashion show in The Point Theatre.
(laughs) I'd probably have done a Naomi Campbell and fallen on my arse. I know Caroline Downey and Ali Hewson quite well as girls, and they persuaded me to come along and present one of the designer awards. I don't usually go to stuff like that in this country, but why not? The fashion world's the same as the rock 'n' roll world. You've got your really sound down-to-earth people and the pretentious assholes who you try to avoid. I went back to The Clarence afterwards, which was great 'cos I was able to gawp at all the really big stars. I stayed there for about an hour and then, realising I was getting obliviously drunk, slipped out. My fear in those situations is that I'm going to end up dancing on a table and giving somebody a headbutt.

Didn't you do something along those lines once in Limerick?
That was a hormonal thing. I'd just stopped breast-feeding, so I was in a weird kind of a mood and not able to hold my alcohol. I don't know if you're aware of this, but after having a baby, women go through a period when they feel really insecure. You go out for the first time, there's this gut of leather hanging off you, and you don't take too kindly to other women giving your man the eye. There was a bit of a scene, but nothing serious.

Do you recognise yourself from the descriptions of you in the paper?
Five or six years ago, I was way too serious. Somebody would ask a question that was, maybe, a bit too personal, and rather than laughing it off, I let it get to me. Now, I'll either answer it straight, make a joke out of it and change the subject, or tell you ever so politely to fuck off! I'm not afraid to let my sense of humour come out or, if needs be, be assertive.

What's the daftest thing that you've read about yourself?
I don't know, really. Sometimes people say "she's a bitch to work with", which I can be when it comes to being on stage. It may be somebody else's fault, but I'm the one who's left looking like a plonker in front of thousands of people. All of my crew know that I'm really, really sound as a person, but if my guitar's out of tune or the monitor's not working, I'm going to blow a gasket. That's just because I'm meticulous about my job. I don't think I'd have gotten this far in life without being that way.

Being branded a bitch is one thing, but didn't you have to take out an injunction against a foreign journalist who was dishing some serious dirt?
We went to court and it was proven that the story was made up. When that happened, the paparazzi guy who'd supplied it started to blackmail (us), so we had to get a lawyer on him.

There was also a German you had to take legal action against.
The guy on the internet? I wouldn't go into that 'cos he was arrested and everything. I don't know how psychologically balanced or unbalanced he was.

I imagine, with a young son, that you're very concerned about security.
Yeah, I am. I mean, God, look out there at all the cameras and infra-red lights. We have full-time security which is essential when you're living this far out in the country. I've had people come up to the front gate and sleep outside, which isn't what you want. They'll ring the buzzer and I'll go, "Sorry, she's in Indonesia". Not that I'm a prisoner, though. If it ever got to the stage where I couldn't go out and do what I wanted, I'd knock it on the head. Band over.

Have you been following the *Angela's Ashes* debate?

The jean genie: Dolores modelling for Calvin Klein.

I didn't read it myself, but from what Ferg (*Lawler*) was telling me, it sounds pretty accurate. God, there were seven kids in my family, and four of us in one bed for a long time. We used to have a big saucepan of potatoes – 30 or 40 of 'em – on the range and eat pig's head, tails and trotters. When you're hungry and a kid, that's grand. I know as well that there was a lot of drinking and stuff. Fathers went out and drank because there was no money and they needed a release and *dah, di, dah*. I mean, how can people say that the author's lying when they haven't been through his experience? Everybody has demons in their closets, but it's from these demons that we learn and become better people. There was certainly poverty around in Limerick, but at the same time I had a lot of spirituality which made up for it.

Do you still consider yourself to be a spiritual person?
I could if I had to be, but I've got a lot of toys now. I love boats and I love motorbikes. The biker culture – like rock 'n' roll – is something that's misunderstood. Harleys, which are my dream bike, are a bit too heavy for me, so I normally stick to four-wheelers.

It doesn't sound like you've got much in common with Meg Matthews.
A new Gucci bag? Nah, get me some more machines! I wouldn't really be into clothes and make-up, except for when we're going on tour and I can't just throw on a pair of jeans. *Calvin Klein* jeans, that is!

Is the upcoming Dublin show a chance to ever so regally wave two fingers at your critics?
There's no agenda apart from wanting to play the best gig possible. It's not going to stick out in my head and be different to Mexico or Malaysia. I'll pick out my clothes, have my massage, do my yoga, meditate and then go out there and kick ass. I've proved anything I've needed to by selling 22 million albums. I'm 28 years of age – I've got a beautiful husband and a beautiful child. It's natural to want to be liked, but if somebody thinks that I'm shit, I'm not going to lose any sleep over it.

It has got pretty personal, though.
There have been a few times when I've had to remind myself that I'm not a murderer or, worse still, a politician. You don't know these people, yet there they are saying they hate you. If you're strong – like I feel now – it's water off a duck's back. If you're in any way vulnerable, though, watch out.

You said the last time we met that you'd suffered something akin to a breakdown. Looking back now, can you understand what brought it about?
What happens is that through a combination of working too hard, and constantly being in the public eye, you start becoming paranoid. You can't see the good things because of all the bad things that are in the way, which is a textbook definition of depression. Everything's sad and bad, which of course comes across in your interviews. If I'd read me five or six years ago, I'd have thought I was a right miserable cow! Having taken the prolonged career break that we did, I realised that there are far more nice people than there are bad asses. It's difficult to explain without sounding all clichéd, but it really is a case of coming out of the tunnel and being dazzled by the light.

Just how fucked-up were you?
I'd accomplished all these record sales which, yeah, made me feel incredibly proud, but I didn't have a home or a car or anything I could really call my own. I was afraid to come back to Ireland. I hadn't come back for years, and when I did I'd be freaked out and hiding under a hat. Basically, I was scared of my crap. Ireland is a small country, which when The Cranberries started was still very Catholic and judgmental. I feel much more comfortable now that the Celtic Tiger's kicked in and things have become more liberal. Eight years ago it was, "Oh my God, she said that!" whereas now no-one gives a damn.

Being in a business where drug-taking is almost mandatory, did you ever turn to chemicals for solace?
No, I just never wanted to be that out of control. I've seen my friends doing mushrooms and they'd be like, "God, your head's gone all furry!" It seems a lot of fun, but with my stomach I'd probably puke. In America, especially, it's harder not to take drugs. The more I was encouraged to try them, the more I thought, "No, I'm not going to give in to peer pressure."

"I think I speak for all women who have small breasts when I say that we can be beautiful too, without getting a big pair of soccer balls hanging off us. "

If I'd wanted to take drugs I would have, but I didn't.

Would you fire a crew member if you knew they were popping pills?
No. They can do what they like as long as they function on stage.

How's your new 'month on, month off' regime working out?
Brilliant. We're flying to Puerto Rico tomorrow to do a show, and I'm really looking forward to it because I know that, in a few weeks time, I'll be back home with my friends and family again. The gigs are better because we're not on such a treadmill and permanently knackered.

Is rock 'n' roll life enough for you, or do you have ambitions outside of music?
Don't laugh, but I'm totally into trees. We're going to set about eight acres 'cos I think everyone should give what they can back to the environment. We're also opening a Benehana – that's a Japanese restaurant where the chef cooks your food in front of you. We've just got the building in Dublin, so that should be open next year. It's something that Don, myself and the lads are doing together – partly for a giggle and partly as an investment.

After your night of debauchery in The Clarence, have you thought about opening your own hotel?
Actually, I have. Not here but somewhere like the South of France. The other thing I'm big into is new beauty treatments and therapies for women. There's a huge need nowadays for stress relief, so I'd love to open a place which would do everything from massage and reflexology to yoga and natural organic highs.

I guess, being into the natural side of things, you'd never consider getting a boob job.
Are you saying that my tits are small?

(acutely embarrassed) What I meant is that you'd be opposed to cosmetic surgery.
I think I speak for all women who have small breasts when I say that we can be beautiful too, without getting a big pair of soccer balls hanging off us. Certain men find us attractive. I'm not insecure about the fact that I've confirmation-size breasts. It's part of me, and I'd feel very strange with a pair of soccer balls. Having answered that, I insist you ask the lads if they've considered getting their penises enlarged.

I'll make a note of it. Before you have me escorted off the premises, a few quick questions. Do you still get trolleyed from time to time?
Yes. Last Friday I did an all-nighter. I began consuming alcohol at approximately eight o'clock and was still standing – well, slouching – at 9AM on Saturday morning. I don't think going on a bender once in a while does you any harm. Except for the hangover, that is. They definitely get worse as you get older.

The best film you've seen recently?
The General's Daughter

Where did you usher in the new millennium?
At home. We fired the pizza oven up, opened a few bottles of Cristal and had a party.

Were champagne corks popped when you heard that Westlife had scored their fifth number one?
No.

Would you regard them as being even more insidious than Boyzone?
Yes.

Do you still think that The Corrs are evil personified?
I've nothing against them, but to me their music's boring. It's kind of squeaky clean. There's not a hair out of place, the lipliner's perfect and they've always got high-heels on to make them look longer and thinner.
  They're very pretty girls and I totally appreciate that other people love them. Guys especially. I was at a party in Dublin with The Corrs and it was like *(does very convincing canine impersonation)* puppies panting all around them.

When are you going solo?
(laughs) Wasn't I supposed to have done that five years ago? Nah, no plans whatsoever.

· **Dolores O'Riordan interview by Stuart Clark, April 2000**

BOYS TALK

The Male Cranberries Have Their Say

Stuart Clark: First things first. Have you given any thought to penis enlargement?
All: What?

Dolores wants to know: if there were any shortcomings on your part — or parts — would you consider having your lads surgically enhanced?
Fergal: I haven't had any complaints.
Mike: Me neither.
Noel: No, but I wouldn't rule out a boob job.

Weren't you meant to be ditching Dolores and going out as a trio?
Fergal: Even before the first album, people were saying, "Oh, she's going to go solo." Obviously she's more comfortable within the framework of a band, not least because there's four people to share the stress among. The big thing is that we all support each other.

Has the dynamic of your relationship changed since Don arrived on the scene?
Noel: It's as good as it's ever been. We realise now that we don't have to see each other every single day. The bond

doesn't weaken just because you go away and do your own thing for a while. Knowing that has definitely made us more relaxed.
Mike: Don's helped us a lot since he came on board. He enjoys telling industry heads to 'fuck off', which is something you need to be able to do in this business.

Have you started thinking about the follow-up to *Bury The Hatchet*?
Noel: There are five or six songs written already, which is about a quarter of what you need to go in to the studio. Dolores and myself are both coming up with stuff, so I imagine we'll be ready to roll fairly soon.

Who's going to be producing?
Fergal: Stephen Street. We met him before Christmas in London and decided that we'd like to work together again.

I thought him and Dolores had a big bust-up?
Noel: That was just a saucy story. It took working with someone else for us to realise how much Stephen gives the band.

WAKE-UP CALL

Dolores O'Riordan may have the highest profile but the others are also here to remind you that The Cranberries are a group, and with the release of their new album *Wake Up And Smell The Coffee*, a happier, wiser, less embattled one than ever before. "All you need is love," they assure Joe Jackson.

PHOTO: ANDY EARL

The Cranberries are pissed off at *Hot Press*. Or, at least, they're pretending to be. Y'see, the guys in the band seem to think that every time they talk to this magazine Dolores gets the bulk of the space and they're sidelined into a box containing a few cursory quotes. Maybe that's why, this time round, we've been told we must "talk to all of The Cranberries or no one at all."

Which would be fine – except that Noel Hogan hasn't turned up for the interview anyway! But Dolores O'Riordan, Mike Hogan and Fergal Lawler have. And as they sit on a sofa near the rehearsal space in Dolores' home in Kilmallock, County Limerick, they're in fine form, buzzing, blissful and anxious as hell to tell the world about their new album, *Wake Up And Smell The Coffee*. But let's kick off by hearing them sound off about the media tendency to focus on Dolores.

Joe Jackson: Are the guys really pissed off at that?
Fergal: No. It is, as you say, a standard media practice.
Dolores: Actually, to be honest, last week we were having a few jars because of my daughter's christening and Mikey got a bit drunk and held my neck up against the wall and told me he was going to bust my ass if I kept hogging the media.
Mike: *(laughs)* That is true. I said, "I've had enough, it's too much, I want some attention!"
That must have been traumatic for the baby. Her first experience of the real world. Or the world of rock 'n' roll!
Dolores: Fortunately, she wasn't there. But I'm telling you, these guys do often grab me, slap me, and say, *(adopts Mafia voice)* "Hey, girl, you're getting too much attention in the media".

But is it only something that happens in Ireland?
Fergal: It varies from country to country, magazine to magazine and even in terms of who does the interviews.
Mike: But people always seem to want to talk to the singer more, in most bands.
Dolores: Plus, there's the fact that girls are far more attractive than boys. Boys are boring!

That's the kind of shite you gave me the last time we talked, Dolores, where you said sexist things like, "All men suck"! Do you still feel the same seven years later?
Dolores: Let me put it this way: girls are more psychological, they're more analytical.

Okay, guys, defend the male of the species.
Mike: I was just listening to the *Gerry Ryan Show*, about women nagging. And they say it's

Into the west: Andy Earl's May 2001 shot of
The Cranberries in Spanish Point, Co. Clare graced
the cover of their 'This Is The Day' promo CD.

"Girls are more psychological, they're more analytical."

scientifically proven that men need to be nagged because it keeps them going! It was the biggest load of shite I ever heard.

Dolores: But women are good at nagging! And I do think women are more analytical. You know that book, by John Gray.

Not *Men Are From Mars And Women Are From Venus* for Christ's sake!

Dolores: Yeah, I read that eleven years ago, when I was only 17. Before it became a big thing! And it helped me realise that men and women are a different species, you can't debate that.

But let's try. Guys, when you read some of Dolores' lyrics on the new album — one is actually called 'Analyse' — would you think, "I'm too thick, too much of a man to analyse things this way'?"

Fergal: I usually relate the lyrics to my life. And all the fans — male and female — do that as well. They often say, "It's as though you guys were singing about my life". So maybe we're not that different after all! Men are more quiet, contemplative, but we take it all in.

All of you have gotten married and had children in the past few years. Though, Fergal, I know your wife is only having her first child as we speak. But do such experiences make The Cranberries even more contemplative?

Dolores: Of course. It's the same for us as it is for every other parent.

Fergal: It's very grounding to become a parent. And you do start thinking about the future more because your children are going to grow up in that world.

How does that affect your life as a rock star?

Dolores: It makes life more difficult in the sense that we all hate leaving our children. So that's one of the hardest things about doing gigs. You try to bring the children with you but that doesn't work. Because when children are three or four they make friends and form their own little secret society and you can't be taking them away from that just because it suits the parents. So one of the challenges for myself — and for the children — is leaving. I brought Taylor, my firstborn, for a time. I'd base him, say, in San Francisco and do gigs in places like Santa Barbara and Arizona then fly back to him. But that, in itself, is hard, because I'm doing all that travelling and I'm tired. So on the last European tour I decided instead to fly out from here, at about ten in the morning, get to Shannon at noon; destination at two; hotel to change my clothes by four;

gig venue by seven; on stage by nine; off-stage by eleven; back in a car; back to the airport; back home here around five in the morning. And I'd be wrecked.

And not in any great condition to be a mother.

Dolores: Right. Because then when you wake up you are too tired to play games, whatever.

That must have been a wake-up call. As in, "I'm too fucked to be a parent to my child" — wake up and smell the coffee indeed!

Dolores: It was a wake-up call for me. So now I structure tours differently. But being a parent is a case of trial and error. You have to learn how to balance things for yourself.

Dolores, the last time we talked, you were insisting "I'm mad keen to have a baby".

Dolores: Well, I didn't want to be some old fossil by the time I got started!

Mike, Fergal, did similar feelings hit either of you or did you just meet the right person and decide to settle down?

Fergal: For everyone, after the third album, *To The Faithful Departed*, things like that hit home because we were just completely exhausted and had devoted the previous five, six years to The Cranberries. As in, touring non-stop.

Dolores, you previously said that, "If anyone in the music business tries to tell me I can't have a child I'll kick their head in." Did any of you ever encounter resistance along these lines? Let's not forget that Sinéad O'Connor's record company suggested she have an abortion because they didn't think having a child at the time of the release of her first album made sense.

Dolores: That's disgusting. I never heard that story. That must have been Jake. He's a beautiful little boy. But no, I didn't get any of that crap and wouldn't have put up with it either, if I had. But then, as you say, they could see me coming and they knew where I stood on this subject. And the point is that I have a very different childhood from Sinéad. I grew up very close to my mother who taught me to be strong, proud and focused. And I know who I am. Sinéad has more vulnerability than I have.

But some girls in my class would say things like, "What are you having a baby for? You're up to 30 million albums, why don't you go on 'till you sell 70 million, first?". And

Does your mother come from Ireland? Noel and Dolores at Dublin Castle in 2000 creating their own variation on the green, white and orange of the Irish flag. Photo by Cathal Dawson.

"Why should I?" Life is about more than selling albums. But they didn't get that. They'd say, "She's all mixed up".

Did both you guys also come to realise life is more than just selling millions of albums?

Mike: That was part of deciding, after the third album, that it's time to do something else, whether that is settle down or whatever. And it wasn't just that we'd been touring non-stop for those five years, the fact was that friends and families had been left behind.

Fergal: And the fun had gone out of being in a rock band.

Mike: True. The same vibe wasn't there at all.

Dolores: And unlike other acts from Ireland, success came quickly for The Cranberries. Our first album sold six million copies and the second, sixteen million. But you're young and naive and green. And the more green you are the more of a shock it is to the system. For U2 their success, massively, came with their third album, I think. But at least they had time to adjust, they were tougher, they were older. Whereas we were a bunch of teenagers and hadn't a clue!

So did it all really end up dark and depressing?

Fergal: It was great fun during the time of the first two albums and recording the third but when we got out on tour it all started to go wrong. Because we basically finished the tour for *No Need To Argue*, went into the studio, recorded *Faithful Departed* and went out on the road with that a few weeks later.

Who was pushing you at this level?

Dolores: Everybody around us.

Fergal: But it was us as well. You see things on paper and you sign it and next thing, you're on tour!

So did you all get greedy?

Dolores: No, you become a robot.

Mike: We thought that was the way things were done, I suppose.

Who was managing you then?

Dolores: Leftbank, a really hot-shot LA company that manage a lot of massive acts such as Meatloaf, Richard Marx, Luther Vandross, Blondie. So they lined up brilliant stuff but the schedule was gruelling.

Mike: We had a lot done before we signed with them. We had toured the first two albums and then said to them, in terms of the third, "We don't want to tour this one" which must have seemed strange to a new management team.

But did anyone in the band ever say, "I'm at the fucking edge here and unless we stop I'm going to go over?"

Dolores: I did. And everybody declared I was anorexic. But it was actually depression. Yet the media love to hop on a story, make it more 'sexy' and marketable and anorexia was a 'big thing' at the time so they said it was anorexia. I was actually clinically depressed.

144

"Music is the one thing that has always kept us bound together."

For how long?

Dolores: Two or three months. And I went off to the Carribbean for three months, basically, to get away from the media. And stayed on one of these tiny islands, with my husband. That was in 1996.

Why did depression hit at that point? You'd found the man you loved.

Dolores: But when I met him all my demons started coming out. I started talking to him and telling him all the things that had happened to me. Relationships that went drastically wrong. One in particular that I really don't want to talk about again. I told Don tons of things. And I'd never really done that because I was too busy working with The Cranberries. I didn't have time to talk to anybody. I was a robot, as I said. But the breaking point really was all the attention I was getting, from the media and otherwise. It also was a case of, say, being in a restaurant and trying to go to the loo and someone comes charging in, banging on the door, shouting, "Are you the singer from The Cranberries?". And, likewise, whereas when we came home the guys could relax, I was being chased to my house by the media. They even chased me to the shopping mall. Because of that anorexia story.

Were you easily able to snap out of that depression after three months?

Dolores: I couldn't go back to the music full-time because I was afraid I'd fall back into the depression. So my next big goal in life was to have a baby. And it took me a while, actually. I wasn't able to conceive, at first, because I was so stressed. When women are stressed it affects the hormones. Then, about six months later, I was pregnant and it was the first real joy I'd had in my life for years. That wasn't alcohol or something like that. It was real. So then I became totally pure, no drink, no nothing for nine months. I really got into the pregnancy and sorted my head out.

And it was a healthy baby?

Dolores: Very healthy.

So after the birth you immediately went back on the alcohol and everything!

Dolores: (laughs) No! Not as much. Because when you have kids you can't.

Do you smoke?

Dolores: Cigarettes? Yeah, once a week, when I drink. But I gave up the cigarettes when I was pregnant.

And did you guys all begin to live healthy lives when you realised you were becoming daddies?

Mike: We're pretty healthy anyway. We all go to the gym and work out regularly.

So when, exactly, did The Cranberries become clean living? Dolores, when you said "no alcohol, no nothing" in terms of the pregnancy does that "nothing" mean you were doing drugs?

Dolores: I never saw alcohol as a drug but now I see it is. Too much of that will mess you up. And, at one point, I was drinking way too much.

Fergal: Drink actually was our drug. We were really fond of the oul' liquor.

Did other drug use ever become a tendency in The Cranberries?

Dolores: No, it was more the drink.

Mike: It was the drink. You'd get pissed most nights.

Dolores: Then you'd wake up with panic attacks, used to hate it.

Panic attacks about what?

Dolores: Drinking and being in the public eye. It was the combination of both. You get very paranoid. You think somebody is following you all the time. That's what I kept thinking. I couldn't get out of the bed. I'd wake up and tell my husband, "I've to go to the toilet" and he'd say, "Go". And I'd tell him, "No, there's somebody out there". And he'd say, "It's all in your head!" And I'd say, "Honestly, there is somebody out there". I was a mess. Really paranoid for that three months. And you can get panic attacks when you are on TV, on camera, doing interviews. Because you've been drinking too much and you get the shakes and you say to yourself, "They're going to think I'm on drugs". And all you're thinking is that you'd love another drink.

Fergal: All of that is magnified when you are in the public eye. Though the worst that could happen to me is a terrible hangover. It never got so bad that I'd think there was somebody outside in the hall. Or following me. Dolores got that, we didn't.

Who took the decision – if the decision was taken – to stay clean in terms of drugs?

Dolores: Nobody really.

Where's the guitarist? Three of the four Cranberries captured by Roger Woolman.

"'Zombie' was written before Dolores even met Don. We all had a metal side to us."

Fergal: We're all pretty sensible like that. And you do read lots of interviews about drugs casualties.

Dolores: In other bands. And crew buses are always pretty wild. But, I think that, at the end of the day, we knew if we started doing cocaine and all that shit we probably wouldn't be here today. We'd probably have killed ourselves.

Fergal: The reason we started the band wasn't to be famous. It was because of the music. And I think if you fall into the drug trap you lose sight of why you started – if you did start out purely to make music. Music is the one thing that has always kept us bound together at the centre. All the rest, surrounding it, was just something that had to be done to get people to hear the music.

So have The Cranberries all rediscovered the absolute joy in making music?

Fergal: At the start of *Bury The Hatchet* that started to return. That's why we went back in the studio. We wouldn't have done that, otherwise. We had a break, then realised we really missed something out of our lives that had been there for years.

You've also recently changed labels so is this another form of war going on in the background?

Dolores: No. It's just that MCA have taken over.

Fergal: Four or five times since we signed to Island it's been sold. And we lost our original point of contact with the label, Denny Cordell, who died. He was a real music guy, great.

Dolores: And we met lots of different record company presidents, and so on, in between. But right now we've another great music guy, Jay Boberg, who started that label IRS, which signed R.E.M. and acts like that. And everyone in the record company really loves 'Analyse', the first single, so we're getting great backing from MCA on this. In fact, as we speak, Don, my husband is over in New York meeting with those guys.

What, exactly is Don's function with the band?

Fergal: Part of the management. We formed our own company.

But did Don have any musical influence on the band? I've heard he teased you towards heavy metal music because that's what he loves.

Dolores: He teased me towards the cot!

"They can write lyrics anytime they want.
But I won't sing them!"

Fergal: 'Zombie' was written before Dolores even met Don. We all had a metal side to us.

It seemed to move to the fore when Don came on board.

Fergal: One of the reasons for this was that we were writing a lot of songs on the road, so they were directly influenced by that live environment.

Dolores: You also figure out how to use your distortion pedal better as you get older. I remember when I started with The Cranberries I saw the distortion pedal and asked Noel, "What's that?'" He showed me *(imitates guitar screech)* and I went, "Jesus, Mary and Joseph!" Now I love that stuff and just say, "give me more distortion".

So did Don have any musical influence on the band at all?

Dolores: No, not really, to be honest. But he would inspire lyrics and stuff.

Mike: He's into Ted Nugent, Aerosmith and all that stuff.

Dolores: And AC/DC!

And you guys can promise that there will be no Nugent or AC/DC derived music coming from The Cranberries?

Fergal: No fucking way will there be!

So what are The Cranberries listening to these days?

Dolores: We all like the new Travis album. Coldplay. The new R.E.M. album. Badly Drawn Boy. And I like Limp Bizkit.

Tell me more about the new album: I see you're back working with Stephen Street who produced the first two albums. Was that to get the old feel back again?

Fergal: At the end of *Bury The Hatchet,* the guy who was mixing it was having problems and we suggested getting Steve in.

It was said that you, Dolores, at one point, were at war with Stephen.

Dolores: I was talking to Stephen recently and he said there's a rumour that he had a fight with Damon from Blur. People just start these rumours. It wasn't that we fought with Stephen. We just went our separate ways. Amicably. You move on. But he was the right person to bring back for this album. And he wanted to come back. So we started from scratch,

again, with Steve, when it came to working on this album.

But there are quite a few mellow tracks on this album, such as 'Chocolate Brown'.

Dolores: I love 'Chocolate Brown' because we did it with one microphone. I went in one morning, thinking I was doing guide vocals – so we get the bass drums and guitar down – and Stephen says, "Actually we're going to do a take on this". And there was one microphone hanging in the middle of the room and we didn't use the 48 tracks at all. Everything was picked up on that mic. You can hear it. The plucking of the guitar and the drum, which we had to keep moving back from the mic. We loved recording that way.

In terms of lyrics, did you guys have any input?

Mike: None.

Why? Are you dummies or what?

Mike: If I wrote something and Dolores had to sing it, I'd find that awkward. So I never even try to write anything. I'd like to write a song sometime. The music but not lyrics.

Fergal: I see it that way, too. If I was a singer and someone wrote lyrics for me, I'd feel strange singing them if they weren't my own.

Isn't the truth that Dolores won't allow you to write!

Dolores: *(laughs)* They can write lyrics anytime they want. But I won't sing them! They can sing them themselves! In fact, they all tried singing in the studio and none of them could!

Mike: I lasted about ten seconds!

Dolores: And it's hard with Ferg because he plays drums and finds it difficult to sing and play at the same time. That's why we got a backing singer to tour with us for a while but that didn't work out, so now we have a guy working with us and he does the really high backing vocals.

Have you, Fergal or Mike, ever read a lyric of Dolores' and said, "I don't want to play on that".

Mike: No that's never arisen.

So, whatever Dolores delivers, lyrically, you will back – in every sense?

Fergal: Yes. Because we trust her. And there is that trust in the band. If someone is doing a guitar part or a percussion part, the rest of us will go off and know that when we come back it will be done. And, at that level alone, we are really

Lady in red: A *Wake Up And Smell The Coffee* promo pic by Andy Earl.

pleased with *Wake Up And Smell The Coffee*. There are new elements involved. The Cranberries have evolved, musically, from the first album to this. It's not that we sit down and say "we have to change our sound". It's more of an evolutionary process. So, to answer a question you asked earlier, we didn't actually say that this album has to sound like the early ones we did with Stephen, or whatever. Because if you do that the music is somewhat artificial. That's another thing I love about the new album. There is a lot of spontaneity on it. We're just going with the flow.

Dolores, tell us about a few of the lyrics on the new album.
Dolores: Okay, ladies and gentlemen! 'Never Grow Old' is a song I wrote with no music whatsoever. I was walking outside here, with my little baby in a pram and my son with me and I started singing: *"I have a dream/ Strange it may seem/ This is my perfect day"*. So I ran home and tried to get down the chords on the piano but didn't because I was distracted. The baby was crying! So I lost it. But the next day I woke up and it came back to me so I wrote it at the piano, then played it with the lads.

'Analyse'?
Dolores: When I wrote that I was actually stuck for lyrics.

I was going, *"Close your eyes/ Breathe the air"* (breathes in and out) looking for lyrics. Then it was, *"We are free/ We can be wide open"*. But as I was trying to think of lyrics, I was telling myself not to analyse, just to let it come and that became the idea of the song. And what that song says is, basically, "Because of you I see beauty I didn't see before so don't analyse, just live for the moment". You know when you analyse, you tend to go "maybe I should, maybe I shouldn't do this?" and you take the spontaneity out of it. This song is about *not* analysing.

And Don is the 'you' to whom you are singing?
Dolores: Yes. Another song, 'Time Is Ticking Out', came as a result of what we were talking about earlier. Your changing awareness as a parent. I'd never have written a song like this before my children came along. But this is talking about how we screwed up our planet, in terms of, say, pollution. And how we sit by and let our governments do that.
Mike: That, too, is what we mean by *Wake Up And Smell The Coffee*.
Dolores: Absolutely. My husband has a house in Canada and I spend a lot of time there. And the Canadians are brilliant when it comes to the environment. Incredibly strict. We're getting better in Ireland with, for example, an organisation like Crann. They're great in terms of preserving trees. I just

"No matter what life throws at you, all you really have to hold onto is love."

planted 300 trees and I am really getting into environmental issues now.

But what world were you guys living on before this that you hadn't been aware of such issues?
Mike: We always were aware.
Fergal: No, let's face it. We were kind of partying on the bus.

Some say that's the general tendency in rock, that as long as its participants are happy on that "bus" they couldn't give a fuck about what goes on in the rest of the world.
Fergal: Until, maybe, they do have children and think about things like "what kind of world will my baby inherit in twenty years?" That may be what it takes. As happened to us.
Dolores: But you do have to wake up to these realities. I can't believe the amount of young people I know who have, for example, skin cancers. So these really are issues that effect everyone. And the song 'Wake Up And Smell The Coffee' is about myself and becoming aware, in a general sense along these lines. On a more personal level, it's also about looking at the face of my daughter, seeing myself in her and hoping she doesn't go through any of the sadness I went through.

She will have to go through some sadness.
Dolores: Of course. But mommies hope their babies won't go through any sadness! Especially little girls. But we do know that girls have to go through more in this world, than boys.

There she goes again, guys! Ending our interview the way it started. Wake up and smell the coffee, Dolores! Boys go through the same heartache girls do!
Dolores: They don't! And what part don't you get, Joe? We have to bear the children. Once a month we menstruate and once a woman comes home from work her work isn't over, because she still has work in the house. For a man life is also not as crazy in terms of the hormones. So, okay, when I look at my son, I think, "I don't want him to go through, whatever", but I honestly do believe it is harder for little girls growing up in this world. I honestly do. And, actually, 'Concept' is about the concept of love and how, no matter what life throws at you, all you really have to hold onto is love. And never lose your vision of love.
Mike: I do believe that is true.
Fergal: So do I. It may sound simplistic but, at the end of the day, all you do have is love...

As John Lennon said.
Dolores: He was right. And, at this stage in our lives, the four of us – fortunately – are in love. And that experience is like having children, in a way. It makes you think of the circle of life. Look outwards. You see children being born and people dying. And you think, "What would I do if I lost this person from my life? This person I love?" Another thing is that, obviously, everyone in The Cranberries is getting older. We're all nearer thirty than twenty so we all are thinking about such things. And that, too, is what this album is all about.

When we were twenty nobody warned us about the illnesses that can be caused by drinking too much. But now I see a lot of my friends have developed those illnesses. I realise, for example, that if you go out drinking heavily your liver collapses. You don't think of things like that when you're a teenager, or twenty. But you do when you're thirty. And have children. 'Carry On', from the new album, was actually inspired by my many friends who are ill and I am just telling them to carry on. Among my friends and in my family I've had an awful lot of people die from cancer and such over the past ten years. That, too, is why I worry about the ozone layer. So this song is to people who are ill. Particularly those who, maybe, have a limited time to live. I'm really saying to them with all my heart: "Carry on".

So, as The Cranberries 'carry on', what's their main goal?
Dolores: Well, getting across messages like that to people is one of my goals.
Mike: But a more simple goal is just to enjoy being in The Cranberries. Which, as I say, we didn't for a while. But right now we can't wait to get the album out, do the tour, play those gigs. Because that is where it all started for us.

And there's no way The Cranberries are going to fuck it all up at this stage in their career, right?
Dolores: No way. Not now. Longevity is the real challenge. To stay true to yourselves over a long period. And stay creative, make great music and still love what you do. At least that's how I see things, in terms of myself and The Cranberries.
Mike: Jesus, Joe, don't give her the last word! Again! Let me have it!

· **The Cranberries interview by Joe Jackson, November 2001**

> "The Cranberries have rediscovered much of what made us love them in the first place."

 THE TRANSFORMATION OF DOLORES O'RIORDAN from shy, tranquil Limerick girl to loud, brash, snarling international rock star is, as well as being one of music's more curious transitions, also a mirror of her band's fortunes. They've moved from the deft acoustics of their debut to the heavy handed, rather boorish rock of recent times. On their fifth album, however, a state of equilibrium seems to have been reached by both parties, resulting in easily their best work for some seven years.

The change is evident from the off. Instead of the expected foot to the floor rocker, 'Never Grow Old' is a sweet, sprightly number built around a *"this is my perfect day"* refrain – a theme that recurs throughout. The lyrics are O'Riordan's most upbeat, optimistic and eloquent for some time, clearly informed by her experiences of motherhood and marriage. The musicians too, have rediscovered their lightness of touch and have produced their most beautiful record (not a word oft associated with the band recently) since *No Need To Argue*. It's a full five songs in before they really cut loose on 'This Is The Day', instead preferring a more subtle, thoughtful approach that gives *Wake Up And Smell The Coffee* huge depth and a pleasing light and shade. Next to the almost lullaby-esque 'Pretty Eyes' then, comes the spirited 'I Really Hope' and the simple, almost Motown pop of 'Every Morning'.

The one snarl at the outside world, 'Do You Know', is still a relatively sunny affair, a 'Linger'-style acoustic strummer that finds Dolores in a defiant mood – *"I will be strong, will carry on and I'll always hold on to my smile"*. They spoil it somewhat by adding three 'special' extra tracks, including two hopelessly tuneless live songs and a surprisingly effective cover of 'In The Ghetto' but let us not be distracted from the matter in hand, namely that The Cranberries have rediscovered much of what made us love them in the first place.

Wake Up And Smell The Coffee **album review by Phil Udell, October 2001**

From Limerick to The World

From childhood to parenthood and from dark times to a new kind of serenity, Dolores O'Riordan had experienced a complex of highs and lows over her life's journey so far – including the dozen or so years she'd spent as a singer in a rock 'n' roll band. So too had her fellow members of The Cranberries: Noel Hogan, Mike Hogan and Fergal Lawler. With the release in September 2002 of *Stars: The Best of 1992-2002* – in effect the first Cranberries 'Greatest Hits' album – it seemed like the ideal moment to look back with Dolores and the guys on their extraordinary first decade in the spotlight. And so we did...

Opposite photo: Kip Carroll

MS. DOLORES REFLECTS

The Cranberries have brought a frantic decade of non-stop recording and touring to a close by releasing their first Greatest Hits. No better woman than Dolores O'Riordan for an honest, and hugely revealing appraisal of where it's gone right and wrong. Interrogation: Peter Murphy.

PHOTOS: KIP CARROLL

It's early November 2002. We're sitting in the library of Dolores O'Riordan's house – or rather, mansion – near the Limerick/Cork border. Three minutes down the road is The Cranberries' production nerve-centre, but here, before a wood fire, with two plush chairs facing each other across a small table holding two cups of coffee, a plate of sandwiches and a tape recorder, it could be any time, any place.

Having introduced her two children, the singer – tiny, fine-boned, dressed casual but smart – sits down to dredge through her memories of 12 years as lead singer of The Cranberries. This month sees the release of the group's *Greatest Hits* album, as apt a time as any to thumb through the back pages of a quartet that have shifted over 40 million units worldwide, are often vilified at home and lauded abroad – frequently confounding both their detractors and supporters. Here, in a four-part suite of interviews, we let the band tell their own story, in their own words.

Therapy time – tell me about your childhood.
I grew up about five miles outside Limerick. I didn't really go into the city that much until I was five and I started school, the reason being we didn't have a car 'til I was about six or seven. My dad had a motorbike and that was our means of transport, basically. If we did go into town we took the bus in – it'd be a big event on Saturday, but generally my mother avoided going in 'cos she'd so many little ones. There were seven of us, so it was difficult to watch them all, everybody holding hands. I remember in those days there was Todd's in Limerick; it's now Brown Thomas. I have one memory of going to see Santa Claus in town every year: the pictures are still there, '74, '75, '76, all the way up, an extra child in the picture every year.

Can you remember the first piece of music to have an impact on you?
There isn't one in particular, but I do remember I always loved Elvis Presley, Bing Crosby and Frank Sinatra and all that because my parents used to play them. My oldest brother Terry, he was really into David Bowie and Gary Numan, that whole scenario, and the Sex Pistols. I remember as a little girl, he had *The Great Rock 'N' Roll Swindle*, the big double album, and when you opened it there was a punk rock girl with no clothes on with some drawing on her body, and there was a dead reindeer. I was only about four or five and I remember it freakin' the crap out of me, I was kind of like, "That's so scary!" Obviously I shouldn't have got my hands on it. I found it in his room.

Was there a moment when you became aware that you were a singer, that you had a voice?
Yeah, I think I became aware when I was about four or five and I used to sing for my uncles. My mother's brothers all moved to London and every summer they'd come home to see the grandparents, and they used to come to our house and bring us presents. They were all wealthy because they moved to London and got good jobs. One of them opened a trucking company or a furniture removal company and

ended up employing a lot of staff, and another one opened a school of motoring. My mum stayed in Ireland and decided to have the big family and to hell with going to London: "I'll rough it out here in Ireland." She loved the country too much – there were only two of the family who stayed and the other six went to England. So, when they came home they'd always bring us really nice lavish gifts or take us out or whatever, and in return they'd always be taken down to the pub. The big novelty was, "Okay, you can go to the pub on Friday night 'cos there's no school in the morning." But I remember when I would sing, everybody in the pub would stop, put their pints down and turn around and go, "Jesus, she has a great little voice, hah? What age is she?" This kind of thing. I kind of knew I could belt it out; I had a really strong voice for a small little thing. I had no problem walking into a room full of people and belting out a bar of some Irish trad tune and capturing the whole room. I was a good copycat: Patsy Cline, 'My Irish Molly' all these kinds of things.

What was your schooling like?
It was like a private school, probably the most yuppie-ish school in Limerick at the time.

Was that a big culture shock?
No, I was quite protected. You see, the school that I went to when I was five was called the Model School, really quite difficult to get into: they took about 50 kids every year, and you had to talk in Irish. There was none of this, "Teacher" 'cos the teacher doesn't answer you: (speaking Irish) *"Cad é? Cad é?" "Eeeeh... a mhuinteor." "A mhuinteoir, sin é."* So by the time you were seven you were fluent. So that was a great asset, plus the tin whistle was compulsory and music was such a huge part of the Model School and the way they developed their children. Still is. I know because I was going to send Taylor there, I had enrolled him and all, but it's probably about thirty miles from here, so the idea of having them in the car for two hours a day while I could be in Turkey or God knows where, I'd be a bag of nerves, so I started them in school up the road here. It's perfect for me 'cos I don't have to deal with any overspill of my career that he might come across; it's nice to try and protect them from that.

Did you pay any attention to the recent stories of a foiled attempt to kidnap David and Victoria Beckham's children?
It's very strange, I had a feeling that would happen about three years ago to be honest with you. I remember when I gave birth to Taylor my initial feeling was, "Oh god, I'm so in love with this child that I would give everything, my fame, my career, every penny to protect this child. How will I protect this child, when I've created this kind of strange

world?" And the answer was keep him out of it. Keep him away from it. Keep him as sane as possible. It's feasible to raise children in this world very healthily as you can see. Obviously, I'm not the first person in a pop band to raise children with respect: you just have to be careful not to expose them to the public eye, not to ever think that they're some kind of fashion accessory. But I think it's a bit sad now, the Beckhams' situation, because I would hate to live in that fear.

You've just come back from playing Turkey. Listening back to 'Dreams' off the *Greatest Hits* album in that context, there was stuff going on in your vocal that was suggestive of Eastern European sacred music.
When I was out in Turkey, at the Mosque at five o'clock in the morning, through the PA system they have this chanting every two hours – the day we flew out of there was the first day of Ramadan. And for me, I'm so taken with that: if I do a solo project I'm definitely going to go into that kind of stuff, ethnic music. I'm definitely going to mess around now after the *Greatest Hits*. I'm definitely not going to go back and do another Cranberries album. I need to do a different project completely, and the boys need some freedom for a while. I'd like to do a little bit more work in the studio, or a little bit more flying out to places like Turkey or Africa and recording some different ethnic things and bringing it back for inspiration. Nobody might ever listen to it, or get it, but these are things in life you have to do for yourself.

You touched on that area before with Jah Wobble's *Invaders Of The Heart*, and it was mooted that you'd work with Brian Eno at one stage. Is that still a possibility?
It would be, yeah. The reason we didn't at the time was because Brian likes to experiment in the studio, he likes to go in with pretty much nothing and just write in there. And we were like, "Aw, but sure we've everything written!" So, with The Cranberries we have a format and we write a certain way and that's that – so it's important for us to go and experiment now.

Reading Eno's *A Year With Swollen Appendices* I noticed that he stuck up for you when everybody else was giving you grief, especially regarding 'Ode To My Family'.
You know who really gets that song? People who've lost their parents. It breaks their heart listening to that song, 'cos they go, "Why didn't I tell them when they were alive?" They go through that weird self-consciousness about certain relationships. It was massive in America first, and it is very

different in America. My husband used to sit down and drink and smoke and party big time with his father – they did everything together. And I was kind of like, "You wha'?" They'd have a spliff and all. But he died very young: they were like best friends.

Do you believe in the afterlife?

I'm one of those people who's an optimist. I like to believe that you die and it's better. Otherwise what's the point, you might as well go out and mug everyone you see. But I mean, I've always had this philosophy that, you know, when you experiment with drugs, they open up certain channels and paths in your mind where maybe you hallucinate or maybe you think you're seeing things that other people are not seeing – but maybe those things are *really* there.

Have you ever taken drugs?

Yeah, a couple of pulls off a spliff. But I never had cocaine or anything hard like that. But I'd get stoned passively now. I haven't had a spliff since I got married. When I was younger I had a couple of pulls, but I never did mushrooms or cocaine or anything. Some of my friends who did told me how it took you over to this other place and you see all these things, and I was going, "God, that's really scary, who wants to be like that, who wants to be so controlled and out of control?" And that's what put me off drugs really. I remember writing *"Salvation is free…"* and thinking, "No, no, no, I'm not doing that, I'm not doing cocaine." I was talking to myself really; it was therapeutic. At the time I was after getting so famous so fast, I had it all, and suddenly I was at the top and there was only one way to go and that's down. You can't stay at the top forever, you start getting burned out, you have to go home and rest. So, I was like, "Will I go down or will I take drugs to get higher?"

Was it that a serious temptation?

Oh *yeah*, Jesus I'm human like everyone else. *Of course*. I was like, "Jesus, I'd *love* to, I'd love to try coke, I wonder what it's like?" "It makes you feel great, it takes all your problems away." I'm like, "That sounds *great*!" But I still kinda knew if I started I would be finished 'cos I knew I'd love it.

Do you have that kind of personality?

Yeah, very addictive.

Do you like your drink?

Love it. I'm the kind of person like, if I've a glass of wine I find it hard to stop. I try to have one and be nice

THE SOUL'S IN THE RIGHT PLACE

They haven't gone away you know. The Cranberries are in the building, brewing up their own little weather system. And, tonight, the storm has hit Detroit.

No, they're not giving a workshop on how to survive life off the rock fashion-rails, after selling more than 30 million albums worldwide. They're onstage at Oakland University, playing to a crowd of 6,000-plus. And both band and audience are on their feet and loving every minute of it.

Contrary to belief in certain circles, this is full-on rock and roll, Cranberry-style, fuelled by more than ten years of songs and a million miles of touring.

Opening with 'Wake Up', followed by 'Analyse' and then 'Zombie', it's clear that The Cranberries have moved on from being a band of intense, quiet little stage creatures to a band of intense, loud motherfuckers – aiming to reach ears and souls on the other side of the state of Michigan as well as those at the very back of the venue.

Backed by the driving rhythms of Fergal Lawler – one of the hardest hitting drummers behind a kit – and the wall of noise provided by Mike and Noel Hogan, Dolores O'Riordan paces about the stage like it was

hers. And it is.

She's full of ease both with the audience and with a state of mind that once threatened to overcome her public persona, as well as the rest of the band. Fears and inhibitions have been sent packing. And she is now free to deliver 30 songs in two hours with a passion and vibrancy that would surprise many a doubting Tom.

The soul's in the right place. The anguish is in a box in some rock museum, and the hunger is still in the playing. Bring it home.

Oakland University, Detroit live review by Paul Russell, May 2002

Dolores O'Riordan pays her second visit to the Vatican on December 14th for the Pope's Annual Christmas Concert. Ahead of that, she and The Cranberries are playing The Point Theatre, Dublin (December 6) and appearing on *So Graham Norton* (9).

Meanwhile, worldwide sales of *Stars: The Best Of The Cranberries* have just passed the million mark, with gold or platinum certifications in 13 territories. This week also sees the band releasing two DVDs – *Stars: The Best of The Videos 1992-2002* and *Beneath The Skin: Live In Paris*.

Hot Press Newsdesk, November 2002

"When you're famous, your life is not real, there's no structure, there's no routine, everybody loves you. You *seriously* don't need drugs when you're famous."

and go to bed and then I'm like, "Ah sure fill 'er up again, man!" Cigarettes, I've to try really hard not to smoke if I go out and have a few drinks. And then when you're famous, your life is not real, there's no structure, there's no routine, everybody loves you. You *seriously* don't need drugs when you're famous.

For a hit band on tour in America the coke must be like a blizzard.

Oh yeah, but the funny thing is, if people know you don't do it, they hide it from you. I've been in that situation. But for me I was too into my career.

1996 was a tough year for The Cranberries. The band had been on the bus for five years; you were tired of the road and of each other; you got married and became a tabloid target. And then *Songs For The Faithful Departed* got slaughtered in the press – some of the reviews were like hate mail, and there was no end of rumours and Chinese whispers.

About us? I was out of the country; I think I was in Australia. Fortunately, I didn't read a lot of them. My husband was very protective and he told everybody on tour, "If anybody lets anything out to Dolores, you're out. Do not talk about what's been said back in Ireland and England to her. If we're doing a show it doesn't matter, it's not going to help her, it's only going to hinder her, so let her do her show and don't say anything." All rock stars have to deal with that. I'm still hearing stuff. It's like, "Did you hear about that one?" And I'm like, "No." It just goes over your head. At that stage we were finishing up a tour and stuff, but I think I was quite aware of where I would end up now at 31, which is here – so who's laughing? What matters?

Do you think some of the problem was that you didn't have any real allies in the business, having pretty much bypassed Dublin and London for America?

Probably, yeah. There's definitely a kind of a scene in rock 'n' roll where if bands don't hang out with journalists and brown-nose a bit, it's going to fall back on you. We've never done that. We just came off stage and if we were to have a few drinks, we'd have them with our friends. We felt like, why should we start acting like different people? Why should we walk into a room with 50 strangers and start going, "Yah, I'm Dolores man, how's it going?" It just seems so false. We

were really just not into the scene.

It wasn't just the press though: you didn't really establish any links with other artists or filmmakers or musicians. Even between bands like U2 and Boyzone and The Corrs, they mightn't necessarily be best buddies, but there's still some sort of support system in place.

Yeah, but they're all from Dublin you see, we're from Limerick.

The Corrs are from Dundalk.

Sure, yer all the one up there, man! *(Laughs)*.

On *The Faithful Departed* tour there were all kinds of reports that you were anorexic, sick, stressed out, suffering from nervous exhaustion. What exactly was going on?

Pretty much all of the above except the anorexia. The minute I stopped touring it just got better. But it was pretty much exhaustion and, "Where is my life? Do I have a life? Where are my friends from school?"

How come you got so thin?

I was just depressed. Like, usually even now on show days, I don't really eat a lot 'cos you can't go jumping around on stage with a full tummy. What I usually used to do was eat when I came offstage or whatever. And then I used to come offstage and just drink instead, drinking like a hog. For the longest time I didn't smoke, but then around about that point I started smoking like a trouper. When it first started it was great: touring, success, six million sales of the first album, it's all exciting and everyone loves you and then suddenly it's schizo. Tuesday it's wonderful, Wednesday it's like, "Now, can they do better?" It was like waking up and Christmas was over, and all the decorations were gone: "Time to move on, next album, when are you going in recording? We have to do much, much better than the first one." So we went in and worked really hard at *No Need To Argue*, and that's when I screwed up my knee in a skiing accident.

Tell us about that.

I ended up in a hospital bed with bedsores on my ass. It all catapulted from this: I was dreading food 'cos it would make me go to do a number two and I didn't want to 'cos I couldn't get out of the bed. It was a big, big operation, a ligament was replaced, not operated on but *replaced*, they

But I guess those nightmares were like flashbacks of those periods. Any problems I ever had in my life were just put to the side because of The Cranberries. So suddenly they all started coming at me, at once, after *Faithful Departed*. I knew that I'd a lot of demons that I'd not dealt with and needed to, 'cos they were going to kill me if I didn't stop and confront them. I was just getting thinner and thinner and couldn't sleep. And I was drinking a lot and you get to the point where you can't go to sleep without a drink 'cos you start getting the sweats. It was just wine, but it was my way of coming down after a gig, slap back a bottle or two on the bus and go to sleep. And I knew I had to go to sleep 'cos I'd have an interview in the morning and I'd have to get up and look good. So, you go to sleep after two bottles of wine, wake up all hungover, shakes, panic attacks, and then you're on camera, somebody's asking you questions and you're going, "What, who, where, what?"

drilled holes here and here and put in screws and all that. It was so bad I couldn't stand up for three days; you had to let it set. And that's when I think the depression started. I was in bed for two weeks in Devonshire Hospital in London. I wasn't eating properly and my girlfriend used to smuggle in a little bit of vodka.

So, then you finished the album and went straight back on the road.

Yeah, I'd had major surgery, I was on morphine for a long time, I was experiencing a little bit of depression, but there was still the pressure to go out there and perform. I went out on crutches in Finsbury Park. *No Need To Argue* did really well, 16 million, and I toured it really hard for a year and a half, but my knee kept getting bad on the tour. And then we went back into the studio with Bruce Fairbairn, went out touring *Faithful Departed* and I really started losing weight and I was miserable after seven years of recording and touring and nothing else. It really wasn't funny for a long time: it got really bad before it got better. It got dark and demonic and heavy and sad. I was seeing things in the dark and stuff, and I kept thinking there were cameras everywhere because I was in the public eye too much.

What, like classic end-of-*Goodfellas* paranoia?

I was really on the edge of schizophrenic or something. My husband was going, "There's nothing in the room", and I would be bawling, going, "Get out and turn on the light 'cos I can see somebody there with a hatchet."

Were you afraid of stalkers?

Well, put it like this, I had my demons, which I can't really speak about. I had my encounters with evil people in my life I guess. I like to leave that behind and forget about it.

You ended up cancelling the last leg of the *Faithful Departed* tour, going home to lick your wounds. You had kids, the rest of the band tried to get back to some sort of normal life. Then you made *Bury The Hatchet* and *Wake Up And Smell The Coffee*. The songs from those albums on *Greatest Hits* seem to suggest you've come to terms with yourself as a person and as a mother.

I'm 31 now, and I'm definitely at my happiest. I'm more self-aware; I see my vulnerabilities and my weaknesses because of the mistakes I made. Not saying I'm not going to make more mistakes, because I definitely am. I'm sure I'm gonna make mistakes with my kids, I do every day: I make stupid mistakes and my mum kinda tells me, "You just stepped on his little emotions there, you did the wrong thing." And I'm like, "Sorry, I'm only a learner here."

There's that famous line by Phillip Larkin: *"They fuck you up, your Mum and Dad/ They don't mean to but they do"*.

They do. But I'm kinda lucky to have my Mom around, 'cos she's always there and she can point out things to me. But the love you have for your kids is so unlike any other love, it's brilliant. I'm so glad that I did have my kids. I know it changed my career and I know that I'll never be like the way I was in the public eye, I'll never be that famous. I can't tour like that now. I don't want to, I did it, I had it. But there's no such thing as an ideal parent and no such thing as an ideal child. That is the world. Without imperfection there wouldn't be any struggle – and without struggle it would be boring.

• **Dolores O'Riordan interview by Peter Murphy, December 2002**

MUCH HEAT WAS GENERATED in the mid-eighties as to whether Irish rock acts had lost the will to write quality pop hits. This album in retrospect proves that such worries were quite unnecessary. Let's face it, few rock artists from anywhere come up with tracks of the consistent vintage of 'Dreams', with its shimmering guitar intro, or the plaintive opening of 'Linger' before it slips effortlessly into gear, or 'Zombie' through which Dolores O'Riordan vents real rage at the rape of this island above an incendiary backing. And that's just the first three tracks on this impressive compilation.

The Cranberries have always had the uncanny ability to create a taut and compact sound clearly recognisable by the time you get to the second bar. That very uniqueness has often distracted from Dolores' ability to risk writing lyrics that spill from the heart while thereby inviting the misogynistic scorn of rock critics bloated with their own self-importance. In that regard one can offer 'Just My Imagination', 'Ridiculous Thoughts' and 'Ode To My Family' as prize exhibits.

That she has always insisted in singing in her own natural Limerick voice has added fuel to their ire. Of course she's penned the occasional blooper too, but so have Dylan, Lennon, Bowie et al, and some of the lines in 'Analyse' are a little short of Nobel prizewinning stature for a song that attempts to recapture the magic of 'Dreams'.

But the band can pack a punch too, as on 'Hollywood' and 'Salvation', while for 'When You're Gone' she takes the doo-wop philosophy of the fifties and catapults it right into the new millennium. The love-song 'You And Me' is appropriately less frantic and 'Time Is Ticking Out' is sublime in an R.E.M. sort of way.

The previously unreleased 'New New York' rattles and hums with stuttering guitars and thundering drums, while the equally new 'Stars' has Dolores at her most vulnerable on a beguiling love song. And then there's the five track bonus CD of a live gig to prove the 'Berry formula works just as well on stage too.

What The Cranberries have proved above all is that by setting their controls for the heart of the song they can take willing listeners to new territories. So this compilation is not merely a fitting celebration of one of the most underrated Irish bands of recent times, it's also a convincing raspberry to all those begrudgers.

Stars: The Best Of 1992-2002 **album review by Jackie Hayden, September 2002**

"The Cranberries have always had the uncanny ability to create a taut and compact sound clearly recognisable by the time you get to the second bar."

The Live Adventures of The Cranberries 1990-2002

Mike Hogan uses a figure of 8 to remember the big moments...

1. EARLY DAYS...

The first show with Dolores, it was a hotel in Limerick that's actually knocked down now, Cruise's Hotel. That was down in a basement, like a nightclub thing. We had about six songs. When we'd done them, people were shouting for more, and we had to come back on stage and play two of the same songs again. That was around 1990. We played with They Do It With Mirrors, who were kinda well known around Limerick. There was about four Saturdays in a row that we did the gigs with them – and after that we started talking about making a demo tape. Looking back, I'd say we were pretty bad at the time. We'd only been playing about a year together.

2. THE A&R STAMPEDE...

There was one show we did in Limerick supporting Something Happens, a college gig in a warehouse on the Ennis Road, and there was a plane that came over from London direct to Shannon, and apparently there were 30 or more A&R people on it. They were all slagging each other saying, 'We're gonna get them first'. So, they all came to the show and we met them all backstage. We met Denny Cordell from Island Records: he seemed to be the coolest of the lot of them to us, so we stayed in contact with him and with Geoff Travis from Rough Trade.

3. THE FIRST LONDON SHOW...

Terrible. Imago Records brought us over to London to do a show: they wanted to see us play live and see if we were competent. So, we pulled up in cabs straight from the airport and got out and thought, 'Oh my God, this place is amazing' — we thought we were playing the Town & Country. This guy started grabbing the guitars and bringing them in, and then some guy came running out of a place called The Pop Club, right next door to the Town & Country, and he says, 'Oh no, it's not there, you're actually playing here next door'. We looked up and it was a bit of a kip. And the guy carrying the guitars dropped everything and walked away. The show

Merch of the day: collectibles from The Cranberries' various tours.

in there was terrible; it was like, one man and his dog, and the record company people at the back of the hall checking us out. We were never so nervous as then. We met them the next day and had a meeting and they said, 'Look, go back to Limerick and we'll have a think about it and maybe take another year 'cos you're not ready yet'. We thought that was the end of it at the time, we were never gonna get signed. But we went back home, and all the interest started coming in from other record companies.

4. AMERICA FOR BEGINNERS...
We were out touring with the Hothouse Flowers in Europe when we heard that 'Linger' had taken off on college radio, so basically the record company said, "Get your arses over here and we'll start working on this". So we went over with a few club shows booked and they all sold out – there were even some nights we had to do two shows. There was definitely something happening. People kept saying to us, "It's because you're Irish",

but a lot of Irish bands never did take off. Maybe it was just a new sound we had at the time. But we kept touring, for six months on end sometimes, and forgot about Europe in a way.

5. ARENAS FOR BEGINNERS...
We were supporting Duran Duran, thinking, "Jaysus, are they still goin'?!" But it was a great tour, it really got us well-known. But when it came around to ourselves doing those types of shows it was just amazing, we couldn't believe it. It makes it so much easier to tour doing those shows rather than clubs, where the dressing-room is a shithole and you wouldn't get looked after as much. It suddenly went from the four of us on a bus with three crew guys and a sound guy, to us and 20 other crew guys, two or three buses and a couple of trucks. When the second album, and 'Zombie' were doing really well we thought, "My God, this is getting really big". But at the same time, we were working so hard we had very little time to think about it – any days off we were doing videos or press or recording or TV.

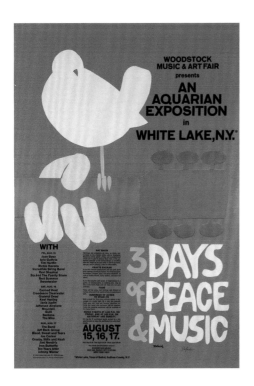

Peace of the action: The Cranberries played to their biggest ever crowd at Woodstock '94, and Dolores at April 2000's Dublin Castle gig by Cathal Dawson.

6. WOODSTOCK '94

I remember the guys coming to me and going, "There's only two ways into Woodstock 'cos the roads are so busy; we either have to get a helicopter or a boat". And I just can't stand flying, I hate it, so I was the only one on the boat. Joe Cocker was on it too. We were the first on that morning: there was a hundred thousand people, the biggest audience we ever played to. The rain started to come down just after we finished. We hung around backstage for a while and had a few beers. Trying to get the bus out of there was a nightmare, because the place was destroyed. But it was a great show.

7. THE CRACK-UP TOUR, '96

It was becoming more like a job, where you would just have to get up there and do it. We weren't enjoying the shows. Basically, there should've been a break after the *No Need To Argue* tour before we went in to record the next album, even to get six months off. But the problem with us was that we used to record albums really quick, five or six weeks and then straight back out on the *Faithful Departed* tour. It was like, "Jesus, not all over again". And there was the pressure of *No Need To Argue* selling about 15 million copies: "Is this one gonna do as well?", it was all coming to a clash. The buzz wasn't there any more: people would just go straight to the bus or wouldn't even hang out. It wasn't the same feeling. We said, "Look, if we don't stop we're gonna start arguing and the band's gonna break up and we don't want that" – so we decided to call a halt for a while.

8. BURYING THE HATCHET 1999-2002

We do two or three weeks of touring at a time now, and then we have about ten days off and go away again. And also, if the gigs are spread out, one-on, one-off, it's well manageable. Once you get a week or two weeks off in between, it's great. You get home and see family and friends and relax, and then you go out and you're looking forward to it.

• Mike Hogan, December 2002

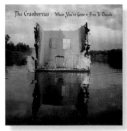

TURN IT UP TO ELEVEN

When The Cranberries were asked to pick ten tracks for their first Greatest Hits album, *Stars*, they decided to slip an extra one in. Fergal Lawler gave *Hot Press* his personal track-by-track guide...

'DREAMS'

When we were writing it, Noel brought in the chords and as soon as it started I said, "This is different". There isn't really much changed between the demo and what ended up on the album. The album version is a bit more poppy, a bit more uptempo. Around that time, we were listening a lot to Peter Gabriel's *Passion* album and to a lot of world music. That was definitely an influence on that song.

'LINGER'

That was the very first song we ever wrote. That string line just hooks you in straight away. We had a tape of it for a few months before Dolores arrived. She came in the first day to the studio and played some stuff that she had on her keyboard and we gave her the instrumental 'Linger'. That was a Sunday – she came back the following Tuesday with the string line and basically the whole song was finished. She had

most of the lyrics and the melody was there – it was incredible. I suppose that would've been the one that got us signed. As soon as people heard that, they kind of said, "This is one of those classic songs". It just has that sound, it could've been from any era, from the '50s or '60s, and even if you hear it now it still sounds good on the radio.

'ZOMBIE'

We had been doing about two years of touring and had learned not to become afraid of distortion. In the early days, the association was distortion = heavy metal. But by the time the second album came around we had done some stuff with Suede and The The, and spent basically two years touring and gained a bit of confidence from that. It was heavy without being heavy metal. Just expressing the anger of that song, you need a ballsy sound. I remember when they were reviewing it on Sky News on the entertainment section at five o' clock, they had some guy on from a local band in London and he was like, "Oh yeah, record company ploy, the Peace Process and all that", but we had planned to release it months before. We had to fight the record company to release it. They thought it was too aggressive, but we put our foot down and eventually turned them around.

'ODE TO MY FAMILY'

Did Dolores have any reservations about that song being so personal? No, she never has. We've often spoken about that and it's like, she just writes the song and gets out whatever's on her mind and then it's released – and you don't really think about the consequences until you start getting the backlash or whatever. If you start worrying about what people will say if I do this or that, then you won't be yourself and you won't be honest, and

that's why we do what we do. Basically, there are no rules: that's the whole great idea of rock 'n' roll; when you're 17 or 18 it's like, fuck them, I can do what I want. You just have to not care what people think.

'SALVATION'

It was an anti-drug song when Ecstasy was taking over the world. Some people picked it up wrong as a preachy thing: *'Don't do it, don't do it'*, like, "Who's *she* to tell *me* don't do it". It wasn't like that, she was kinda talking to herself really. 'Cos we'd been on tour with lots of different bands and you see different things and hear the stories of people fucking themselves up. It's something we've always been wary of and kept an eye on, and we kind of steer away from that, 'cos it's the old cliché of ending up at the Betty Ford Clinic. What's the point of that?

'FREE TO DECIDE'

That was basically because we were starting to get a bit of a backlash in the press – not all of it obviously, but you read the reviews and stuff and you start taking them personally. That's a song saying "Fuck you" to the begrudgers – I'm entitled to my opinion, and if you don't like it, fine, don't listen to it, but don't make a personal attack on me just 'cos you don't like what I'm saying.

'WHEN YOU'RE GONE'

Before we recorded it we thought of that timeless thing again, like the almost Spector vibe of 'Linger'. I remember recording the finger snaps – and cheesy as they are, they had to be there. They suited it perfectly, so we had to do it. I love that song, still love playing it live – especially when you're on tour, it just says it all.

'HOLLYWOOD'

I suppose when you're 17 or 18 you imagine being in a band and what it would be like being really successful and all that – but in '96 it had been six years of non-stop touring, and then our time off was spent recording or writing and then you're back out on the road again promoting it. We had no break or holiday really, just a couple of weeks here and there in the whole six years. We were all disillusioned by the whole thing, because it wasn't what we expected it to be and we weren't very happy. That's kind of where that song is coming from, the whole idea of Hollywood being this myth.

'JUST MY IMAGINATION'

During that period after *Faithful Departed*, Dolores wouldn't actually sing in the shower. She'd stop herself singing, it was like, "Singing got me into this state, and if that's what it did, I never want to do it again". It took a long time for her to come around and say, "You can still do it, but at a slower pace". After about a year, Noel started sending some tapes over to Dolores in Toronto and she came back home to Ireland for a while and we did some rehearsal down in her house in Dingle for a month. Then we decided, "Why don't we do some demos?", so we went over to Toronto and started demoing what eventually became the songs on the *Bury The Hatchet* album.

'YOU AND ME'

That and 'Animal Instinct' were probably the first songs that Dolores wrote after she had kids, so that was kind of a love song for her son. Parenthood really does ground you a lot. When you come back off tour, it takes a few days to adjust to being back home, but with kids it's like, "Tough shit, get used to it!" It brings you back down with a bang. It's brilliant.

'ANALYSE'

Bury The Hatchet was more going back into the fray warily, whereas with *Wake Up And Smell The Coffee* we'd done a tour and everyone was feeling pretty good, pretty normal, nobody was burnt out and we were ready to go for it again with more confidence. And we worked with Stephen Street again – it was just what we needed really, that passion that he got out of us as players, 'cos anyone we've worked with since then hasn't really managed to do that.

· **Fergal Lawler interview by Peter Murphy, December 2002**

We've got a live one here: a collage of shots from the *Stars* album artwork.

GETTING BEHIND THE MUSIC

The release of the Limerick foursome's *Stars: The Best Of 1992-2002* was the perfect moment for guitar wizard Noel Hogan to offer his own, unique insights into the story – so far...

To start at the start, do you think the management deal with Pearse Gilmore giving you almost unlimited access to Xeric Studios allowed you to mature at a much faster rate than other bands around that time?
The fact that we had a studio at our disposal meant that we could write a song on a Tuesday and record it on a Wednesday, and there's very few bands who ever had that. We didn't know how lucky we were at the time.

There was a period around 1991 when The Cranberries were a hip band in the UK press – hard to believe in light of what happened later.
Basically, what happened was we'd demoed every song we'd written at that point, and the demos were given to a guy called John Best who was our press agent at the time. John was great – when we met him he said he'd get us the cover of whatever magazines were hip at the time, which he did by basically giving the journalists demos that were pretty much the entire first album. Of course, at the time we thought this was magical, not a bad word was ever written about us. Then came the time to do the album, and we handed the album to the press, who had lived with it for a year already in the form of demos – the songs hadn't changed dramatically, they were better produced but basically the same songs. So, then the press decided, 'Well, we've heard all this already'. I think they were expecting twelve other brand-new songs, so that's

when it all kind of turned sour.

It's been said that The Cranberries were pretty much ignored by the Irish rock press, with the exception of people like Jim Carroll and Colm O'Callaghan.
Without sounding swollen-headed, there was a certain jealousy that we bypassed Dublin at the time. It wasn't a deliberate thing, it was that we got an agent in the UK who, no disrespect, but he had no interest in us doing gigs here. We borrowed money, hired a van and started touring.

The American tour with Suede is regarded as a landmark, the point where it became obvious something was happening for you in the US at the expense of the headliners.
We'd done a bunch of tours before the Suede one and had built up momentum at that point. We had a pretty big following, and they were pretty much non-existent at that stage. People were leaving after we were finished, so we suggested to them – not trying to be awkward or anything – we said, "Look, if you want to go on first, we'll still say it's a double headliner or whatever way you want to put it". But certain members of the band weren't having any of it, they were still living on the high from the success they'd had in the UK. It wasn't until we got home afterwards that we knew Suede got slated for it and it really hurt them. And as well, to be fair, they were going through some problems within

"It might've been DOLORES that came up
with the idea of getting a *ROCK PRODUCER* in. She had
always been a FAN OF AEROSMITH and METALLICA
and all that stuff."

✳

Strumming attraction: Noel Hogan on stage in Florida by Jim Leatherman, and in the studio with Dolores and Stephen Street.

the band. Bernard would come on our bus. His father died at the beginning of the tour, and himself and Brett weren't getting on at the time, which is fair enough, shit happens. But the whole thing kinda snowballed then. For them, I think it was a nightmare, but for us it was a giant stepping stone.

Around this time you switched management from Geoff Travis to the West Coast-based Left Bank Organization.

They were around when we did the Duran Duran tour, which was always a strange pairing in my opinion, it was a bizarre thing. But we met these people – one of the brothers from Left Bank still manages us now, and he often jokes, "I knew you hated me the night I walked in!" Because I just thought they were big American management, not at all what I imagined us to be. But over a few months we met them, and to be honest our record deal wasn't the best when we signed, and nobody had ever done anything about it. You'd all this success and you'd expect to be paid for it, and that's when questions began to arise about, "Are certain managers doing what they should be doing?" We had Geoff Travis for a few years, and I could never say a bad word about Geoff ever. He's an amazing man, his knowledge of music – I always respected anything he had to say. But he's such a nice guy, that's the problem. He'd go into the record company and, instead of demanding something, he'd ask for it. I can't fault him for that, because that's just the way he is. But we met Left Bank, and they told us, "You should be on this, you should be on that", and it made us think a bit.

After *No Need To Argue*, you also switched producers, going from Stephen Street to Bruce Fairbairn. At the time it seemed like a calculated attempt to crack a US market you'd already conquered. The album *To The Faithful Departed* subsequently got a pretty poor reception. Any regrets?

I don't think we ever regretted it. We've regretted very few things we've done. Why him? Mainly because we had done the two albums with Steve, we had massive success, and to us it got to the point where we felt we were being a bit safe. We'd been touring non-stop up to that point, so the third album was totally written at soundchecks: it was very heavy, and we were playing harder than ever before. We thought it had a rockier sound and a darker edge to it. It might've been Dolores that came up with the idea of getting a rock producer in. She had always been a fan of Aerosmith and Metallica and all that kind of stuff. We recorded the whole album and mixed it in just under five weeks – we flew through it 'cos we were pretty tight from being on tour all the time. The songs were pretty basic, we didn't do a whole lot of overdubs. I knew doing it that it was different from the other two, even the songs. We had the attitude – still do — that we'll do it for ourselves and see what happens.

On that tour you were all overworked, overstressed and on the point of burnout. Also, the amount of bad press you were getting was remarkable. Some unflattering quotes about the band were attributed to Stephen Street in a *Sunday Times* article, written by Michael Ross. How did you resolve all this, when it came to working with Stephen again on *Wake Up And Smell The Coffee*?

Well, I had always talked to Stephen. I kept in touch with him since the second album, and he read the thing and swore to me on the phone that he was misquoted, and he didn't know the guy was out to do a hatchet job. That's something only he and that journalist will ever know for sure. But I know Stephen pretty well outside of work – we go out a

"Dolores felt like shite and had to go to a lot of head doctors to tell her, 'You're not going insane, you just need some time off'."

lot together when we meet up in London or whatever, so it seemed out of character to me. Like, if Stephen has a problem with something he usually tells you straight up front. He wouldn't go the back way around it. It was just something that was read in a bus someday by someone who had a copy of it and then kinda forgotten about to be honest. Between the second album and the last album there was a good six years in between. It wasn't brought up.

The cancelling of the last leg of the *Faithful Departed* tour seems like the point where you said, "It's not worth it". How did the decision to blow out those American shows come about?

One day we did a soundcheck, and the four of us were sitting down at the back of this gig out on the grass, and one of us said, "Look, are we actually happy doing this?" And everybody kind of agreed that they weren't. Y'know, everyone was thinking the same thing, but who wanted to be the one to pull the plug on

the whole thing? You're having success beyond anything you ever expected. It obviously wasn't the easiest decision, but for our own sanity we had to do that. To be honest, if we'd had a couple of months off it probably would've solved the problem, but it was just non-stop. We didn't even have homes. I was still living with my parents because it wasn't worth my while buying a house because I was never there. Dolores felt like shite and had to go to a lot of head doctors to tell her, "You're not going insane, you just need some time off". She was just withered, mentally sick of the thing. I didn't really notice her not eating, the massive weight loss, because when you're looking at somebody every day it's gradual, you just think that's the way they are. And now when I look back at photos I think, "Christ, she was skinny alright". But that was it then, basically we called it a day.

The last three albums have failed to match the sales of the first two, and you're no longer guaranteed magazine covers or MTV airplay. How do you deal with functioning outside the machinery?

Ever since *No Need To Argue*, no matter what we've done it's kind of been overshadowed by that. People go, "Do you not feel disappointed 'cos you're not selling 12 or 15 million?" – or whatever – and you're kind of going, "Well, what am I gonna do about it? It's just one of those things! It happens!" Once you've been part of the machinery, which we very much were at the beginning, when you first kinda get rejected, you go, "What the hell's going on here? Why aren't the fans buying the album?" Then you see that you're still selling whatever amount, and if you do a tour, you still sell it out. Then you start to wonder is it all worth it to be part of the machinery; can you still play the game without having to lick all that ass? Which we've somehow managed to do. When *Bury The Hatchet* came out, I never saw one poster for the whole tour of the States. Completely the opposite of what it used to be for us. But still the tour happened, people still came to see us, and people still bought the record. I dunno, it's still a mystery. We haven't really done anything in the UK in a long time – it's been years since we had any kind of success there – but the *Greatest Hits* came out there a few weeks ago and it went in at, I think it was 25, and I was thinking, "How?" because I thought people in England reckoned we were practically broken up at this point. But somehow there seems to be this underground word going around that we're still there and people still seem to come and see us.

• **Noel Hogan interview by Peter Murphy, December 2002**

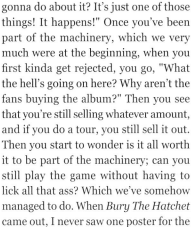

Free To Be Me

Rumours of them taking a break had previously been denied, but after fourteen years on the rock 'n' roll hamster wheel, The Cranberries decided in 2003 to go on an open-ended sabbatical. Dolores wasted little time in starting work on her debut solo album, *Are You Listening?*, and collaborating on projects with the high-profile likes of Angelo Badalamenti and Zucchero. Not to be outdone, Noel forged solo plans of his own.

Opposite photo: Andy Earl

I've A Few Things To Look After
I'll Be Back In A While

There is a time in any successful band's career when the best thing to do is step back and take a break. That's what was happening in Camp Cranberries this year with Dolores O'Riordan working on a number of solo collaborations and meeting the man they call Il Papa. Words: Stuart Clark

I t's thirteen years since I advised a fresh out of school Dolores O'Riordan to put college on 'hold' and give this rock star malarkey a go as one quarter of The Cranberry Saw Us.

Since then, the re-christened Cranberries have sold upwards of 35 million albums, graced some of the world's biggest concert stages and helped to soundtrack such smash hit TV shows and movies as *Mission: Impossible, Click, You've Got Mail, Beverly Hills, 90210, Charmed* and *Clueless*.

With fame has come wealth – the platinum Am-Ex card was secured when their debut album *Everybody Else Is Doing It, So Why Can't We?* went Top 20 in America – along with the chance to hang out with such top celebs as U2, The Rolling Stones, Kate Moss, Naomi Campbell, Pavarotti and, er, The Pope.

"I'm not sure if anyone gets to 'hang out' with The Pope but, yeah, I've sung for him a couple of times which is a big deal for a good Catholic girl like me," O'Riordan chuckles. "You've no way of realising how special the atmosphere in The Vatican is until you've been there. Part of it may have been that my grandparents, who I was very close to, worshipped him – but he's the closest thing to a saint I've ever met.

"It was great when I went back last Christmas because I was able to bring my mum and son Taylor with me. The best moment was when The Pope walked in and Taylor whispered to me, 'It's kind of like Santa Claus, isn't it?' He was expecting him to produce a big red sack and give him a present! My Mum went up then and was so happy she started crying. It was a wonderful day."

VERY STRANGE PEOPLE
They say a gig's a gig, but one imagines that The Pope and his entourage are a little more sedate than your average rock crowd.

"It was a tough audience, I tell ya!" she laughs again. "There were 20 bishops in the front row who I wanted to shout 'Come on, let's see you dancing!' to — but I chickened out. Unlike Lionel Richie who was running round going, *'We're going to have a party ... all night long!'* With the choirs and orchestras that were there, there must have been 200 people on stage.

"The only thing that compares to that in the oddness stakes was when The Cranberries played at the Nobel Peace Prize ceremony. I looked down at one point and there was the King of Norway bopping away!"

Has Dolores, who sang in church and went to convent school, had her faith dented by the almost daily reports linking this priest and that nun to child sex abuse?

"Not at all. I grew up in Ireland, so I was aware that there were some very strange people in the church long before these revelations appeared in the newspaper. I think older people have found it hard to deal with – my Mum, for instance. Her world caved in for a while, but I don't think you can blame God for the actions of the people claiming to represent him.

"My main reason for enjoying church was the singing and the services, which sometimes were very beautiful, but I was never the sort of person who sat there in awe of every word the priest said, taking it as gospel. There are some bits I accepted, others that I didn't, which makes it my own personal faith."

> ## "I had to give Ron a scolding when I was wearing my hot pants and he roared, 'Nice legs, darling!' down the corridor at me."

Jaggered edge: The Cranberries joined The Rolling Stones for the European leg of their 2003 *Hot Licks* tour with the San Siro among the stop-offs.

A MAGICAL TIME

Heads of state and churches were noticeable by their absence, but nevertheless Dolores and her bandmates had a corking time in the summer, when they went on the road with The Rolling Stones.

"I was doing my yoga one night when there was a knock on the door and there was Mick Jagger come to say 'hello'. I didn't want to let him in at first because I was in an old T-shirt, but my husband Don told me to stop being silly and we had a great chat.

"What people don't realise is that compared to his reputation, Mick's quite shy," she adds. "Ronnie, Keith and Charlie are nice guys as well. Every time you saw them they were laughing and hanging off each other like naughty school kids. I had to give Ron a scolding when I was wearing my hot pants and he roared, 'Nice legs, darling!' down the corridor at me.

"I made a bit of a mistake at the Milan gig, which was in a 100,000-seater place called the San Siro. There was this walkway I ran down, not realising that it's only Mick who's supposed to use it. Everyone backstage was freaking, thinking we were going to be thrown off the tour, but he was cool and said, 'She can do whatever she wants!' The Stones know that however on fire you might be, you're not going to blow them off stage."

The end of 2003 finds The Cranberries announcing that they're taking time out to pursue solo projects. Dolores is adamant that this isn't another way of saying, 'We can't stand to be in the same room as each other any more'.

"We've been together for 13 years," she observes. "Everybody needs a bit of space because we're at that different place in life. We're not a bunch of kids just starting."

Never one to let the grass grow under her feet, she's already recorded a song for Mel Gibson's controversial new film *The Passion*; duetted with Italian superstar Zucchero; and talked to AC/DC's Brian Johnson about participating in his rock opera version of *Helen Of Troy*. Her immediate priority, though, is making sure that the O'Riordan clan has a fantastic Christmas.

"Having two Rugrats – well, three, including Don who's a big kid! – it's still a magical time of year," she enthuses. "We're going to be in Toronto, which means a lot of running around in the snow and hot whiskies afterwards. There are bears in the woods near us, but they'll be hibernating. God, I can't wait!"

· **Dolores O'Riordan interview by Stuart Clark,
December 2003**

THE CRANBERRIES **ARE NOT**, *Hot Press* can confirm, splitting up! Despite the fact that she stressed that all is well within The Cranberries, an Irish tabloid has managed to turn what Dolores O'Riordan said in a recent *Hot Press* interview about her prospective solo album into a "band splitting" story.

Concerned that some fans may be confused, an official spokesperson has now clarified where things stand. And the fact is that The Cranberries are still very much a band.

"The situation is exactly as you reported it," the spokesperson told *Hot Press*. "The band are on family holidays now, following their summer mini-tour and initial writing and recording schedule. The band are all happy and planning to reconvene for rehearsals of new material for 2004. No record companies have been decided yet, but many discussions have taken place with companies all over the world. All is good in The Cranberries camp. The rumours of a band crisis are simply untrue.

"Dolores is collaborating on solo material, as noted previously," she continued. "She has written many songs and is also writing with Noel Hogan on others. They are both working on a variety of material, which is expected to be released in the coming years.

"This material is Cranberries-related and may also be solo. No specific determination has really been made, as the songs are not finished. As noted previously, the band members have been approached about films, TV, soundtracks, collaborations etc. They have worked with Stephen Street, Cenzo Townsend, Matt Vaughan – and others to be decided in the coming months."

As for her solo activities, the spokesperson revealed: "Dolores has already recorded a duet with the Italian artist Zucchero for his next album. This song, 'Puro Amore', will be featured on a collection of duets. No release date has been confirmed – it may be this autumn at the earliest. The song was written by Zucchero, with adapted English lyrics by Dolores and another lyricist. She also sings in Italian.

"Dolores is also waiting to hear songs written by Brian Johnson of AC/DC with others, for his play *Helen Of Troy*. Brian has been working on this idea for a number of years. The musical is expected to feature many artists and may be ready for its debut in London later in the year."

***Hot Press* Newsdesk, July 2002**

ZUCCHERO FORNACIARI
on Dolores
SEPTEMBER 2021

"My friend Dolores will always have a special place in my heart. We shared many emotions together. She had a beautiful and unique voice, a great personality, strong and fragile; but authentic, genuine, blood and tears, heart and soul, love, nerve and sweetness. A true Irish person. I loved her very much. And I want to remember her the way she was, thinking she still lives in a special place at the bottom of my heart."

Above: Zucchero in concert by Eleonora Rubini/ imSocial.

Me, Myself & I

In a world exclusive interview, Dolores O'Riordan tells Stuart Clark about her upcoming debut solo album, a return trip to the Vatican and why there's been radio silence with the rest of The Cranberries.

Dublin. A November drizzle outside. Dolores O'Riordan is talking exclusively to *Hot Press* – and becoming increasingly animated. The Cranberries singer reveals that her as-yet-untitled solo debut LP will emerge in late spring/early summer 2006 – and be accompanied by a worldwide series of live shows.

"I've just finished a week's worth of recording in Dublin's Pulse Studios, which is the third or fourth session we've done," she enthuses. "Other parts of it were recorded in Los Angeles, and Metalworks in Toronto. I'd start the songs off at home on piano and then bring a programmer to the house to take care of the Pro-Tools side of things. Once I had three or four songs like that I'd go into a bigger studio with my musicians."

These include ace Kilkenny drummer Graham Hopkins (My Little Funhouse, The Frames, Therapy?) and bassist Marco Mendoza (Ozzy Osbourne, Whitesnake, Ted Nugent).

"Before you ask, no, I haven't gone heavy metal," Dolores laughs. "Graham, I love for his energy, and Marco, who's been friends with my husband for 15 or 20 years, creates the most amazing sounds. He's a Mexican dude, so he's got that Latin rhythm thing going on as well as the rock. The main guitarist is Steve DeMarchi, who used to do live session work with The Cranberries."

In addition to finishing her album, Dolores is heading to Rome in December for the annual Vatican Christmas Concert.

"It's my third concert and second Pope! There are about a thousand people on stage, including the Vatican Orchestra, so the vibe's amazing. I tend to stick to the traditional Latin Gregorian songs I sang in school, but I imagine The Black-Eyed Peas, who are also on the bill this year, will dance things up a bit."

Does Dolores think that the new Pontiff is as rock 'n' roll as the last one?

"John Paul used to work the crowd a bit whereas Benny's only new in the gig," she laughs again. "He probably needs a few lessons and a pair of shades from Bono!"

Living in the rock 'n' roll spotlight hasn't always been easy for Dolores who, at various times during The Cranberries' world-conquering exploits, had to contend with stalkers, kidnap plots and the sort of tabloid intrusion that even Pete Doherty and Kate Moss would balk at.

Add in trying to raise two kids while on the album/tour/album/tour treadmill, and it was no surprise in December 2003 when she called a temporary halt to band activities.

Fast-forward two Christmases, and it's a much more relaxed and cheery Dolores who's sitting down for a chinwag with *Hot Press*.

"As wonderful and great as being in The Cranberries was, we'd been together 14 years and things had gotten a bit predictable and boring," she reflects. "Having released and toured a Greatest Hits, it seemed a natural time in the band's life to take a break."

A few tweaks short of completing her solo record, the 34-year-old admits that she finds not being in a group liberating.

"John Paul used to work the crowd a bit whereas Benny's only new in the gig. He needs a few lessons and a pair of shades from Bono!"

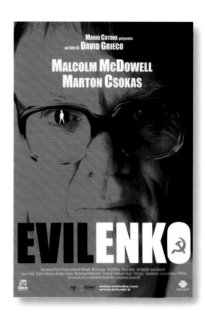

"I no longer feel the pressure of three people waiting on me," she resumes. "I'd have a baby, nurse him or her for three months and then have to break the bond because there was an album to record or a tour to go on.

"As soon as the band was finished, I thought, 'If I have another baby, I'll be able to enjoy this one for six months', which is exactly what happened. We also moved house, so I got to live my life for a change."

Amidst all this domestic bliss, Dolores rediscovered the passion for making music that had evaporated somewhat with The Cranberries.

"I've been able to write songs in my own time and in my own way," she enthuses. "There are lyrics on this album that I'd never have sung in a boys' band that happened to have a girl singer. This time I could go anywhere and say anything without having to worry about the lads being comfortable with it. There's just so much more freedom."

While her approach to making it may be upbeat, the record deals in some decidedly dark and adult themes.

"There's a very intricate and eerie song, 'The Black Widow', which is about watching my husband's mum die of cancer," she explains. "You might think, 'Oh, that's the same singer', but otherwise it's completely different to The Cranberries.'"

Dolores' mother-in-law also appears to be the inspiration for 'Letting Go', another emotionally-charged song that includes such couplets as, *"She'll be with your father/ And they will be the one/ In heaven, in heaven."*

No mere studio project, Dolores will be giving it a live airing in the New Year.

"We'll decide on the plans after Christmas, but I imagine we'll start in America with a promotional tour and then do some theatre shows there. It won't be a marathon Cranberries-style trek, but we'll get to as many places as possible."

In addition to her own album, Dolores has been indulging in some extracurricular activities with *Twin Peaks* and *Blue Velvet* composer Angelo Badalamenti.

"I've been working with him for the last two years, although we've never actually met!" she laughs. "We started talking on the phone, and then he asked me to work on some music for a film called *Evilenko*, which interested me because it wasn't a big Hollywood glamour thing. It was a low-budget film noir about a cannibal, very dark and scary but fun to do because it was so completely different.

"He sent me these music parts on CD, and I added the vocals in the studio I have downstairs in my house. We're now working on another script with David Grieco called *Secrets Of Love*. Again it's weird and dysfunctional but dead interesting."

I'd be guilty of gross dereliction of journalistic duty if I didn't ask whether Dolores has been in contact recently with Mike, Ferg and Noel.

"Not for a while," she admits. "We used to talk every now and again on the 'phone, but we've all had our own music and families to concentrate on."

Sadly for Cranberries fans, internet reports that the band gathered recently in a Dublin restaurant to discuss a reunion are totally false.

"Other than releasing my own record I've no plans for next year or the year after that or the year after that," Dolores laughs again. "It really is a case of seeing what happens."

At Home With Noel Hogan

Currently on sabbatical from The Cranberries, Noel Hogan has been working on a new project, Mono Band, in his large period house in Limerick. Though not without keeping abreast of developments in *The Sopranos* and *24*, of course. Words: Colm O'Hare.

PHOTOS: LIAM BURKE

Quietly spoken with an easy going, laid-back manner, Cranberries guitarist Noel Hogan is the very antithesis of the hell-raising rock star. He lives with his wife and two young daughters in a large period house close to the heart of Limerick City.

"It suits me fine living here," he says. "I had toyed with the idea of moving out to the country somewhere, but there's so much more maintenance and work involved in keeping a big place going and you're a bit far away from things."

After living in London during the height of The Cranberries' initial success, he moved back to Limerick about five years ago.

"I actually used to live about ten doors down from here so I knew the area well," he says. "The house was in a really run-down state when we saw it first. We knocked out the whole inside leaving just four walls standing and the staircase is all that survives of the original interior. It's nothing too fancy, it's got five bedrooms with a basic garden with a hedge around it. But it's 150 years old and we discovered an old shed at the back with a row of coat-hooks up on the wall, so we think it might have been used as a school or an institution at some point in the past."

When not on the road with The Cranberries, Hogan can usually be found at home either working on new songs, listening to music or watching DVDs.

"I have a pretty big CD and DVD collection," he says. "I started buying records when I was about 12 and I've kept everything, even the really crappy ones that you get given for free. It was worthwhile hanging on to them – I had a massive library to choose from when I got into sampling. And I have old cassettes of early demos that we did with the band, songs that are now well forgotten. Once in another house I tried to put things into alphabetical order but it didn't last long. I've recently fallen prey to the whole iPod thing. I have one of those multi-room systems so I can set up the iPod and hear music all over the house."

Hogan is a huge fan of the silver screen and devours DVDs – both movies and TV series.

"When DVD came out first I went completely nuts on it," he says. "The quality was so unbelievable compared to video. A few years ago my wife bought me

Left: Noel Hogan at home with his beloved guitars.

That's entertainment: Noel with his extensive music and film collection.

"It's not the end of The Cranberries, we'll get going again when everyone's ready – we never put a time limit on it."

a present of a 52-inch plasma screen with the surround-sound speakers. I watch a lot of different stuff but I like sci-fi things like *The Matrix*, horrors and thrillers and the odd comedy. I love getting an entire TV series like *The Sopranos* or *24* and watching it through from the start. "I don't have a whole lot of music DVDs – we tend to watch those on the tour bus. For instance, I remember we had the *R.E.M. Tourfilm*, which I must have watched about 100 times. And we used to watch things like *The Office* and *Phoenix Nights*. We had a bunch of Canadians on the bus with us once and I didn't think they'd get *The Office*, but they absolutely loved it."

After almost thirteen years of relentless touring and sales in excess of 38 million albums worldwide, The Cranberries have been understandably quiet of late. The birth of Dolores O'Riordan's third child means they'll be off the road for the immediate future. But for Hogan – guitarist and co-writer of many of the band's hits including 'Dreams' and 'Linger' – this sabbatical has presented him with the opportunity to get down to work in his home studio on a solo project, which goes under the title of Mono Band . An album is due at the end of May, with a handful of gigs also in the pipeline.

"It's just me with a bunch of different people singing," he says. "There's about seven different singers in all. I didn't think calling the project 'Noel Hogan' would make any sense. Out the back of the house we'd built a garage with a room overhead, and I was thinking at some point it would be some kind of studio. I had bits of gear I'd bought over the years and I got it into one space. The album was largely done on a laptop, although we did bits in the studio, but I wouldn't consider myself an expert. I taught myself how to programme through trial and error. I spent a lot of time on the phone talking to friends, looking for advice."

The band recently appeared at the SXSW industry showcase in Austin, Texas and will be doing some more live gigs over the coming months.

"I was a bag of nerves and got pretty drunk afterwards but it was really good fun and I got some interest going," says Hogan. "We're going back to LA for some more gigs, including one in the Viper Room, and there's been a bit of radio interest too. But it's not the end of The Cranberries. We'll get going again when everyone's ready – we never put a time limit on it."

· **Noel Hogan interview by Colm O'Hare, May 2005**

 ASIDE FROM THE OBVIOUS, one of the benefits of being in an outfit that sells 38 million albums, I should imagine, would be the chance to work with a reassuringly pricey roll-call of producers. For his first solo project, Cranberries guitarist and writer Noel Hogan has recruited an impressive line-up of sonic doctors, among them Marius De Vries, Stephen Street and Matt Vaughan.

Herein lies the rub; armed to the teeth with the world's foremost knob-jockeys, Mono Band is styled to within an inch of its life, yet it's not an agressively stylish work. Then again, nobody can ever accuse Hogan of not having an ear for an anthem; rather than being modern, despite the chattering of various studio toys, *Mono Band* boasts a nicely-honed feel for the timeless.

Effectively, the album is a nifty platform for various collaborators, among them Richard Walters and Woodstar frontman Fin Chambers. As the album moves from style to style with little forewarning, there's no denying Hogan's unique, fluid pop sensibility; call it, if you will, adult-oriented pop with a ticklish melange of quirks. 'Why?' is a hazy slice of wondrous chill-out bliss, evoking the likes of Zero 7, while 'Waves' packs a hefty punch as a swoonsome, heart-on-sleeve moment. 'Miss P' also stands out as a gorgeously spring-fresh, space-age ballad.

At once unassuming and affecting, *Mono Band* is essentially a powerful exercise in understatement. Hogan pushes buttons and boundaries, becoming experimental and playful – more so than anyone with an illustrious career already under their belts need have any inclination to be. For that, I applaud him.

Mono Band **album review by Tanya Sweeney, May 2005**

"Hogan pushes buttons and boundaries, at once becoming experimental and playful."

Flying Solo

Having surrounded herself with a crack squad of musicians, Dolores' debut solo album,
Are You Listening?, more than lived up to expectations, with nods to Bjork, Bowie and Sinéad
O'Connor – and some of her most intensely personal lyrics yet. But that was just the first chapter in
a solo adventure that would reveal another aspect of the Cranberries singer's remarkable creativity.
Then the rumours about a reunion began in earnest...

Opposite photo: Graham Keogh

Above: Producer Dan Brodbeck and
Dolores in concert at Festi'neuch 2016.
Photo:Pierik Falco

The Producer Who Helped Shape Dolores' Solo Vision

It was good fortune – and a little white lie – that led to Dan Brodbeck producing Dolores O'Riordan's first solo album, *Are You Listening?* The Canadian quickly became one of her closest musical allies, and later contributed to three of The Cranberries' latter-day records. Here, Dan provides us with a powerful insight into Dolores' creative process, during her solo musical adventures.

"It was 2003 when I got a call from a studio manager I knew in Toronto. Dolores had been working in the studio with another producer and clearly everything wasn't exactly going according to plan. I don't know what it was, but something had happened and this woman wanted to know if I was *au fait* with two particular pieces of software.

I'm expert in one of them, but lied and said I was expert in the other one too! She asked would I go and see Dolores in her holiday home outside of Toronto. Despite the fact that it was a four-hour drive from where I'm based in London, Ontario, I said "Yes" immediately. To be honest, I was excited. I always loved Dolores' voice and the possibility of working with her was intriguing.

Before making the trip, I got the software I didn't know how to use and over the weekend created a song with it, so I wouldn't be totally rumbled! We met, had dinner and barely talked about music. My impression is that she was more interested in discovering whether we'd click personality-wise. As me and my wife were leaving she said, "We'll get together next week at the studio and if it doesn't work out you'll never hear from me again." I'm still not sure to what degree she was joking, but I liked her directness.

So we met again at the studio. Dolores played a few notes on the piano. She added a few chords and then left telling me, "I'm going to work with this other producer now." As soon as Dolores was out of earshot, I turned to my assistant and said, "What the hell am I supposed to do?!" Anyhow, I took those bare bones and messed around with them. Two hours later she got back. "Oh, that's lovely" she said. And then she asked for a microphone and started making the lyrics up on the spot. That ended up being a song on *Are You Listening?* called 'In The Garden' – though of course I didn't know that at the time!

It was a sort of slow burn effect. Dolores went off again to work with another guy, who she'd lined up to produce and engineer her vocals. That might have been that, but she called me a month later saying, "I think I want you to do it." Dolores kept giving me more and more things to do, which was great – and after a while she asked me would I come to Ireland with her for two or three days. In effect, that turned into a twelve year gig!

IN WHATEVER DIRECTION

Everything on *Are You Listening?* started from barely nothing – a note, a chord, a couple of lines of lyric from Dolores – which I'd then go and work on. It was like a kind

London, Ontario calling: Dan Brodbeck with Dolores.

"If I came up with something Dolores didn't like she told me, but 90% of the time she *did* like it and so the whole process was painless. I really enjoyed it."

of relay. Dolores would take it forward again, until it was ready to add instrumentation. In other words, the writing session turned into a demo session, which turned into the real recording.

The studio we used in Dublin was actually this tiny vocal booth downstairs in Windmill Lane, out in Ringsend. Upstairs in the big room was Van Morrison, who was re-mixing everything he'd ever done. He had it booked out for two years, and then eventually bought it. The assistant snuck me up there one day when Van wasn't around and the whole floor was littered with these master tapes of his. It was an extraordinary sight.

Anyway, we'd squeeze a drum-kit into our little booth, and then take it out so the cellist was able to fit in. We ended up doing some supplementary recording in another place in Dublin called Pulse, which gave us a little bit more flexibility. It wasn't your usual album-making process. I'm not sure what the right word for it is – 'eccentric' maybe. But we got there.

One of the songs she did with the other producer, 'Black Widow', sort of pointed the way for me (*production on the track is credited to Dolores and Matt Vaughan, with mixing*

by Richard Chyski – Sub Ed). It's about Dolores' mother-in-law tragically dying from cancer and it's really dramatic, almost *cinematic*. It wasn't written with a band in mind, so we were able to do what the heck we wanted with it, which was the whole point of her making a solo record. We were free to take it in whatever direction appealed to Dolores.

If I came up with something Dolores didn't like she told me, but 90% of the time she *did* like it and so the whole process was painless. I really enjoyed it.

Are You Listening? came out on an independent label called Sanctuary, which also had a management division. It was up around the 500,000 sales mark and really starting to take off when Sanctuary was bought by Universal Music – who, as far as I could see at the time, only wanted it for the managerial side of the operation. Certainly, the effect on projects that were happening at the time was very disruptive. As a result, the album pretty much disappeared from stores overnight. Dolores, who'd paid for all the recording herself, tried to get it back from them – but they said "no". Rather than letting that demoralise her, she said to me, "The momentum's too great, we have to make another record now."

Continued on p.194 »

Family Life Had Taken Over – Now Dolores Was Back With *Are You Listening?*

ADVICE TO HER SON, TAYLOR

"I don't want him to be a rock star. It's far too tough! No life for anyone… If he wants to, he can. They can do whatever they wish. But rock 'n' roll is a difficult lifestyle. You have to have a very strong head on your shoulders. You know, it's fantasy, it's not real. Whether you can deal with that or not depends on the individual and the character. You're travelling so much and living out of suitcases, you don't know what time it is or even what time zone you're in, and all that stuff. I was very unhappy for a long time. Being in a band, I mean. Just constantly on tour. Always moving, never settling, never stopping."

WHY IT'S GOOD THAT *ARE YOU LISTENING?* WAS DELAYED…

"It was going to come out last year. It just got delayed. But I'm glad it did now, because my youngest is two-years-old, and if I'd released it last year, I don't think I would have been ready. I've now had the extra year to get my body back in shape. And the little one's a bit bigger – she can talk a bit now so I don't feel so bad. It's harder to leave them when they're twelve months, so it's a good thing really."

ON THE POSSIBILITY OF ADDING TO THE FAMILY…

"I often think three is plenty but, then, you never know. You can't tell the future, can you? So many people say, 'Oh, we're not having any more kids ever again' – and then something happens. So we'll see. But I've no immediate plans. 'Ordinary Day' was inspired by the birth of my daughter, but it's more like for both girls really. It's about the girls growing up and the challenges that life presents them and the unpredictability of life. There's so much that they don't

know that I can't really tell them, that they have to figure out for themselves. So sometimes you look at them and you have a flash of yourself when you were a kid and you see yourself in them and it's quite an emotional thing as they grow older."

ON THE RESPONSE TO THE BIG WEDDING

"Do I regret it? No – definitely not! *(laughs)*. I was a 21-year-old and I was living the life I was living. And you know what – it got people talking. Ha, ha! It gave people something to talk about. And if people liked it or didn't like it, it didn't really matter. It mattered how I felt: it was my wedding day. I think that's what they say for all women getting married – 'It's her day!'"

OPEN-MINDEDNESS IS BEST…

"There's a lot of judgemental people in the world. Human beings are the same wherever you go. There's people who point the finger, and there are those who choose to be open-minded and not to judge so much. There are those who have interesting lives themselves so they don't really have to probe into other people's lives."

DOLORES' VOICE IS THE STAR OF THE SHOW

"Thank you, that's flattering. I always find it flattering when people give you comparisons to great singers – whether it's with Björk or Annie Lennox or Kate Bush or whatever. People say so many different things and it's always nice to hear. But, luckily, I know I have my own unique sound. That's a great thing to have, but it's always complimentary to me to be compared to such great female singers."

• Dolores O'Riordan interview, *Hot Press*, June 2007

WITH THE CRANBERRIES NO MORE (or at least on an extended sabbatical) it was only a matter of time before their crystal-voiced singer struck out on her own. Or was it? Nearly four years in the making, *Are You Listening?* is the eagerly awaited first solo salvo from the Limerick siren. Recorded in Dublin and Canada with co-production from Youth, it's an intriguing prospect sonically, especially given that O'Riordan could quite easily have gone down the singer-songwriter route and produced a pleasant acoustic backdrop to her distinctive vocal style. Or she could have recruited a slew of session guns and come up with a faux-Cranberries sound, keeping the fans and the record company happy until the inevitable reunion comes around. But instead, she's done something far more ambitious by releasing this multi-layered collection of songs that traverses styles and genres.

There are echoes of her recent past; the guitar-driven 'When We Were Young' could sit comfortably on any Cranberries album, while 'Human Spirit' recalls early Sinéad O'Connor who she's been compared with over the years. Inspired by the birth of her daughter Dakota, the opening 'Ordinary Day' is a terrific mid-tempo pop song with a keening chorus and enough melodic hooks to guarantee it radio play and potential hit status. Another tale of domestic bliss, 'In The Garden' starts out with playful piano before evolving into a big production number – one part guitar-rock, one part electronica grounded by a metronomic snare.

Her current state of marital bliss hasn't dulled her lyrical potency and there's an undercurrent of anger and frustration on the guitar, bass and drum dominated 'Loser': *"I'm sick and tired of people like you/You think you're clever but you haven't a clue."*

On the other hand 'Stay With Me' is almost pastoral, with gentle acoustic strumming, reverb-ed piano and contemplative singing, while 'Apple Of My Eye' takes a similar approach. The quirky, ethereal 'Black Widow' is Björk-like; 'October' has a Bowie (circa *Scary Monsters)* texture; and the album closes the way it opens with another mid-tempo ballad, 'Ecstasy' – with O'Riordan's multi-tracked vocals providing the dreamy backing to another winning melody.

She's been describing this in interviews as a "new awakening", the start of a fresh journey and she hits the road for an extensive tour in support of it. Don't be surprised if it takes off!

***Are You Listening?* album review by Colm O'Hare, April 2007**

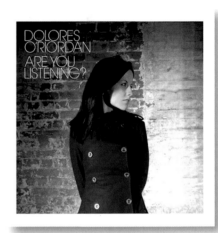

> **"'Human Spirit' recalls early Sinéad O'Connor who she's been compared with over the years."**

Continued from p.190 »

"She was never the big 'I am' and loved to have a laugh in the studio. I'm four years older than her, but she'd start mothering me – 'Are you eating properly?'"

LOVED A LAUGH

We kept going after *Are You Listening?* so we quickly had loads of things stockpiled, some of which made it onto her second solo album, *No Baggage*.

We were going to blast through the demos in Ireland – but I found out one day that my Dad had a brain tumour, so everything had to be done in London, Ontario. Dolores was there maybe five days in total, but for three months I spent my days in the studio and nights at the hospital. It was a really strange, difficult time. A track on the album that's really personal to me is 'Tranquilizer', which is partly about all that. Dolores asked if I minded her writing about my father and I had absolutely no objections.

We re-recorded 'Apple Of My Eye' from *Are You Listening?* That was an unusual thing to do but a few producers had worked on the track and it was never exactly what Dolores wanted. She loved the song and so she said, "Can we pretend the other version doesn't exist and do a joint take on it?" It's the song I won the Canadian Juno Award for, so I'm glad she did!

Again, it was all incredibly spontaneous. That was how Dolores worked creatively. 'Be Careful' is another example: it was written in immediate response to a call she'd gotten. It was amazing. Dolores put the phone down and started scatting the lyrics to a piece of music I'd just presented her with. Often with singers, you have to convince them that the most important thing is getting the emotional part right, but all you had to do with Dolores was turn the microphone on. That was her natural instinct.

On top of that, the people she had playing on those two records were just outstanding musicians. I've never, in my entire musical career, encountered a bass-player who's as intuitive as Marco Mendoza is. Steve DeMarchi had been The Cranberries' touring guitarist for seven years so there was already chemistry there, and his brother Denny went on to work with the band after playing keys for Dolores. They were really top players.

As had happened with me, they immediately warmed to Dolores. She was never the big 'I am' and loved to have a laugh in the studio. I'm four years older than her, but she'd start mothering me – "Are you eating properly?" and all that sort of stuff. She was so kind and caring.

IMMENSELY PROUD

We eventually set up a studio at her house in Canada, which is where most of the vocals that made it on to The Cranberries' *In The End* album were recorded. Dolores would collect ideas in her head, get a little bit stir crazy and ask me to come up for the weekend, during which we'd bang off five or six ideas at a time. I often had it in my head what direction they were likely to go in – but she was extraordinary. What came out of her mouth was totally different.

One of those ideas turned into 'Summer Song', a co-write between me and Dolores, which The Cranberries included on *In The End* – and that's what earned me an invitation to the Grammys in Los Angeles in January 2020.

For the most part I was sat with Dolores' boyfriend Olé at the very, very back of the room – but then the Cranberries guys left and we snuck down to their table, which was to the left of Lil Nas X's crew and ten metres away from Billie Eilish – who, of course, kept getting up because she won everything that night. They didn't win Best Rock Album, but it was really nice that, after close to thirty years, The Cranberries finally got that recognition. And it was great for me to be even a small part of that.

I really hope that *Are You Listening?* and *No Baggage* are re-released and reappraised because there are songs on there that Dolores was immensely proud of – and rightly so."

· Dan Brodbeck in conversation with Stuart Clark, September 2021

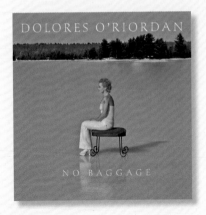

Sanctuary Messed Up With *Are You Listening?* What To Do? Dolores Rocked Back With *No Baggage*!

PHOTOS: CARY 'SLIM' RICHTER

HER HOPES FOR *NO BAGGAGE*

"It'd be great if it does well, but to be honest with you, I'm not really all that worried either way. I'm not one of those mad greedy guts or anything. I've had a lot of luck, and made a lot. At the end of the day, I love making music anyway, to inspire people."

ON THE DEMISE OF THE SANCTUARY LABEL

I signed to Sanctuary right after being with Universal for years and years and years. And after 17 years with The Cranberries, I took a four-year break from music. I didn't know that I'd ever go back, but I did. So I signed to Sanctuary Records. They started off as a management company for Iron Maiden, maybe 25 years ago. But they've been around forever and now they'd become a record company, and I thought, that looks grand and solid – they're indie and they'll be good. Jesus, six months later they get bought out by Universal in the States and they became defunct and everyone gets fired, and my record gets taken off the shelves. What a pain in the arse, man!"

... AND STILL *ARE YOU LISTENING?* DID WELL

"I didn't really look at the numbers, to be honest with you, but it did pretty well – but it was only beginning, really. Because you bring out your first single and then you get your second one out. You start here and then you try and get it up and up. But, sure, there were no CDs in the shops so what was the point being out there breaking my arse touring, you know?"

ON ILLEGAL DOWNLOADING

"The music industry invented all that stuff, right? So again, you know, they should have thought about it, shouldn't they? It's not really my problem. There's nothing you can do about it. It's just the way the world is. Keep your fingers crossed and if the music helps people through their journey and comforts them at the end of the day, whatever happens, happens. I can't be in control of that stuff. And I don't really go around worrying about it. So I don't really mind. Music is supposed to be free anyway."

OPPOSITES ATTRACT

"I was in a really, really, bad relationship. But when I met Don (Burton), he helped me to get out of that relationship, and he looked after me. And he took me and all my broken goods underneath his arm, and he promised me that he would mind me, basically. I said to him, 'You know what? I'm not going to fall in love with ya. I've just had my heart broken, I'm actually afraid to get into a relationship again. So if you want to have anything with me, it's all or nothing'.

"I always liked Doc Martens with really messed-up style, but at least I was thinking that my mind was more important than my body, anyway."

It was kind of, 'We get married, or see ya'. And he was like, 'Okay, let's get married'. And with that, I was like, 'What? Are you serious?' And he was like, 'Yeah'. I remember thinking he was just gorgeous, but completely out of my league. Completely unattainable. I mean, I'm a small little punk with no tan, you know. I've got a little skinhead, I'm kind of, in my opinion, okay looking. I'm not exactly a supermodel with these huge... *melons*. I was a little quirky, punky kind of girl. And I thought, there's no way he's going to go for my type. But actually, he liked quirky girls, he liked quirky people. So maybe opposites attract."

MESSED UP STYLE

"I had this little pink quiff of hair. And then his style was different to mine. He had these big snakeskin cowboy boots. And he steps in and he's six-foot-four and I'm, like, five-foot-two, so he's massive! I'm like, I couldn't. What would I do with him anyway? Sure he'd break me! Throw me off the roof, you know. But actually, it was really funny, because sometimes really big men like really small girls. And he liked that kind of girl, he liked my personality an awful lot because I was a little bit eccentric and I wasn't trying to be high-heels and all that. I always liked Doc Martens with really messed-up style, but at least I was thinking that my mind was more important than my body, anyway. And he liked that, because I'm sure he grew up in a massive city and sometimes people can become overly obsessed with how they appear, and lose their spiritual side, you know. There's a balance. You can look nice and all that, but by the same token, you have to look after your spirit and your soul, too."

THE BIG MOVE TO CANADA WITH THE FAMILY

"We'll kind of play it by ear – I mean, Jesus, we're always travelling. We are travellers, m'dear! As they say, it's in the blood. So what happened was, the 12-year old is going to high-school and he wanted to go there. And with the kids, really, I always try to move wherever it's more appropriate for the children."

WORKING WITH DAN BRODBECK IN CANADA

"We recorded most of *No Baggage* in London, Ontario, where Dan has his studio. It's two hours west of Toronto. I did everything first creatively at home, and then I flew in, the lads played, and that was it. Very quick. All the pre-production and the creative stuff was done at my place. And so, in London, I'd say the whole thing was done in the studio in about twenty days."

ON SONGS LIKE 'FLY THROUGH' AND 'STUPID'

"It's very confessional and dealing with my true emotions. Everyone, through their experiences or their background, has had terrible moments where they think they can't handle it. With this record I'm trying to show that, no matter how bad things may seem, it's not that bad in the big picture."

WRITING CAN BE A FORM OF THERAPY...

"Well, I guess it was therapeutic, really. It's like my therapy now. I've been to *loads* of shrinks. They are nice guys, but they can get a bit pricey so now, instead of going to the shrink, I just write songs."

BE CAREFUL WHAT YOU WISH FOR

"Life's kind of funny because sometimes we think that we want something, right? For me, when I was a little girl, I always thought the idea of being a successful singer, being in a band – man, that's what it's all about! But then when it actually happened, it almost destroyed me at a certain point. So you know, you have to be careful of what you wish for because for every action there is a reaction; for everything we do there is a repercussion. So if you think about that, you don't necessarily know what the repercussion is going to be – but you learn down the road, obviously."

AS THE SONG SAYS, "ALCOHOL AND COCAINE, I THINK IT'S DRIVING YOU INSANE"

"I've got loads of friends who went to the edge and ended up in rehab and all that stuff, and nearly destroyed themselves. But they get better, they live to tell the tale and you learn from them. Most of them would go around to talk in classrooms and what-not, to try and inspire children to know about the dangers of addiction."

SYMPATHY FOR AMY WINEHOUSE

"She is a very, very talented girl. She has such a beautiful voice. And when she sings she has a lot of soul in there. She sings from her heart. I have no idea what that girl's life is about or anything. It's not for me to judge others. Hopefully, she will shine through."

NAIVETY CAN BE GOOD
"The Cranberries' success was very overnight. But we weren't going out there and saying like, 'Hey man, cool rock stars. Check out my shades!' and all that. We were the opposite, we just loved making music. And maybe we stuck out because of that freshness. I mean, they didn't get much more fresh than we were. We were totally like 'twigs'! We just cut this bunch from the hedge a minute ago, you know. We were really naïve."

LEARNING TO LOVE YOURSELF
"Anger comes from the fact that you're angry with yourself. Hatred and all that stuff is coming from inside yourself, so as you get older and you learn to get to know yourself more and more, and why you might have certain issues, you learn to confront them and you learn to stop judging others because you also learn to stop hating yourself, or being mean to yourself, or running from yourself. At the end of the day, everybody has elements of themselves that they don't like, that they really hate. But as you get older you learn to love everything, warts and all, scabs and everything."

... WHICH IS WHAT *NO BAGGAGE* IS ABOUT
"It's really about that self-healing when you get to know yourself. And you learn to love yourself and all your weaknesses. The last album was kind of about evolution. And this one is more philosophical, I would say."

A CRANBERRIES REUNION BECKONS
"We all got together last Saturday week. My son had his confirmation so all the Cran-babies got together. There's eleven in all. Eleven kids between the four of us. They're all really cute. We took a picture of them and gave it to each other. It was really nice, actually. Down the road, definitely getting back together would be something that I would look at. But not straight away. My plate is full now because I'm moving, and I've got a lot going on with the kids starting school and all that stuff – settling in. And then releasing the record and, if it catches on, I'll go out on tour. And if it doesn't, well then I won't, and then I'll see what I'll do next year, because I'm not really sure enough to see that far ahead."

STILL: THE GLASS IS MORE THAN HALF-FULL...
"Life is about really enjoying the sense of things. Like every morning that you wake up and you get out of bed, if you can see, and you can walk and talk; you've got your hands; you've got your feet; you've got beautiful children that are perfect. Is the glass half-empty or half-full? It's always half-full when you look at your blessings. So we are really blessed and it is really important to enjoy each moment and to focus on the beautiful things, and then you don't get depressed and you don't get stressed – because stress is bad because it makes you sick, anyway. It means that trying to stay positive is really important."

· Dolores O'Riordan interview, *Hot Press*, January 2009

FANS WANTING TO KNOW WHAT the latest iteration of Noel Hogan's post-Cranberries project, Mono Band, sounds like can find out by downloading the two tracks he's made available through European iTunes.

While the service is not yet available in Ireland, people in eleven other EU countries can cop an earful of 'Release' featuring Woodstar's Fin Chambers and the Kate Havnevik-assisted 'Invitation'.

Although unlikely to shoot to the top of the Belgian gabba charts, the tracks are as reliant on loops and samples as they are Hogan's trusty Fender Strat.

"The Cranberries deciding last year to take a break means that I've been able to work on my own stuff full-time, but even before then I'd been listening to a lot of Beck and Moby and wondering, without going hardcore dance, how to incorporate the electronic side of things into my writing," he explains from his Limerick abode. "There was something very liberating about being in my own little studio rather than a formal band environment. I'd go in there after breakfast and refuse to come out until the rough mix was finished!"

Having decided to assign vocal duties to other people – "Anyone who's heard me sing will know why!" he quips – Noel MP3ed those mixes to eight guest vocalists including Eagle-Eye Cherry.

"It wasn't so much a recruitment process as me randomly coming across singers I liked and asking them to come on board," Noel explains. "They're more collaborators than featured vocalists because, although I did all the music, the melodies and lyrics were down to them. The really exciting part, which reminded me of being 15 and waiting to hear how your first demo had turned out, was getting the songs back. Some were pretty much as I imagined they'd be, while others were completely different."

Although predominantly a DIY affair, Hogan had occasion to call on Alabama 3/XTC programmer Matt Vaughan and his old producer friend Stephen Street.

"There were a few tracks where I felt my production wasn't doing the vocal justice so I contacted Stephen and he said 'Come on over!' He told me the other stuff I'd done was really good, which coming from the man responsible for all those classic Smiths albums was a big confidence booster!"

Currently shopping the album round the majors, Hogan is lining a series of Mono Band gigs up for the New Year.

Hot Press Newsdesk, November 2007

THE CRANBERRIES — WELL, THREE QUARTERS OF THEM — reunited last night in honour of Dolores O'Riordan joining the likes of The Edge, Al Pacino, Helen Mirren and Salman Rushdie in being made an Honorary Patron of Trinity College's Philosophical Society.

After being interviewed in front of 300 wildly appreciative Trinners students by *Hot Press*' Stuart Clark, Dolores and the brothers Hogan, who hadn't been on stage together for almost six years, performed string-quartet assisted versions of 'Linger', her 2007 solo hit 'Ordinary Day' and that other Cranberries chestnut, 'Zombie'.

"When I was asked a few weeks ago if I was up for it I thought, 'Oh, it'll be a nice simple acoustic job', but Dolores being Dolores she decided she wanted to make a real occasion of it and have a string section as well," Noel Hogan told *Hot Press* beforehand. "I kept leaving it, but finally got my old notebooks out last night and slipped right back into it. We rehearsed this afternoon and, I have to say, it sounded pretty good."

It certainly did. Despite professing to some pre-gig butterflies, the band were

Above: Noel Hogan at home in 2005 by Liam Burke. **Opposite:** Dolores hits the ceiling in this *No Baggage* portrait by Cary 'Slim' Richter.

The holy Trinity: Dolores performing with Noel and Mike for the first time in six years in the same room that Oscar Wilde, Samuel Beckett and Bram Stoker frequented during their college days. Below: Dolores with her Phil Soc award. Photos by Ruth Medjber.

as note perfect as they were back in their '90s heyday prompting the inevitable question – are The Cranberries going to get back together?

"Definitely down the road, but not right now," Dolores says, "because we've all got kids and babies. You can't really do both – be on the road all the time and be a good parent. To bring kids into the world, you need to be there for them. I'm really enjoying taking things at my own pace."

Which means local newspaper talk of The Cranberries playing Thomond Park in Limerick is, for the time being, wide of the mark.

Fans will be pleased to hear though that Dolores' second solo album, *No Baggage?* is due in May with 'Skeleton', 'Tranquilizer', 'Lunatic' and 'Switch Off The Moment' among the stand-outs.

Also in the can and awaiting summer release is the first album by Noel Hogan and Oxford singer Richard Walters' collaborative project, Arkitekt. It's trailed on March 1 by '14 Waves', a song that packs the most potent of pop punches. The duo are planning to spend a goodly part of 2009 on the road which, laughs Hogan, "will surprise my three kids who are too young to remember The Cranberries and think their dad's job is hanging around at home. We're both excited about playing these songs live and building things from the ground up. It really does feel like a new beginning." He also has a compilation of Limerick acts ready to go on his own Gohan Records label.

Hot Press **Newsdesk, January 2009**

AS HINTED AT LAST WEEK ON HOTPRESS.COM, the original Cranberries line-up is to reform in the near future. Dolores O'Riordan has confirmed that the band are planning a tour for later this year.

"I've decided to reunite with my former band members in The Cranberries and we will be writing new songs and performing tracks off my new album as well as our greatest hits during the shows," O'Riordan stated.

According to guitarist and co-songwriter Noel Hogan: "Over the last few years, each member of the band has had time to work on different projects and learn so much from their experience. Now the time is right for The Cranberries to bring all of this together and move forward."

Touring will begin at the end of the year in North America and make its way to Europe in early 2010, with dates to be announced shortly.

Today also marks the release of Dolores O'Riordan's solo album, *No Baggage*.

Hot Press **Newsdesk, August 2009**

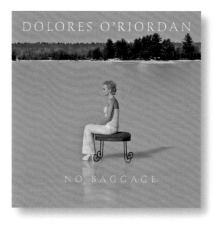

 THE ONLY DOWNSIDE TO THE AUGUST **2009** confirmation that The Cranberries were getting back together was that it overshadowed the release of Dolores' second solo album, *No Baggage*, which just happened to come out the same day as the news broke.

With everybody understandably diving excitedly into the band's back catalogue, there was no way her latest musical creations were going to be allowed to compete with the likes of 'Dreams' and 'Zombie'.

It's a shame because freed from the shackles of band democracy, the twelve-track collection found Dolores going off on all sorts of musical tangents, which underlined how her influences and reference points were constantly evolving.

Dolores laughed when I told her that she made a rather good benign dictator!

As *Hot Press'* Peter Murphy pointed out at the time, the wall of sound production meant that some of the subtlties of the songs were lost – if anyone's got the bare bones demos of 'In The Garden' and 'Throw Your Arms Around Me', I want them! – but he was also correct in highlighting what he described as the "fragile and perfectly pitched 'Stupid'"; and "'It's You', a gem of a song, which with its directness of sentiment allied to 4AD/indie charm is a dose of Prozac."

No wonder Mr. Murphy went on to write a string of novels!

Listening back now, I'm struck by the graceful love/lust song 'Apple Of My Eye'; the psychedelic swirl of 'The Journey', which follows Led Zeppelin to Marrakech; and 'Lunatic', which is the aural equivalent of waves washing over hot sand.

If any of Dolores' musical endeavours deserve a reappraisal, or indeed a fresh remix to give added currency, then *No Baggage* is up there at the top of the list.

No Baggage **album reappraised by Stuart Clark October 2021**

> "I'm struck by the graceful love/lust song 'Apple Of My Eye'; the psychedelic swirl of 'The Journey', which follows Led Zeppelin to Marrakech; and 'Lunatic', which is the aural equivalent of waves washing over hot sand."

There Will Be Some Turbulence Along The Way

In 2009, The Cranberries re-united for a major live touring stint. That productive period on the road led to the recording of *Roses* – which became the band's first new album in eleven years, when it was released in 2012. But all was not well in Dolores' personal life, and – in what was a harrowing time for her personally – the difficulties she was experiencing spilled over into the public domain. But that the band and Dolores were still greatly loved was confirmed with the inclusion of The Cranberries' 1993 Limerick homecoming show in the *Hot Press* Greatest Irish Gigs of All Time list.

Opposite photo: Jess Baumung

THERE'VE BEEN LIVE ALBUMS AND GREATEST HITS in the intervening eleven years, but *Roses* is The Cranberries' first brand new album since 2001's *Wake Up And Smell The Coffee*. After taking a sabbatical in 2003, individual members diversified into solo projects. Most notably, Dolores O'Riordan released two stand-alone records in 2007 and 2009.

However, given their enduring popularity, a reunion was all but inevitable, and the band duly went out on the road together two years ago, playing to packed houses across Europe and the US. And why not? If everybody else is doing it why can't they?

Many band reunions are a damp squib, of course. But *Roses* is different. From the outset, it is clear that this is no bargain basement catalogue-filler to wring a few more dollars from an established brand name. What we get instead is a full-on Cranberries offering, chockful of the kind of tuneful alt.rock that has seen the band's most enduring work ('Linger', 'Dreams', 'Zombie') become radio staples, where many of their contemporaries – and detractors – have faded into insignificance.

Long gone are the early influences of acts like The Sundays: the band have established their own trademark sound, not least via-tight but tuneful band arrangements topped off with Dolores' fine, emphatic vocals. Far from stagnating, the thoughtful use of guitars and drums on *Roses* serves as a timely reminder that there are still areas to be explored within the idiom by those with the appropriate creative instincts. There is lots here that fans will enjoy – but more than a few surprises too.

Stephen Street is again in the producer's chair, which has to be a good thing. The album starts with the decidedly languorous 'Conduct', suggesting a renewed confidence: great bands know that you don't always have to go for the jugular straight away. It heralds an optimistic feel that is evident throughout the new album, perhaps best exemplified by the crisp and infectious 'Tomorrow', with its carpe diem lyrics and Dolores in top vocal form as she sings "*I know that you're mad/ You spend a lot of time in your head.*"

'Show Me' is vintage Cranberries, sturdy percussion and evocative guitars dressed in warm strings setting the perfect aural backdrop for Dolores' muscular vocal. Her hushed reverence on 'Fire And Soul' evokes Sinéad O'Connor, a comparison that has raised its head in the past, but here with the overdubbed *doo-doohs* revealing a light-hearted playfulness. The track is fleshed out sweetly by an accordion, which re-appears for the laid-back 'Astral Projections'.

But the real charmer is the presumably autobiographical 'Waiting In Walthamstow' in which O'Riordan's wonderful voice is wrapped lovingly in autumnal strings. It's a deeply affecting rocker, full of aching melancholy. Those strings are in evidence again on 'Show Me', confirming that The Cranberries can do lush as well.

Not that it's all perfect. 'Losing My Mind' still has some convincing to do and the mainly acoustic 'So Good' is more filler than killer. While you might question the placing of the title-track after the more strident anthems that precede it, there's no gainsaying its enchanting folksy quality, complete with deliciously sinewy electric guitar.

All told then, *Roses* showcases a band reinvigorated by their time off – and eager to re-enter the fray with renewed determination and energy. Time to wake up and smell the roses, perhaps?

***Roses* album review by Jackie Hayden, January 2012**

"The thoughtful use of guitars and drums on *Roses* serves as a timely reminder that there are still areas to be explored within the idiom by those with the appropriate creative instincts."

DOLORES O'RIORDAN IS JOINING *The Voice Of Ireland* line-up. The Cranberries singer will take her seat for October 18–20's blind auditions, tickets for which can be applied for at audiencetickets@shinawil.com.

"It's great to be back in Ireland and to be taking part in one of Ireland's most popular TV shows at the same time," Dolores said, after jetting in from Canada where she has a family home. "I know a good voice when I hear one and I'm out to find the best star in the country."

Having sold 40 million-plus records, Dolores O'Riordan certainly knows her way around the music industry. Her addition to the *Voice Of Ireland* team was welcomed by fellow judge Jamelia who tweeted: "Whoop whoop. Very excited about having Dolores joining us on the big red chairs. Gonna be a good 'un I think."

An old pal of *Hot Press'* O'Riordan released two solo albums in 2007 and 2009, before reconvening The Cranberries for a major tour and the recording of the *Roses* album, released in 2012.

Incidentally, the promo video for 'Zombie', from the *No Need To Argue* album, has now been viewed a staggering 91,975,849 times – and counting!

***Hot Press* Newsdesk, October 2013**

NOEL HOGAN IS TICKLED PINK – and several other colours – that The Cranberries' 1993 homecoming show is number 18 in the newly published *Hot Press* Greatest Irish Gigs of All Time list.

"It was either the second or third year we'd done a Christmas gig at the Theatre Royal," he recalls. "The previous ones had been a bit quieter though, put it that way!"

The band jetted in from the States for the sweatbox of a show, which sold out in mere minutes.

"We'd been away for nearly a year, starting with a few weeks around Europe supporting Hothouse Flowers in February," Noel remembers. "Our album had come out, but done nothing – it charted in the late hundreds – and we thought we were going to get dropped. Then, we got a call saying 'Linger' had taken off on US college radio, and off we went to the States. It was nine months later when we got home.

"We had no idea what was coming. Shannon Airport was stuffed with photographers and press. I'd heard from my parents that they'd read things were going well, but we didn't know that it had been picked up back here to that extent.

"My dad was waiting at the airport, and he was as surprised as we were! I'll always remember how rammed the Theatre Royal was that night. At the back door, there were old schoolmates you hadn't seen in years banging on the door looking to get in: all of a sudden, you had a lot more cousins than ever!"

It was a very special sort of homecoming for The Cranberries.

"To play a home gig is always a buzz," Noel says, "but to have everyone know every song, and to get the reaction we did that night made it totally special. You felt like you'd arrived. If it had ended the following day, we'd done what most bands hope to do."

***Hot Press* Newsdesk, July 2015**

"I know a good voice when I hear one and I'm out to find the best star in the country."

Above: Dolores being the judge of that on *The Voice Of Ireland* in 2014.

LIMERICK LADIES

A massive Cranberries fan growing up, Kellie Lewis couldn't believe her good fortune when she made it through to the blind audition round of the *Voice Of Ireland*, which Dolores O'Riordan had joined as a judge. She was even more delighted when her TV show mentor became a firm friend!

"I'm from a little village in the Limerick part of the Galtee Mountains, which also extend into Tipperary and Cork where I went to school. My Mam put me into music classes when I was four. I did piano, singing, the recorder and speech and drama and by the time I made it into my teens would've been playing in a dozen or more competitions a year. Letters were sent home from school urging that I do other studies in the evening and not just piano!

I started to perform and write my own songs when I was seventeen, and started gigging when I went to college in Cork. I took science and hated it so Mam, who's an angel, paid for me to do music again.

I loved *The Voice Of Ireland,* but it was a very guilty watch and I had no interest in being a contestant on it. That changed when I came home from the nightclub I was working in, checked to see who the new *Voice* judge was and started bawling when I saw it was Dolores O'Riordan.

I was like, "This isn't happening, you're joking!"

At this stage Dolores was like an ethereal, mythical creature – albeit a music obsessed one from rural Limerick like myself, which is why I totally identified with her. Dolores was *way* too big a star for me to ever meet, but suddenly there was an actual possibility it might happen. I barely slept that night and in the morning contacted everybody I knew to try and get me in front of her. Somehow the planets aligned and I made it through to the 2014 series blinds.

I almost levitated during that audition. The only reason I was getting my butt up to Dublin was to be in the same room as Dolores and get her to turn around before I'd finished my version of Kate Bush's 'Running Up That Hill'. Everything else was just white noise.

If you watch the video of it, I'm emotionless when Jamelia and Kian Egan turn round but punch the air in victory when Dolores joins them.

We had to leave immediately after auditioning, so my only other interaction that day with Dolores was her giving me a big hug – the most special hug I've ever gotten!

> **"Dolores set the tone for the positive way people were treated on *The Voice*."**

Going for it: Kellie Lewis photographed by Virginia Thomas, and backstage with Dolores on *The Voice Of Ireland*.

The first time I properly got to meet her was a few months later in the Helix Theatre bathroom where we were filming.

I was in one of the stalls and heard a zip being pulled down. I was like, "Jesus, am I in the men's?", came out and saw it was Dolores getting changed. I said to her, "Thank God, I thought you were a fella!" which had us both roaring laughing.

The two of us were late going down into the recording, which was the start of the mischief between us. She had a really wicked sense of humour! Any time we got the chance, we'd hang out with each other just messing and having the craic. Oh my God, I miss her so much!

Dolores set the tone for the positive way people were treated on *The Voice*. She'd be all jokey backstage and skipping down the corridors, but when it came to the performance side of things she was deadly serious.

What used to drive her mad was the band, who are unbelievable musicians, being too loud. They'd have been rehearsing the arrangement all week but she'd come in and go, "No, no, no, no!" and then excite everybody with her ideas as to how it should sound, which were always spot on. There'd be a joyous "Yes!" then when the band got it right, which is a lovely way of getting everybody on board.

Dolores had all these little tips like, "When you're standing there at the start of a song waiting to come in, just focus on the first couple of words you're going to sing. Get those out and the rest will follow."

Another week I was doing Florence's 'Cosmic Love', which has this massive note that I didn't think I was going to get. I'd come up with a Plan B to sing it lower, but seconds before the performance started she grabbed my shoulder, looked me straight in the eyes and said, "Go for the note!" So I went for it – and got it!

I still hear Dolores saying "Go for it!" whenever I'm nervous about a performance.

Realising during the battles that it was my birthday, she disappeared for a few moments and then came back in with a cake, a card and balloons that her daughter Molly, who was with her, had blown up. Dolores sang 'Happy Birthday' to me and gave me a pair of vintage Jeffrey Campbell shoes as a gift. When they fitted like a glove, she said we had a cosmic connection, which meant the world to me.

I thought after *The Voice* ended that that would be that, but she made a point of keeping in contact. I'd get the odd phone call and emails and texts for Christmas and New Year's.

Later in 2014, Dolores sent me down to Limerick to do five demos with a lovely guy called Dave Keary, who plays with Van Morrison and has his own Red Door Productions Studio. The plan was that I'd go over to Canada and re-record them in her home studio. We were going back and forth with the songs when she became unwell and wasn't able to do it. I totally understood: her health was primary.

The last time I heard from Dolores was the December before she died. I wrote to her ten days before the awful news broke in January, but never heard back.

Dolores was a beautiful soul who touched us all in so many way different ways – and still does."

· **Kellie Lewis in conversation with Stuart Clark, September 2021**

WALK ON THE D.A.R.K. SIDE

Dolores had no idea when she was obsessing over The Smiths as a teenager that she'd one day end up playing in a band with their bassist Andy Rourke. He tells us about their friendship and musical adventures.

PHOTO: JEN MALER

"I love Manchester, but I wasn't living a healthy lifestyle there and had to get out. I'd been infatuated with New York since the first time The Smiths played there on New Year's Eve 1983. I made this promise to myself that if ever I were to change locations, I'd make my home in Manhattan or one of the other boroughs.

Anyway, I was DJ-ing at a Britpop night in Washington D.C. with Mike Joyce, and there too was a fella from New York called Olé Koretsky. He wasn't staying in our hotel, but nevertheless ended up splashing around in the pool after the gig.

I'd gone off to bed reasonably early, and was drifting off to sleep when, at around 4am, there was a knock on the door. I thought there was a fire or something but, no, it was a full-of-beans Olé, who'd been sent up there by Mike. He had a CD with all this graffiti on it in his hand, and said, 'You have to hear my music.'

Normally, I'd have gone, 'What the fuck are you doing? Piss off!' but he worked some voodoo magic on me and I let him in.

Because I was DJ-ing, I had a little music system with me, and we listened to his CD and some other stuff until the sun came up. Olé was very charming and intriguing and we've been best friends ever since.

I was equally as intrigued by the music on his CD, which was very different to what I'd played or even heard before. I'd been wanting to push my boundaries, so when he said, 'Let's do something together', I was like, 'Yeah, absolutely.'

At that point I was travelling to New York five or six times a year and staying in the Soho Grand Hotel as an escape from Manchester, which was starting to close in on me. Having mentioned to him that I was thinking of moving here permanently, I got a call from Olé saying, 'I'm in a brand new building and the apartment above me is up for rent. I know the landlord, he's English and really cool and won't want all your documents' – which was great because back then I didn't have 'em. I said, 'Fuck it!', put a load of stuff in storage and moved over with a couple of suitcases. The music-making started even before I'd unpacked.

One of the people I told all this to was Dolores. A mutual friend of ours from The Cranberries' record company had suggested that we exchange phone numbers, and before long we were talking to each other at all hours, two or three times a week.

I don't drink anymore, but back then I'd open a bottle of wine and we'd shoot the breeze about music, life, *anything* for an hour or two. That went on for months and months, so when we first met I felt like I knew her already.

Dolores, who was a bit of a techy, would ask me questions

> ## "When she laid down the harmonies it would literally give you goosebumps. Dolores' voice was so unique and from the heart."

about the music we were making, and being a Luddite I couldn't answer them. She wanted me to send her some WAVs, so I said, 'Look, here's Olé's number, sort it out between yourselves.'

When she got the files she messed around with them a bit in her home studio in Canada, and then invited myself, my wife and Olé up for a few days. After that, we went to another studio in London, Ontario and recorded what were the first D.A.R.K. songs.

Again, there was an instant rapport and chemistry between us. One of the things that was a constant when we were together as a band is that we'd laugh so much. We were like naughty schoolkids, giggling at stuff all the time.

Dolores didn't really like crowded places, so instead of going to gigs in New York, we'd eat out in restaurants four or five times a week. The relationship between her and Olé evolved naturally – it was a beautiful thing to see them so happy together.

I was aware of the Stephen Street connection, but I didn't know what big Smiths fans The Cranberries were until Dolores told me. It's only as time passes that you realise just how big an impact you've had on younger bands. I must check out 'Desperate Andy' – not about me, although I've been desperate lots of times – which was apparently her 'Smiths song' with The Cranberries.

While she did occasionally bring The Smiths up, it was Bob Marley who Dolores was really into and played nonstop. She was definitely attracted to things that had that spiritual element, and was a very spiritual being herself.

When it came to her own music, Dolores had a crystal clear vision of what she wanted in the studio; she was in her element in there. She used to carry around lots of pieces of paper with lyric ideas on them, but could also make things up on the spot. She'd say, 'What do you think of this?' and, of course, it'd be brilliant every time. It was magical watching her. When she laid down the harmonies it would literally give you goosebumps. Dolores' voice was so unique and from the heart.

We did a lot of rehearsing using a full stage set-up, but sadly because of Dolores' back, and her being taken from us, we never actually gigged – which is a shame because it was sounding really good.

I'd played there with The Smiths and Sinéad O'Connor, but only got to properly spend time in Limerick when I went over with Olé and Dolores. I have to say it's a beautiful city.

I remember Dolores being very maternal towards us whilst we there. She'd disappear off to Dunne's and come back with socks and warm pyjamas for me and Olé. She was Mother Earth!"

· **Andy Rourke in conversation with Stuart Clark, October 2021**

While the concept of unlikely musical team-ups is always interesting, the results are often unpredictable. For every Bowie and Bing there's a Metallica and Lou Reed: the experiments usually yield more misses than hits.

D.A.R.K., featuring The Cranberries' Dolores O'Riordan, ex-Smiths bassist Andy Rourke and DJ/producer Olé Koretsky, buck that trend with their '80s steeped debut *Science Agrees* and, while there are a few wobbles ('Steal You Away,' 'Underwater'), it's a strong offering.

There's a huge New Order influence throughout ('Curvy', 'Watch Out'); the Bowie-informed 'Gunfight' is superb; and the record is crammed with hooks and slick studio trickery. O'Riordan's vocals are understated but effective, and much of the material sees her sing alongside Koretsky ('Miles Away'), while Rourke's basslines steer the ship.

The ghosts of The Cranberries and The Smiths rarely make an appearance on *Science Agrees:* all concerned have created a project that genuinely stands on its own.
Science Agrees album review by Edwin McFee, August 2016

NOEL HOGAN HAS TAKEN TO TWITTER TO CONFIRM the surprise return of The Cranberries who are appearing alongside Skunk Anansie at the Festi'neuch festival in Neuchatel, Switzerland on June 9th.

"This is one of a few shows planned for this summer," Hogan says tantalisingly. "More Cranberries dates coming..."
The announcement has caused much excitement locally with our friends at the *Limerick Leader* hoping for a homecoming show.

"The prospect of the group playing a gig in their native Limerick will raise excitement levels, with the 2,000 capacity King John's Castle – soon to play host to The Coronas – appearing to be a natural fit for The Cranberries, who have not played in the city since a short performance at the 2010 Special Olympic Ireland Games opening ceremony," they speculate.

Hot Press **Newsdesk, April 2016**

IT'S FRIGHTENING TO THINK THAT THE CRANBERRIES' early hits 'Linger' and 'Dreams' are almost a quarter-of-a-century old. While, in one sense, Dolores and the boys seem to have been around forever, they still appear strangely contemporary. These songs and other gems from their breakthrough years are re-imagined on this instantly appealing album – their first in five years. Recorded over two weeks in Limerick, with the Irish Chamber Orchestra providing a suitably lush backdrop, they return to those triumphs with the benefit of maturity.

The good news is that the aforementioned brace of classics have never sounded better – fans of the originals will be happy that the arrangements haven't been tampered with too much, apart from the fact that the jangly guitars have largely been replaced by sweeping strings. 'Dreams' in particular is utterly gorgeous, the staccato punch of violins and sweeping textures adding even more romance and nostalgia, while Dolores's vocals have never sounded sweeter.

The new interpretation of 'Zombie' might even be an improvement on the original, with the backdrop offering a more restrained antidote to the insistent, repetitive vocal. Meanwhile, the doo-wop melody of 'When You're Gone' reminds us just how good they were at coming up with melodic indie-pop gems. Then there's overlooked tunes like 'Just My Imagination' and 'Ode To My Family'.

A couple of new songs are added to freshen things up, though you'd barely notice a difference among the classics – underlining perhaps how much they've remained faithful to the sound that first launched them into the big league.

***Something Else* album review by Colm O'Hare, April 2017**

"The new interpretation of 'Zombie' might even be an improvement on the original, with the backdrop offering a more restrained antidote to the insistent, repetitive vocal."

Above: It's hand in glove as The Cranberries play the 2016 Festi'neuch Festival in Switzerland. Photo by Pierik Falco.

Tour De Force

Kodaline were barely out of musical nappies when in 2012 they got the call to open for The Cranberries on their French arena tour. Eight years later they were joined on stage by Noel Hogan for a rousing festival tribute to Dolores. Add in the Dublin band's appearance on the new *Salvation – Inspired By The Cranberries For Pieta* tribute album and there's lots for guitarist Mark Prendergast to talk about!

PHOTO: MIGUEL RUIZ

> "We were in our tiny rehearsal room in Swords when totally out of the blue we got the phone call saying, 'You're going on tour with The Cranberries. They've heard your stuff and they're happy to bring you with them. Also the fact that you're an Irish band as well.'

So straight away we took out our phones, typed in the venues and went, 'What the fuck? The Zenith in Paris: that holds 15,000 people!'

At this point we'd only released one EP, *All I Want,* and played just four tiny gigs – Oldcastle, Longford, Whelan's in Dublin and another I can't remember – around Ireland.

We were like, 'Oh, fucking hell!' because when you're playing small clubs you can kind of hide your little mistakes. I don't know which emotion was stronger – the fear or the excitement!

We'd never travelled outside the country or stayed in hotels before as a band so it felt like the real rock 'n' roll deal. You only get to do your first tour once and that was ours.

It kicked off somewhere in northern France, gradually working its way to the Zenith, which was absolutely crazy, and the last stop, Lyons, which was another massive gig.

After a couple of years it starts blending into one, but from my first time hearing Benny's drums through the PA at soundcheck, and the roar of the crowd when The Cranberries walked on to the catering and our various dressing rooms, that tour is tattooed onto our brains.

We were simultaneously shitting ourselves and thinking, 'Wow, this is what your life could be like one day!' It gave us a real hunger to be successful.

We thought they were bonkers opening every night with

214

"She came out looking how you want a rock star to look wearing all white, and made the hairs on the back of your neck stand up with her singing."

'Dreams', but when you've so many other great songs you can get away with playing your most famous one first. We're still not at the level where we can do that and probably never will be.

Nothing prepares you for just how massive those arena stages are – Jay, our bass-player, was so far away I needed binoculars to see him!

Normally everyone heads to the bar when the support band is on but the Cranberries fans were very supportive. It was my first time watching a big show from the wings, and I couldn't believe the control Dolores exerted over the crowd – they were in the palm of her hand from the first note.

She came out looking how you want a rock star to look wearing all white, and made the hairs on the back of your neck stand up with her singing. I can't think of anyone who has a purer voice than Dolores'. It seemed effortless but of course it wasn't. To operate at that level, you have to raise every aspect of your game.

I was very intimidated because I only knew her as Dolores, the rock star who stands up in front of thousands of people, but when four or five shows in I met her, I felt like I was just talking to an Irish girl. She made us feel very, very welcome: the whole band did.

It's incredible to think that 'Linger' and 'Dreams' were respectively the first and second songs she wrote with Noel. There's genius in the naivety of those songs where she probably didn't even realise what she was doing. You can spend the rest of your career trying to recapture the magic and freshness of those first songs, but Dolores and The Cranberries did it again and again and again.

We really hit it off and stayed in touch with Noel who gave us lots of advice when he came up to Dublin to just hang out for the day.

Eight months or so after Dolores passed away, we had this huge slot at the Electric Picnic and thought, 'Fuck it, why don't we ask Noel to do 'Zombie' with us as a tribute?' When to our amazement he said: 'Yes!' we rehearsed it a bunch of times on our own and thought it sounded pretty good. Then Noel turned up, plugged in and it sounded a hundred times better. When he said, 'You play Dolores' part and I'll play mine,' I was like, 'Holy shit, these are big boots to fill!'

When we played 'Zombie' at the Picnic, it took off like a fucking rocket. I've never heard a crowd sing that loud: every person in the field was feeling it. It was Noel's first time back on stage since Dolores' death and he loved it – so much so that we did it again with him and the RTÉ Concert Orchestra for a New Year's TV show, which is the version on the *Salvation* album.

You only have to hear the *'It's that same old theme since 1916'* to go, 'We own that song!' As Irish people, you just identify with it.

The word 'timeless' tends to be overused in relation to music, but the Cranberries songs are as fresh now as when they were released. There will be people jumping around to 'Zombie' in fifty, a hundred, probably a thousand years time. As a musician it's like, 'That's it, job done!'"

· **Mark Prendergast in conversation with Stuart Clark, August 2021**

Redemption Songs

Released at the start of November 2021 through Universal Music Ireland, *Salvation – Inspired By The Cranberries* is intended to raise awareness and money for Pieta, an Irish charity providing a therapeutic service to people who are in suicidal distress, engaged in self-harm or have been bereaved by suicide.

Along with a 2fm radio session of The Cranberries performing 'Chocolate Brown' and Noel Hogan teaming up with Kodaline and the RTÉ Concert Orchestra on a swooping and soaring 'Zombie', there are eleven lovingly crafted covers by the likes of Sinéad O'Connor ('No Need To Argue'), Hozier's pals Wyvern Lingo ('Salvation'), Dublin indie hotshots Pillow Queens ('When You're Gone'), the thirty-nine strong Irish Women In Harmony ('Dreams'), Adele guitarist Moncrieff ('Free To Decide'), brothers-in-arms True Tides ('Ode To My Family') and other Irish acts whose world was rocked by Dolores, Noel, Mike and Fergal.

I Read The News Today, Oh Boy

Limerick and the rest of the rock 'n' roll world went into mourning on Monday January 15, 2018 when it was announced that Dolores O'Riordan had died suddenly in London. Tributes poured in from across the globe, and closer to home from the President of Ireland, Michael D. Higgins. Her old friend Stuart Clark and *Hot Press* editor Niall Stokes both reflected in depth on what was a desperately tragic accident, as the inquest heard. Later, meanwhile, Noel Hogan sat down with us and spoke of life without Dolores.

Opposite photo: Kip Carroll

Life is a cabaret: Dolores in 2010 in Motril, Spain by fan Javier Patón Melgarejo.

"Dolores is beautiful. Her art is beautiful. Her family is beautiful."

I was chatting to one of my *Hot Press* colleagues about the Shane MacGowan 60th birthday gig we were going to that night in the National Concert Hall, when at five o'clock an email pinged in from Lindsey Holmes, U2's Dublin publicist, who also looked after The Cranberries for the majority of their career.

With the subject header reading "Dolores O'Riordan, The Cranberries" I thought it was a gig or album announcement, but unfortunately not. It was something else entirely: something profoundly shocking.

Opened, it starkly read: "Irish and international singer Dolores O'Riordan has died suddenly in London today. She was 46 years old. The lead singer with the Irish band The Cranberries was in London for a short recording session. No further details are available at this time. Family members are devastated to hear the breaking news and have requested privacy at this very difficult time."

I read it again and again, but it just wouldn't sink in.

The shock had been infinitely worse for Noel Hogan a few hours earlier, when he'd received the news at home in Limerick. The Cranberries guitar player and co-writer of so many songs with Dolores, had been getting ready to head off on a promo trip to China for the band.

"Her brother, PJ, rang me and said, 'Will you tell the boys?' because obviously the family was devastated and needed to be dealing with their own thing," Noel tells *Hot Press*. "So, um, I rang the lads... I can barely remember it. The shock is impossible to explain. The whole day is just a blur. It felt like somebody had made a mistake. It still does sometimes. You think you're going to get another call in a minute saying, 'Oh, there's been a mix up, she's fine'. It all feels so... unfair."

With Bono, Nick Cave, Imelda May, Cerys Matthews, Johnny Depp, Glen Hansard, Bobbie Gillespie, Clem Burke, assorted Pogues and President Michael D. Higgins among the celebrants, there were plenty of other things to talk about at Shane's birthday bash, but the conversation kept returning to Dolores. At just 46, and in a great place again

both professionally and personally, it all seemed, as Noel said, so totally fucking unfair.

Reading the room just right, Bono threw in a line from 'Linger' at the end of his and Johnny Depp's cover of 'A Rainy Night In Soho'. I wasn't the only one who suddenly had tears streaming down their cheeks.

GORGEOUS MEMORY

Getting home at around 3am – there's always a Shane after-party – I was stunned by both the volume and heartfelt nature of the tributes to Dolores.

In Limerick, fans had gathered spontaneously at Arthur's Quay for a Cranberries singsong at which lots more tears were shed.

Before heading to the Concert Hall to present Shane with a Lifetime Achievement Award, that rock 'n' roll President of ours, Michael D. Higgins, had written: "I recall with fondness the late Limerick TD Jim Kemmy's introduction of Dolores and The Cranberries to me, and the pride he and so many others took in their successes. To all those who follow and support Irish music, Irish musicians and the performing arts, her death will be a big loss."

The word from Bono and the rest of U2 was, "The band are floored, but it's of course her family we're all thinking of right now. Out of the West came this storm of a voice – she had such strength of conviction, yet she could speak to the fragility in all of us. Limerick's 'Bel canto'."

A shocked Stephen Street, who produced those classic Cranberries records, messaged: "I have just heard the news regarding Dolores. I need a little time to process what has happened. Suffice to say, I am very sad to lose someone who meant so much to me and many people across the world. RIP my songbird."

Speaking on behalf of R.E.M., her old pal Michael Stipe said: "We are all saddened to hear the news. Dolores was a brilliant and generous spirit with a quick humour and a stunning voice. Our love to the band and to her family."

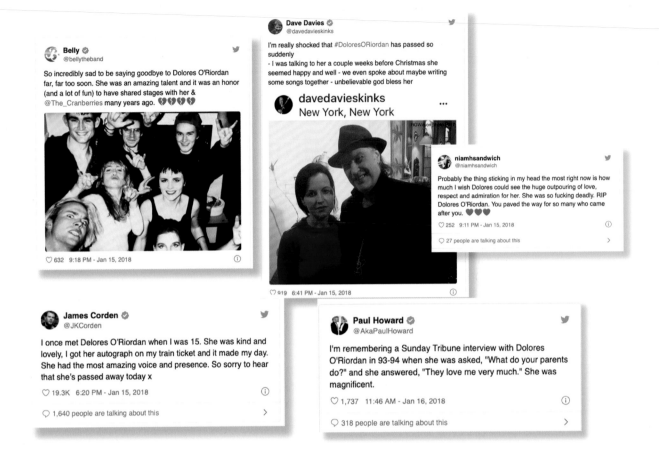

Belly ✓
@bellytheband

So incredibly sad to be saying goodbye to Dolores O'Riordan far, far too soon. She was an amazing talent and it was an honor (and a lot of fun) to have shared stages with her & @The_Cranberries many years ago. 💔💔💔💔

♡ 632 9:18 PM - Jan 15, 2018

Dave Davies ✓
@davedavieskinks

I'm really shocked that #DoloresORiordan has passed so suddenly
- I was talking to her a couple weeks before Christmas she seemed happy and well - we even spoke about maybe writing some songs together - unbelievable god bless her

davedavieskinks
New York, New York ...

♡ 919 6:41 PM - Jan 15, 2018

niamhsandwich
@niamhsandwich

Probably the thing sticking in my head the most right now is how much I wish Dolores could see the huge outpouring of love, respect and admiration for her. She was so fucking deadly. RIP Dolores O'Riordan. You paved the way for so many who came after you. 🖤🖤🖤

♡ 252 9:11 PM - Jan 15, 2018

○ 27 people are talking about this >

James Corden ✓
@JKCorden

I once met Delores O'Riordan when I was 15. She was kind and lovely, I got her autograph on my train ticket and it made my day. She had the most amazing voice and presence. So sorry to hear that she's passed away today x

♡ 19.3K 6:20 PM - Jan 15, 2018

○ 1,640 people are talking about this >

Paul Howard ✓
@AkaPaulHoward

I'm remembering a Sunday Tribune interview with Dolores O'Riordan in 93-94 when she was asked, "What do your parents do?" and she answered, "They love me very much." She was magnificent.

♡ 1,737 11:46 AM - Jan 16, 2018

○ 318 people are talking about this >

Another old friend of hers, Tanya Donnelly from Belly, added: "So incredibly sad to be saying goodbye to Dolores O'Riordan far, far too soon. She was an amazing talent and it was an honour – and a lot of fun – to have shared stages with her and The Cranberries many moons ago."

Kinks legend Dave Davies posted a photo of himself in New York with the accompanying message: "I was talking to her a couple of weeks before Christmas. She seemed happy and well. We even spoke about maybe writing some songs together. Unbelievable, God bless her."

US talk show host James Corden shared this gorgeous memory: "I once met Dolores O'Riordan when I was 15. She was a kid and lovely. I got her autograph on my train ticket and it made my day. She had the most amazing voice and presence. So sorry to hear that she's passed away."

BREATH-TAKING TALENT

Closer to home, former Fight Like Apes and Le Galaxie singer MayKay noted that, "Dolores O'Riordan has had such a huge impact on me in so many ways. Watching the light and shade in her performances, her voice, her attitude. She's the reason so many young girls saw a place for themselves in rock music. So, so sad."

Hozier reflected that, "My first time hearing Dolores O'Riordan's voice was unforgettable. It threw into question what a voice could sound like in that context of rock. I'd never heard somebody use their instrument in that way."

Smiths legend Andy Rourke, who'd been working with her as one-third of D.A.R.K., said: "I am heartbroken by the unexpected passing of Dolores. I've enjoyed the years spent together and am privileged to call her a close friend. It was a bonus to work with her and experience her breathtaking and unique talent. I will miss her terribly."

Most poignant of all were these words from Olé Koretsky, the New York-based DJ and producer who completed the D.A.R.K. lineup and was also Dolores' boyfriend.

"My friend, partner and the love of my life has gone," he said. "Dolores is beautiful. Her art is beautiful. Her family is beautiful. The energy she continues to radiate is undeniable. I am lost. I miss her so much. I will continue to stumble around this planet for some time, knowing well there's no real place for me here."

· **Stuart Clark, January 2018**

Dolores O'Riordan is buried in Ballybricken, Co. Limerick

David Raleigh attended the funeral mass and reports on what was a sombre occasion.

St Ailbe's Church, in the Co. Limerick village of Ballybricken, with a capacity to hold just 200 people, was thronged.

At first there was silence, and then that gorgeous Limerick accent filled the building to the rafters.

"Aaaaavvvvvvveee Mariaaaaaaaaa"... Dolores O'Riordan's voice echoed through the church, in the most extraordinary way.

Tears flowed, as they had done in 1995, when together with Luciano Pavarotti, Dolores had performed a stunning version of the hymn to an audience – which included Lady Diana, Princess of Wales – at a Children of Bosnia concert. There was much crying and weeping in this little valley of tears, as locals came to sympathise with O'Riordan's mother Eileen, and the singer's children, Taylor (20); Molly (16); and Dakota (12).

Ali Hewson, Bressie, Dave Fanning, and his 2fm colleague Eoghan McDermott also came to say their last goodbyes.

Members of the Irish Chamber Orchestra (ICO) played soothing Quartet music as Dolores' loved ones brought symbols of her short, extraordinary life to the altar: a guitar and a platinum disc award, by her niece, Eileen, and life-long friend, Teresa; a picture of Our Lady of Dolours, after whom Dolores was named by her nephew, Patrick; and a poetry book by Breffni, a life-long friend.

Dolores had spoken publicly about her own ongoing battle with mental health issues. But she ventured recently that she had found joy again in performing her music, which touched so many.

"It must be added that the numbers she rescued from the darkness of depression are impossible to count," her friend Fr. Liam McNamara said. "No words are adequate to describe Dolores or to accurately state the influence for good she has been over the years."

O'Riordan's partner Olé Koretsky – who performed alongside Dolores in her new band D.A.R.K. – was also there. President Michael D. Higgins – who travelled to Limerick yesterday to meet the family and to offer his condolences – and the Taoiseach were represented by their Aide-De-Camps.

Fr. McNamara revealed how Dolores had "loved" to visit monasteries, including Mount Mellery, Glenstal, and Roscrea "to listen to the monks chant." Expressing his "sincere sympathy" to her fellow Cranberries bandmates – Mike Hogan, Noel Hogan and Fergal Lawler – he added: "We all share in the deep pain of your bereavement. We shall miss her gentle handshake, her loving smile."

Archbishop Kieran O'Reilly SMA, Archbishop of Cashel & Emly, also spoke.

"She was an inspiration and source of encouragement to many young artists over the years," he said. "Her singing voice was unique, far reaching and distinctly Irish."

Ex-husband Don Burton (a former Duran Duran tour manager) and his son Donny Jnr (26) helped shoulder Dolores' coffin out of the church, as The Cranberries song 'When You're Gone' was aired.

The world's media had waited in anticipation of other music icons rocking up to the church. In the end, they stayed away. This was no circus. It was a final farewell for those who knew "Dolly" best. Family, friends, and neighbours came to say their personal goodbyes. Dolores was leaving Ballybricken for good, on her final solo tour, before joining the big choir in the sky.

In a last, gentle tribute, her coffin paused, as nephews Daniel and Andy, who pipe with the City of Limerick Pipe Band, performed 'Hard Times (Come Again No More)'.

There was no further time to linger. Dolores O'Riordan was carried to her final resting place, alongside her beloved late father Terry.

• **David Raleigh, January 2018**

THE FUNERAL ORATION

"Since we heard of the sudden death of Dolores O'Riordan, many hearts in Ireland and around the world are heavy with sadness on hearing the news. Indeed, the great outpouring of sympathy and love for Dolores, which we have seen since her death is a witness and a tribute to her great musical talent and very special voice by her many fans and lovers of music.

"Dolores put her God given talents at the service of others. From an early age she had a passion and love for music. She has been an inspiration and source of encouragement to many young artists over the years. Her gifts have resonated in the lives of many and will continue to do so as her music and her songs will continue to be played and listened to. Her singing voice was unique, far reaching and distinctly Irish.

"In an interview after meeting the now Saint Pope John Paul II, Dolores stated that her faith was one of her greatest musical influences. She said the Church had nurtured her development as an artist and musician and, for her, her faith was always important – a source of strength in her life.

"Dolores will be sadly missed by all who knew and loved her, particularly her family, friends and the people of her native Limerick who held her close to their hearts.

"Our thoughts and prayers are with her mother, Eileen, children, sister, brothers and wide circle of friends, especially in the music world, who have worked with Dolores over the many years of her career. We commend Dolores to the loving and tender care of our God. *Ar dheis Dé go raibh a anam dílis.*"

Archbishop Kieran O'Reilly, Limerick, January 2018

Remembering
AN IRISH ICON

R ust never sleeps. Death is only ever down the road. The inescapable question is: how far away is the long black car and how quickly is it moving?

It is inevitable, of course, with the passage of time, that people we know, and among them people we revere, will have to say their last goodbyes. For music fans, 2016, which began with the death of David Bowie and ended in the loss of the inestimably great Leonard Cohen, was an especially crushing year.

And so it came as a relief that 2017 proved to be less brutal. Tom Petty died in October and the sense of loss was immense. But we were spared the kind of Bowie-Prince-Cohen triple-whammy that had robbed the world of three of the all-time greats the previous year.

We don't want our heroes to die. Their success, and by extension their stardom, carries within it intimations of immortality. When Elvis scandalously shook those shapely hips of his on the *Ed Sullivan Show* back in the 1950s, he had the look of a young man who might just live forever. Of course he couldn't and didn't. Elvis died in 1977, the year that *Hot Press* was launched. At 42 years of age, he was a young man still, carried to his final resting place long before his time.

The same is true of a litany of rock stars and leading music lights, who died, often tragically, far too young: Buddy Holly, Otis Redding, Jim Morrison, Jimi Hendrix, Janis Joplin, Brian Jones, Sandy Denny, Keith Moon, Tim Buckley, Marc Bolan, Nick Drake, Luke Kelly, John Bonham, John Lennon, Philip Lynott, Bob Marley, Joe Strummer, Laura Nyro, John

Borrowman, Freddie Mercury, George Harrison, Donna Summer, Michael Jackson, Kurt Cobain, Jeff Buckley, Rory Gallagher, Michael Hutchence, Amy Winehouse, Lou Reed, Gary Moore, Tupac Shakur, Philip Chevron, Biggie Smalls, Whitney Houston, Aaliyah, Guy Clark and so on, up to more recent high profile departures like George Michael, Bowie, and Prince.

That list is, of course, only scratching the surface of the surface. But it is long enough, and most of those on it were young enough to confirm that the world of music takes a grim toll. Well, now another Irish name can be scratched onto the memorial stone.

The news, thundering across the wires, came like a hammer blow. Later that night, the National Concert Hall in Dublin would play host to the incomparable Shane MacGowan, and a cast of musicians and celebrities, who were there to celebrate the great Irish songwriter's 60th birthday. People have been predicting Shane's demise for years, but so far they have been proven wrong: he may not exactly be hale and hearty in 2018, but he is still battling through, fighting the good fight. And there are others around whom the grim reaper has been circling. We know this: it is in the nature of things.

But in the run up to Shane's big night we heard the words being spoken aloud, and on the radio: Dolores O'Riordan, lead singer with The Cranberries has died. It was worse than a hammer blow. It was like an explosion, and the immediate reaction was to look around to see if anyone else had been caught in the blast, or what might be shrouded by the debris.

As it turned out, Dolores was alone. Her body had been

David Rooney's *Hot Press* illustration

Psycho thriller: Dolores captured in 2001 by Mick Quinn.

found by staff, in her room in the Park Lane Hotel in London. Police said quickly that foul play was not suspected. The rest of the day raced by in a blur of rumour, hard information and requests for different members of the *Hot Press* inner circle to say a few words on radio and television about the loss of a great Irish artist.

In circumstances like these, there is hardly time to think. You marshal your ideas to the max, put your best foot forward and answer the questions which are asked. Almost inevitably, you are left with the feeling that there was more to say, that you might have done better, that you are not quite articulating the profound sense of loss that is creeping up on people and mugging them, over and over again, whether individually or as a community. And so for clarity, you ask yourself the same questions.

What was it about Dolores O'Riordan that made her special? What, in the cold, terrible, light of the morning, of the day after she died, was – or is – her legacy? It is easy to offer glib answers. But we need to do better than that, if we are to honour her work and her memory in the way that we should. Which is why we are gathered here today...

DE FACTO LEADER

I remember Colm O'Callaghan and Mick O'Hara and Kevin Barry writing passionately in *Hot Press* about the wonderful music of this extraordinary new band from Limerick; the early rush of excitement, hearing tracks like 'Linger' and 'Dreams'; newcomer Stuart Clark offering seminal insights into the Limerick scene. In early reports like these, as a fledgling band emerges from their cocoon, there is a sense that everybody is feeling their way. There may be something special afoot. Then again there may not. But Dolores certainly didn't answer to any rock 'n' roll cliché. That was a good start.

She wore Aran sweaters to photo shoots. With dark Irish hair, she looked like the girl from down the road who was a good bet to do well in the Leaving Cert. And she was serious with it. Or that was how it seemed at least. Some of the boy critics fell madly in love, precisely because she wasn't a 'glamour chick', putting on the rock 'n' roll style. A certain innocence shone through. It was a lovely quality.

The Cranberries were serious young men too. They recognised Dolores' potential from that first audition. They heard in her voice a unique quality that would later captivate the world. Ireland had a tradition of strong female singers on the folk and blues scene, with people like Mary Black, Moya Ní Bhraonáin, Maura O'Connell and Dolores Keane to the fore. For the most part, they were interpreters, singing songs written by others or that were part of the canon. Clodagh Simonds of Mellow Candle and Gay Woods of Auto Dá Fé had made the transition from folk to rock, but they were exceptions.

On a Swiss roll: Dolores getting the crowd to sing it back to her at the 2016 Festi'neuch Festival. Photo by Pierik Falco.

Arriving in the latter half of the 1980s, Sinéad O'Connor was the first to indisputably break through the glass ceiling. But there were precious few precedents for what Dolores O'Riordan set out to do: to be a woman fronting a rock 'n' roll band in Ireland, who was also the primary songwriter. She was a late-comer to the band. An opening was created by the fact that her predecessor vocalist, Niall Quinn, was also The Cranberries' main lyricist. But it took courage and strength of character to take up the mantle in the way that she did.

From their debut album on, she was the band's lyricist, with composer credits on *Everybody Else Is Doing It, So Why Can't We?* for the most part shared with Noel Hogan. By the time of *No Need To Argue*, the number of songs credited solely to Dolores had increased to six, including the record's megahit, 'Zombie'.

Nothing, you can argue, really happens in isolation. While Sinéad O'Connor created the blueprint in a rock context, other female songwriters were also breaking through at the end of the 1980s and the beginning of the '90s, notably including Enya and lyricist Roma Ryan, whose *Watermark* album, released in 1988, was an international bestseller, as well as Eleanor McEvoy – around whose original song, 'A Woman's Heart', the hugely successful album and tour of the same name were constructed in 1992.

But what Dolores was doing with The Cranberries was different. She became the de facto leader of a rock band, capable of making a loud, grungy and occasionally angry noise – who with the release of *No Need To Argue*, shot to global recognition and acclaim. She was the front woman. The star. And the songs reflected what she wanted to say.

VITAL CONTRIBUTION

For ambitious female musicians all over Ireland, this was a vindication. There were ways in which Dolores' view of the world was conservative, but her effect on young Irish women was radical. It made a huge difference here to see a convent girl from Co. Limerick, transformed, within a few years, into a global rock icon, leading an otherwise all-male band from the front.

There was something extraordinary too about the way Dolores approached the whole process. It was possible to disagree with what she said and still be impressed by the way that she said it. *Hot Press* always had a good working relationship with The Cranberries, and we interviewed Dolores whenever the band were heading out, into the rock 'n' roll trenches.

Looking over those interviews, you can see why people enjoyed talking to her so much. She was open, straightforward and honest. There was nothing she wouldn't discuss. She didn't give a damn if what she was saying was fashionable or otherwise. What you saw was what you got. There was a lot to admire in that.

She approached the task of lyric writing in the same way. Dolores had no illusions about being a literary heavyweight:

> "She didn't give a damn if what she was saying was fashionable or otherwise. What you saw was what you got. There was a lot to admire in that."

Bob Dylan could rest easy on his future Nobel laurels. But she thought of herself as a poet, and the directness and lack of pretence that shone through when she spoke was there in the lyrics too. As far as she was concerned that lack of artifice was a strength – and her fans loved it.

In a moment like this, it is important to acknowledge the huge part that the other members of the band played in creating the noise – The Cranberries' sound – that resonated so widely. But the fact that Dolores was out front, singing songs that came from the heart – from her heart – and being hailed across the world, and played constantly on the radio at home, was exactly the kind of inspiration that younger Irish female musicians needed back then.

To describe that as a vital contribution to Irish music is to understate it. Sinéad O'Connor was pivotal. But Dolores O'Riordan was in the vanguard of the next wave and she went on to scale extraordinary heights. She offered another role model. There was no need for anyone to argue or apologise. Far from it. Irish women were more than capable of doing it for themselves. Dolores did – and in doing so she helped hugely to break down the barriers that had, until then, restricted women in music. Following her example, dozens more have stepped to the fore in Ireland over the past 15 years, bringing a different and often vital sensibility to their craft.

DISTINCTIVE VOICE

And then there was that voice. Here again, Dolores set out her stall early and emphatically. A lot of singers start by copying well-known performers, following their intonation and phrasing, and even their accents. They end up in that swampy middle ground, where the universal voice of pop or rock prevails. Dolores wasn't interested in that. She was a Co. Limerick girl and that was the accent she sang in. There was a richness to it. But there was also an emotional honesty. And the distinctive yodel which she practised and cultivated gave it an even more haunting, spectral quality. She really was a very special singer.

When The Cranberries were a huge band, they generously agreed to do an intimate show for us, at a *Hot Press Yearbook* launch. I remember watching Dolores in real close-up that night in the Sugar Club, just a few yards away from me, and becoming aware afresh of just how good she was: she lived the songs, her phrasing was beautiful and she used the microphone superbly, to add a further dimension of expressiveness and control. And the sound of her voice was gorgeous too: haunting and mesmerising. It was the kind of performance that had you thinking that she could sing the phonebook and make it sound soulful.

It is easy to miss the point, if we try too hard to break music down, or attempt to nutshell what it is that makes it appealing or successful. Often, it defies rational analysis. Songs, hooks and riffs sneak up on us and seize hold of a part of the brain.

Sometimes we do know why. Other times it is harder to explain. But with The Cranberries, there is little doubt that Dolores O'Riordan's extraordinary, thoroughly distinctive voice, and the way she used it so often to thrilling effect, was vital to their music – and ultimately to their legacy.

OVERWHELMING SADNESS

Of course, Dolores was vulnerable. She talked about having been abused as a child. And in interviews, she explained unselfconsciously to *Hot Press* how the demands of fame and being in the public eye were hard, and sometimes nearly impossible, to handle. She found solace in becoming a mother. But too often we fail to acknowledge that raising a family creates its own pressures and difficulties.

Life can seem like an obstacle course. She wrestled for a time with anorexia. Depression dragged her down and she had to rise back up again in spite of it. More recently she was diagnosed as bipolar. There is relief, sometimes, in being able to name the source of our disturbances. But it doesn't make it any easier to deal with the turbulence we experience at the core of our very beings. Dolores always did that with the best of intentions. When she was knocked down, she'd get up again, and battle on.

The sun shone in her life too. Of course it did. She loved her family and her children. She was, we knew, a good and generous heart – the kind and lovely person that her friends from Limerick knew and speak about, who should have been free to live her life without the trials and tribulations that visited themselves on her. At a later date, it will be possible to reflect on all of this, and on what she herself said about the pressures she felt, and the difficulties she experienced personally, along the way.

But for now there is just the overwhelming sadness that crashed down around us, when family and friends have to say their last goodbyes to someone they loved, and still love, madly and deeply. And with good reason. Dolores brought so much joy into the lives of people all over the world. Her voice, and the music she made with The Cranberries, as well as in a solo guise, are her gifts to the world. They will resonate, off into the future in a way that none of us will ever fully know.

Because we too will receive the call. The long black cars will take us to the place from which none of us can escape, in the end. Cremation or burial: it doesn't matter really, does it? Beyond our small concerns, the sun will continue to rise. The seas will roar. The trees will grow. The winds will blow. The birds will sing. And amid this ageless living, someone somewhere will press play.

Dolores O'Riordan's voice, like a light against the darkness, will reach out into the void. Timeless – and beautiful...

· *Hot Press* **Editor Niall Stokes, January 2018**

"She thought of herself as a poet, and the directness and lack of pretence that shone through when she spoke was there in the lyrics too."

Niall Stokes, February 2018

Opposite Photo: Kip Carroll

There Is A Light That Never Goes Out

The death of their friend and bandmate knocked the wind out of them at first, but as the weeks passed Mike, Noel and Ferg decided that the best way to pay tribute to Dolores was to finish off the record they'd been working on together at the time of her tragic death. Aided and abetted by 'fifth Cranberry' Stephen Street, the prophetically titled *In The End* was everything fans had hoped it would be... and more! Prior to that, there had been hometown honours and a 25th birthday re-release of the album that started it all for Limerick's very own fab four.

Opposite photo: Jim Leatherman

Something Else...

As their groundbreaking *Everybody Else Is Doing It, So Why Can't We?* album gets a box-set re-release, Noel Hogan joins Stuart Clark on the sofa to talk about The Cranberries' formative years, and the pain of losing Dolores O'Riordan.

PHOTO: JIM LEATHERMAN

There's a tendency among musicians to romanticise their early years, but Noel Hogan is brutally honest about The Cranberry Saw Us' live prowess (or lack thereof) when they played their first few local Limerick gigs with new singer Dolores O'Riordan, a true rock 'n' roll ingénue who'd previously only performed with her church and school choirs.

"We were absolutely terrible," Noel winces. "We'd write and record these songs and then try and recreate them on stage, which didn't work because we were using lots of reverb and effects in the studio that ended up being empty space when we did them live. Dolores was really nervous and would stare at the floor, the ceiling, Mike playing the bass, Ferg

drumming – at anything other than the audience who mainly got to see the side and back of her head.

"A turning point was being flown to London by this American label, Imago," he continues. "We naively thought, 'This is it, we're going to be signed', but after playing in a room next-door to the Town & Country Club, the main guy said, 'You're just not ready yet. Go away and develop.' So, tail between our legs, we went home, bought a proper amp and a distortion pedal and started to beef it up. It was a combination of that and Dolores and I getting to know each other a lot better. At the beginning, you're gingerly dancing around things because you don't want to insult somebody you've only just met."

Those early gigs may have fallen way short of The Beatles in The Cavern or Nirvana in The Vogue, but it wasn't long

"Up until the very end, the biggest buzz of writing was hearing what direction Dolores would take it in lyrically."

before Noel and Dolores were making beautiful music together in the studio.

"The very first song we wrote together was 'Linger'," he recalls. "I'd come up with the music before she joined but there were no words, so we got used to playing it as an instrumental. It had something about it, so I gave a cassette version to Dolores and only a few days later she came back and said, 'I've got something for that.' Not having proper equipment, she was plugged into my guitar amp and all I could hear was the melody and the word 'linger'. It was only when we went in to do the first demo that I got to hear all the words and realise it was a break-up song. Up until the very end, the biggest buzz of writing was hearing what direction Dolores would take it in lyrically. It was like, 'Here's a bunch of music', and she'd go, 'I like this one and this one.' I loved going over to rehearsals and then, as things went on, she'd email me ideas and stuff. Even after being in a band together for 28 years, I couldn't predict what Dolores would come up with, which kept things fresh."

'Linger' was promptly followed by the penning of another of their globe-conquering tunes, 'Dreams', which for a brief period had a spoken word intro.

"God, I'd forgotten that!" Noel remarks. "It's only this year that I've properly listened to 'Dreams' – playing it every single show we became numb to it – and I'm like, 'Wow,

these are the thoughts of a 17-year-old!' Dolores' lyrics are so good!"

What they accompany isn't bad either…

"Thanks! Sitting in my bedroom writing it, I had no idea that the song would grow and grow like it has. I'm still pinching myself and wondering, 'How did we come up with 'Dreams'?' because it's on ads, it's on movies, it's on the radio – it's constantly there."

The reason for all this fond reflection is the 25th anniversary box-set re-release of the debut Cranberries album, *Everybody Else Is Doing It, So Why Can't We?*

Produced by Stephen Street who went on to become their George Martin-like fifth member, it's a record that still dazzles from plaintive start ('I Still Do') to heartbreaking finish ('Put Me Down').

Does the making of it feel like a lifetime ago?

"It does and it doesn't," Noel reflects. "With the year we've had it can seem very distant, but I still remember, plain as day, sitting in my bedroom getting 'Linger' together. My first time hearing *Everybody Else…* from start to finish in over 20 years was when I went to master it in Abbey Road. It was a month after Dolores passed away and my first day back at work, so to speak. Obviously, I've heard 'Linger' and 'Dreams' a gazillion times, but there's so much else about the record – the little nuances – that I'd completely forgotten.

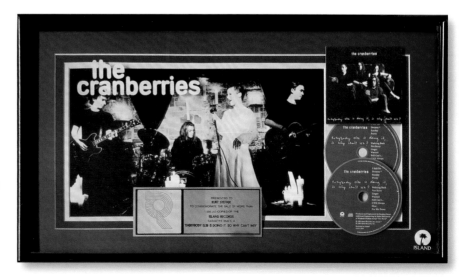

Every end has a start: The Cranberries' RIAA Award for selling a million copies of *Everybody Else Is Doing It, So Why Can't We?* in America. Photo by Sören Szameitat. **Opposite:** Dolores at a 1993 gig in Jacksonville Beach, Florida. Photo by Jim Leatherman.

"We went from playing THE PSYCHIC PIG in TROWBRIDGE to RADIO CITY HALL in NEW YORK in the space of about twelve months. It was PURE CRAZINESS."

*

Pressing engagement: The Cranberries with Mayor of Limerick, Jan O'Sullivan, at their 1993 Civic Reception. **Opposite:** The same year's Christmas homecoming show in the Theatre Royal. Photos by *Limerick Leader*.

I don't mean it in a cocky way, but I was really pleased how well it's held up and sounds now."

Among the treasure trove of bonus tracks is 'Íosa', an *Everybody Else...* outtake that has gained mythic status among Cranberries fans.

"It's Irish for 'Jesus', which at the time I didn't know because I'm brutal at all languages – including my own! We played it once or twice live and rehearsed it now and again, but the general feeling was that being in Irish it wouldn't travel well. It had never been mixed, so I said to the Abbey Road guy, 'I don't want it to sound big and flash and modern. Give it a bit of EQ and leave it at that.'"

The result is 4mins 10secs of exquisitely crafted pop, which had me welling up the moment Dolores starts singing her heart out *as Gaelige*. What's often forgotten in the telling of The Cranberries story is that *Everybody Else...* came within a whisker of being binned along with its creators.

"We'd started the album with Pearse (Gilmore, their original Limerick mentor) but that fell apart after we'd spent a lot of Island Records' money," Noel explains. "They weren't willy-nilly going to go, 'Here, take two, lads' so we were given a trial period of about six days with Stephen Street, who I'd asked for but didn't think we'd get because he'd had all that success with The Smiths and the first Morrissey solo album, *Viva Hate*. After working very long hours for a week, the guy who'd signed us, Denny Cordell, flew from New York to Dublin to see how we were doing. We were shitting ourselves playing him the three or four songs we'd recorded – I think 'Dreams' was in that first batch – because he could've pulled the plug on it there and then, but he looked at us with a big smile and said, 'Just keep going.' That's when we realised that the combination of us and Stephen was working."

Asked whether Dolores was nervous or confident working with such an A-List producer, Noel smiles and says, "Again, a bit of both. Dolores had this telltale thing of biting her jaw if she was nervous – I remember her even last year doing it. She wasn't the girl that used to have her back to the audience any more, but still needed to be told, 'Yeah, that's great!' by Stephen. We knew what we wanted, but didn't know how to get there. He definitely shaped the sound of The Cranberries. Stephen wasn't a dictator – I don't think that would've worked with us at all – and made sure things kept flowing. We laughed a lot making that album, and ended up even better friends as a result."

239

One for the road: (l-r) Dolores, Noel, Mike and Fergal touring *Everybody Else Is Doing It...* in the States. Photos by Jim Leatherman.

"If ever an Americanism crept in, he'd say it to Dolores and she'd switch back into Limerick mode!"

They didn't know it at the time, but The Cranberries were the catalyst for Stephen Street also getting to produce Blur's *Modern Life Is Rubbish*.

"Yeah, he only told me the story when we were doing our latest album," Noel reveals. "When Denny rang Stephen about doing *Everybody Else...*, he said, 'Come down and see us play next week in the Marquee.' At the gig, which thankfully he really liked, he bumped into Graham Coxon who was also there, and they got talking about working together. Stephen had done a couple of bits with Blur already, but that was the first time the idea of him producing *Modern Life Is Rubbish* was floated. I think, like us, they'd started on it with somebody else and it wasn't really working out. So, basically, Stephen was two-timing us going between Blur and The Cranberries!"

While the fashion then was for either London or mid-Atlantic twangs, Street made no attempt to tame Dolores' accent.

"In fact, as we travelled and her accent softened, as it does, he'd push her back towards the more Irish thing she was known for. If ever an Americanism crept in, he'd say it to Dolores and she'd switch back into Limerick mode!"

The thrill of *Everybody Else Is Doing It, So Why Can't We?* hitting the racks on March 1st, 1993 was tempered by the British inkies giving it a lukewarm reception.

"The *NME* and *Melody Maker* had had the demos for two years, so by the time the record came out they'd lost interest. If it charted it was in the hundreds, which left us feeling totally gutted because we'd put so much work into it. We always got a good crowd in London, but elsewhere we were playing really crappy venues to five people. After doing a particularly awful gig at a club in Newport called TJ's, we were sure the record company was going to drop us. Around that time we were offered a Hothouse Flowers tour in Europe, which we treated as a paid holiday before Island got rid of us. We went off with the Flowers without a

penny to our name, relying on their catering for meals and the promoters for a few beers after the gigs. They were doing well and really looked after us. A few weeks into the tour we got a call from somebody in Island's New York office saying, 'You need to drop what you're doing and come to the States.' Basically, 'Linger' had taken off mainly through college radio, and MTV had picked up on it too. We left the Flowers a week early, and flew straight from Spain to our first US show in Denver. Everything changed overnight."

Seven million album sales later and The Cranberries were vying with U2 for the title of Biggest Irish Rock Band.

"We went from playing the Psychic Pig in Trowbridge to Radio City Hall in New York in the space of about twelve months. It was pure craziness." In addition to overseeing the *Everybody Else...* re-release, Noel has also been applying the finishing touches to the album the band were recording at the time of Dolores' death in January. Noel admits that completing it without her is one of the hardest things he's ever had to do.

"Yeah, it's been weird," he says, voice faltering slightly. "Once the dust had settled a bit, I started going through the drives and everything Dolores had sent me during the previous six months and put some rough mixes together.

I sent them to Mike and Fergal to see what their thoughts were and they felt that we had the makings of a really strong album. The obvious thing after that was to contact Stephen and he agreed straight away that it was something that had to be finished. He had another project he was meant to be starting, but moved it back because we all felt the momentum was there.

"We went back to Stephen in May and did the strings and extra guitars and keyboards. I'm delighted to have had the opportunity to do it, but it's been a very emotional experience. After a day in the studio, I'd go to wherever I was staying and think, 'This just isn't fair.'"

Has it given him and the rest of the lads a sense of closure?

"Kind of, yeah," he nods. "It also meant a lot to us that we did two months of gigs last year that were really well received. We obviously didn't realise the symbolism of it at the time, but it was us stripping the songs back to how they were originally written – acoustic guitars and Dolores' voice. It was smaller venues, and we all really enjoyed ourselves, so it was a good final tour."

· Noel Hogan interview by Stuart Clark, September 2018

Dolores O'Riordan and Mike and Noel Hogan receive honorary University of Limerick doctorates

PHOTOS: SEAN CURTIN

There were smiles, laughter and tears in almost equal measure yesterday as the University of Limerick conferred honorary doctorates on Mike and Noel Hogan and Dolores O'Riordan.

Dolores' scroll and the robes she would have worn were accepted by her mother, Eileen.

"UL had initially planned to present these doctorates to The Cranberries in April 2017, however promotional and rehearsal commitments prevented the band from being available to accept the honour at that stage," UL President Dr. Des Fitzgerald explained. "It is with very sad regret that since that time the world and more importantly her family and band mates have lost Dolores O'Riordan and her incredible voice. We very much appreciate her family's presence here today."

Talking before the conferral ceremony, Eileen O'Riordan said that it was "a sad day for the family but we have to move on, don't we? I know that she's happy and in heaven and that makes me happy. She's here for this in spirit."

Asked how the family were coping with Dolores' anniversary, Eileen reflected: "You know, Christmas was a bit harder than the anniversary. Since she was a child, she'd have spent Christmas Eve singing. We had the anniversary mass last Sunday night. The week's been very, very busy and once you're busy you don't have a lot of time to think about it.

"Today is a great honour," she continued. "I feel awed, really. I find it hard to comprehend and take it all in. When I go home I'll relax and think about it. I'll realise how good it all is. Dolores loved Limerick. She was happier here than any place else. I didn't realise how much she was loved. I keep telling the children how much everyone loves her. It's very comforting to the family that people are so good."

Noel admitted to being equally in awe of the occasion.

"It's amazing to be back here because, in many ways, we began out in this university playing what was The Stables to a handful of people. It's come full circle as we near the end of The Cranberries' career. It feels like the thirty years of hard work has brought us to this moment. The way to look at it is that it's a celebration of Dolores and the band.

"I think she'd get a great kick out of this," he chuckled. "These kind of things she used to get a real skit at. It was four years ago that the university first approached us.

The timing was just never right for it. I remember her telling her brothers, who've different degrees, that she'd be more qualified than them! That was her personality. She'd be really, really loving this today."

Mike spoke of how difficult a task completing The Cranberries' swan song album, *In The End*, had been without Dolores.

"We had to put our emotions to one side and just get on with the job. There's been a great reaction so far to the single. We're very proud of it."

Hot Press also got to chat to PJ O'Riordan, Dolores' brother who helped take care of the business side of things for The Cranberries; former Student Ents Officer Ber Angley who was responsible for that first trip out to UL in 1991; local promoter Bob O'Connell who gave them a middle of the bill spot alongside Cry Before Dawn, An Emotional Fish, The Blue Angels, They Do It With Mirrors, Those Stilted Boys and Colours at that same year's Lark In The Park which, with 6,000 attending, was their biggest hometown gig ever; Lindsey Holmes, The Cranberries' publicist for much of their career; and tour manager Sett Neiland who's now on the road with Celtic Woman.

Earlier in the day, our man Stuart Clark took a nostalgic stroll round Limerick which took in Savin's, the music shop where Mr. and Mrs. Hogan bought young Noel and Michael their first guitars; the scene of their legendary 1993 Christmas homecoming, the Theatre Royal; one of Noel, Mike and Ferg's favourite indie disco hangouts, Costello's Tavern, which was (and still is) renowned for the stickiness of its carpet; the site of another very early gig, the Glentworth Hotel; and Laurel Hill, the school where Dolores did her Leaving Cert and was in the school choir. Her classmate Catherine Hayes suggested she audition for The Cranberry Saw Us when original singer Niall Quinn quit. The rest was most definitely history.

Hot Press Newsdesk, January 2019

Doctors in the house: (from left) Noel and Mike with Dolores' Mum Eileen, and their wives Catherine and Siobhán at UL; Dolores' posthumous award; and the Shannon riverscape that would have been so familiar to her. Photo: Miguel Ruiz

"It feels like the thirty years of hard work has brought us to this moment. It's a celebration of Dolores and the band. "

THIS IS THE END,

Beautiful Friend

Few Irish rock stars have shone as brightly as Dolores O'Riordan did. As they get ready to release the album they were working on at the time of her death, Mike and Noel Hogan and Fergal Lawler talk about what made their friend so special and recall some of their fondest band memories. Interview: Stuart Clark

PHOTO: MIGUEL RUIZ

The man hugs, backslaps and well-intentioned lies about none of us looking a day older as I meet Ferg Lawler and Mike and Noel Hogan feel reassuringly familiar. I've known the lads since 1989 when I reviewed the first Cranberry Saw Us cassette demo, *Anything,* for the now long-gone *Limerick Tribune.*

"Do you still have that tape?" asks Ferg who winces when I answer in the affirmative. "God, it was awful. How much do you want to destroy the evidence?"

They'll have to prise it out of my cold dead hands! Not only do I have a copy of the C45 in question – ask your grandparents – but courtesy of the *Cranberries World* fansite and their exhaustive archives, I was also recently reunited with the critical musings in question.

Contrary to what Mr. Lawler would have you believe, the four-tracker showed great potential with the cub reporter me describing 'Throw Me Down A Big Stairs' as "a quivering song that smacks of good ideas"; 'How's It Going To Bleed' being praised for "its measured moodiness flowing nicely alongside a delicate refrain"; the "bright playful pop" of 'Storm In A Teacup' earning them a Monkees comparison; and 'Good Morning God' displaying "a Cure-ish guitar riff and a Stunning-type line in lyrics."

"If they give it a bit of time, who knows?" I concluded, which was sufficiently positive for their then lead singer Niall Quinn to buy me a pint of Bulmers after their November '89 gig in the Speakeasy with A Touch Of Oliver.

By the time they stuck another demo in my paw, Quinn had been replaced by Laurel Hill sixth former Dolores O'Riordan who'd promptly dashed out the lyrics for 'Sunday', 'Linger', 'Chrome Paint' and 'A Fast One'.

"A total newcomer to the local rock scene, the lass sounds for all the world like Kirsty MaColl's younger sister and has a deliciously unaffected, almost innocent style, which wouldn't seem out of place on an All About Eve album," I said in my *Limerick Tribune* review of what eventually became the *Water Circle* EP and, well, I wasn't a million miles wide of the mark.

The band asked me to write the accompanying press release, which this time earned me a bottle of Jack Daniel's. It was and remains the best afternoon's work I've ever done.

"I remember you were also doing the Saturday night rock show on Radio Limerick One, and invited us out for what was our first broadcast interview," Noel reminisces. "We were shitting ourselves with nerves. Dolores borrowed a pair of Doc Martens for the occasion. It was a radio interview but she wanted to look the part."

As Noel mentions Dolores' name for the first time, the mood instantly changes. Beneath the smiles and bonhomie, you can tell that the lads are still grieving for their friend and bandmate who drowned in the bath of her London hotel room on January 15th, 2018. Dolores had started laying down her vocals for *In The End*, The Cranberries' prophetically-titled eighth album which, after much soul searching and consultation with the O'Riordan family, they decided to finish off with producer Stephen Street. Having kept it to themselves for the guts of six months – "We

Stare tactics: The Cranberries backstage at RTÉ's *The Late Late Show* in 1994 by Cathal Dawson.

needed time to get our heads round the record, and what it represents," Noel reflects – they're now ready to share it with the world.

"I have to say I'm finding this part of the process – the interviews, which are obviously going to be mainly about Dolores – really difficult," Ferg says, visibly tearing up.

Talking to *Hot Press* last year at the time of the *Everybody Else Is Doing It...* 25th anniversary re-release, Noel said that having *In The End* to work on is what kept him from falling apart after Dolores died.

"It's hard to imagine what else I'd have done during that period other than get really down," he adds today. "It ended up being therapy for all of us. It was Stephen who said, 'You're emotional about everything but, look, there's a momentum here that you might never regain if you put it on 'hold' for a year.' It was his faith in the songs and the work we'd already done that made us decide to continue with the album."

The bitter irony is that *In The End* sounds more like a rebirth than a full stop with a number of tracks that wouldn't have been out of place on *Everybody Else Is Doing It, So Why Can't We?* or *No Need To Argue*.

"Lyrically, Dolores had a lot to say again," Noel nods. "When you spoke to her, it was always, 'So much has happened to me over the last three years that I want to write

about' – and a lot had happened. It felt like she did five times the living that the rest of us did. There was so much that needed to come out, to the point where I couldn't keep up with her. You'd mail Dolores a rough idea and she'd say, 'You got anything else?' I was like, 'Give me a chance!' She was working at the same furious pace as when she first joined The Cranberries, and was really, really excited about this album and everything that was going to happen as a result of it. Dolores was gutted that we'd had to cut short our tour in 2017 because of her bad back – the shows up till then had been brilliant – and was mad keen to start gigging again."

What was the cause of those back problems?

"It was a ruptured disc or a bulging disc, something like that," Mike answers. "At those last gigs you'd see Dolores being careful about how much she moved, and then forgetting and doing something really physical that left her in a lot of pain afterwards. She'd made a pretty much full recovery, though, and like Noel said, was up for touring."

One of *In The End*'s numerous standouts is 'Lost', which goes from the proverbial whisper to a scream with Dolores sounding not unlike Sinéad O'Connor circa *The Lion And The Cobra*.

"She'd have been thrilled with the comparison; Sinéad was always a big hero of hers," Noel notes. "Dolores' tone changed from exercising her vocal cords so much, which is

"The thing we remember the most about Dolores is the craic we had. She'd be sat on the bus ripping the piss out of you."

really evident if you play *Everybody Else...* and this record back to back. She was screaming over all of us for thirty years – and her brothers before that – so there was a real power to Dolores' voice."

With its opening *"Do you remember?/ Remember the night?/ At a hotel in London"* refrain, *In The End*'s lead single, 'All Over Now' is, like some of the songs on David Bowie's *Blackstar*, almost too painful to listen to.

There's a collective silence before Noel jumps into the void.

"I'd obviously heard it before she died but, yeah, it does take on a whole extra resonance," he half-whispers. "It speaks for itself in terms of how Dolores was feeling about everything. It's also the most old school Cranberries song on the record so, yeah, it's a bit of an emotional one."

Despite its flagrant disregard for health and safety regulations, the cover photo of kids throwing rock 'n' roll shapes in a junkyard couldn't be more striking.

"It was down the road from Dolan's in the docks," Mike explains. "We asked a couple of the managers and they were like, 'Work away'. There was all this heavy machinery driving around in the background. The kids are all family members, so it was nice to get them in on it."

While you could tell from talking to her down through the years that Dolores had her demons, I was shocked in 2013 when she revealed in a *Sunday Independent* interview that she'd been serially abused as a kid by a supposed friend of the family who's since died.

Did the lads hang out much with Dolores when they weren't recording or touring?

"We were all off doing our own things," Noel reflects. "You have family, you have kids. When you're away for nine months out of a year, there's a lot of catching up to be done when you get home. There'd be texts and emails and phone calls, but not a whole lot of hanging out. We were able to sit in Tom Collins' and have a pint without anyone being bothered that we were there, but Dolores didn't have that luxury. Even when she was off she had to be careful because people expected her to be 'Dolores, the Rock Star'. People say, 'What are you complaining about; it's what you wanted' but not being able to do normal stuff like that can be difficult."

It's important to remember that Dolores was also – I'm going to use a technical term here – as funny as fuck.

"A lot of people don't get that," Ferg nods. "The thing we remember the most about Dolores is the craic we had. She'd be sat on the bus ripping the piss out of you."

"What Dolores also had," Noel chuckles, "was a very low boredom threshold. Two days into rehearsals, you'd look over and see that look on her face. She mightn't have said anything there and then but at seven in the evening you'd get a call from her asking, 'What did you think of today?' and before you could answer she'd go, 'It wasn't rock enough.' She was always the metaller in the band."

Tell us more about that look of hers...

"You'd see it and think: 'There's going to be trouble here now; she's going to kick off any second!'" Noel smiles. "If you were doing an interview and somebody asked a stupid question you'd see it. Initially, Dolores was very shy around us because we were strangers, but as we got to know each other better we realised that, 'She's well able to stand up for herself.' She was never the 'innocent colleen' that the British music press made her out to be. She was a very smart person."

I should really be referring to both Mike and Noel as 'Dr. Hogan' following January's bestowing of honorary degrees on them by the University of Limerick. Dolores' force of nature mum Eileen was also there to collect the robes and scroll that would've been presented to her daughter who, but for joining The Cranberries, probably would have gone to UL.

"'Force of nature' is right," Noel says. "Eileen's a rock, you know? She's amazing. You look at her and think, 'Okay, you better get your shit together now.' It's hard for us but, can you imagine? It's her daughter. It's got to be incredibly hard. And yet she shakes herself off and does all that kind of stuff. Especially that day at UL when the press were asking her about Dolores."

I thought the lads rocked the robes very well.

"I wear mine round the house all the time," Noel deadpans. "Saturday mornings reading the paper with that outfit on. Somebody out at UL said to me, 'You fly a lot, don't you? Well, when you're booking a ticket make sure to put in 'Dr. Hogan' because if there's ever upgrades they always give them to the doctors first."

"Which is fine until they ask, 'Is there a doctor on board?' and you're expected to perform mouth-to-mouth

Fade to black: Noel and Dolores in June 2016 at one of The Cranberries' last ever gigs in Barcelona. Photo by Javier Patón Melgarejo.

resuscitation on a sick passenger," Mike cackles.

"Ah, if that happens, I'll just wing it," Noel replies.

The lads aren't sure whether Dolores got to see *Derry Girls*, the first episode of which went out on January 4th, 2018 and starts with a blast of 'Dreams'.

"Then you see Erin's bedroom and there's a picture of The Cranberries on the wall," Noel beams. "*Derry Girls* is like an advert for The Cranberries. They've also used 'Zombie', 'I Can't Be With You' and 'Ode To My Family', which has done wonders for our Spotify plays! *Derry Girls* is absolutely Dolores' sense of humor. She'd have loved it, especially Sister Michael. That episode where she was on the bus reading *The Exorcist*; Dolores would have been howling."

Their bandmate definitely was aware that Eminem had sampled 'Zombie' on the album that returned him to the US top spot last year, *Kamikaze*.

"She always thought Eminem was cool so, yeah, that was a massive deal for Dolores," Noel says. "She knew about it,

but forgot to tell me until just beforehand, so my first time hearing it was the day of release on Spotify. I was expecting a snippet, but it's the whole song. It's almost more of a cover than a sample, which is cool because he did a great job of it."

Does Noel ever get sick of his own songs?

"They're always playing 'Dreams' in the gym I go to," he grimaces, "which is a bit off-putting when you're working out. Otherwise, no, I don't dive for the 'off' switch when one of our songs comes on the radio. It's amazing the places 'Dreams' ends up. The Chinese Olympic team had it as their official walking out music. There's a version of it on YouTube in Cantonese."

In The End promotion duties completed, the lads will be turning their attentions to a major Cranberries documentary.

"You'll be getting a call, Stuart," Noel informs me. "We had done a few small interviews three years ago individually, the idea being that we'd dip in and out of it," Noel reveals. "Those interviews, which of course include Dolores, were never used

> # "It can't be The Cranberries without Dolores. I'm just glad that we had the adventures together that we did."
>
> - NOEL HOGAN

so there's lots of great footage we're going to develop. The original idea was to have it about the first album, how that all came about, but since Dolores passed away we've been in talks with different people who've approached us about doing a full start to finish documentary. You've the bones of thirty years there. If we don't do it somebody else will, and probably badly. We'll do it properly."

From serenading Pope John Paul and appearing on the cover of *Rolling Stone* to collaborating with Angelo Badalamenti and simultaneously blowing Pavarotti and Princess Diana away with her singing, Dolores' career was one of extraordinary highs. What are the lads' own 'wouldn't swap 'em for anything' Cranberries' moments?

"You'll have to wait for the documentary," Ferg laughs. "We opened up for the Stones in the San Siro. I remember looking around and thinking, 'Jayyyysssssusssss!' During 'New New York', I could hear Dolores' vocal just swirling around. It was fucking unreal. Mick does his own thing, but the others came and said 'hello'. I was totally starstruck meeting Charlie Watts. Someone said he hasn't changed his bass drum skin

since the '60s; he's afraid the sound will be different."

"We were on the same Milton Keynes bill as Oasis, Radiohead and R.E.M. who were headlining," says Noel. "Even now thinking back, it was mental to be in that company. When we did the 'Linger' video, Michael Stipe turned up on the set because he was friends with the director, Melodie McDaniel, who'd also done the 'Losing My Religion' video. This was our first time in America – we hadn't long been signed – and this legend just pops in. You never forget stuff like that."

As for what the future holds, the only thing the lads are 100% certain of is that they won't be recording again as The Cranberries.

"It can't be The Cranberries without Dolores," Noel concludes. "I'm just glad that we had the adventures together that we did, and have an album we're all immensely proud of to say 'goodbye' with."

· **The Cranberries interviewed by Stuart Clark, March 2019**

 IT REQUIRED DOLORES O'RIORDAN'S sudden passing last year to convince the unconverted of the depth of The Cranberries' body of work. But just when we thought it was all over, along comes this album: based on fresh demos, it makes for an unexpected gift.

Dolores was blessed with an utterly unmistakable voice, and it never disappoints, especially on outstanding tracks like 'Catch Me If You Can', 'Got It' and single 'All Over Now'. The latter opens like it means business, propelled by solid drums, Noel Hogan's excellent guitar work, and Dolores' deliciously impish delivery. Lyrics about a couple at loggerheads in a London hotel can make for uneasy listening, especially given what we know now, but Dolores was never one to avoid the awkward side of truth. But lines like *"She was afraid the truth would be found"* and *"It's all over now"* sound at the very least intriguing, if not downright eerie.

Indeed, the shadow of Dolores' death hovers over nearly every track – and some words bear a weight of meaning they may never have been intended to carry. 'Lost' is a wistfully atmospheric effort, with the vocals soaring above a band in reflective mood. 'A Place I Know' has a semi-acoustic feel, and a haunting, sliding guitar motif popping up at regular intervals. Elsewhere, 'Wake Me When It's Over' evokes 'Zombie'; 'Got It' has a sense of urgency at the inevitable passing of time; and 'The Pressure' – fittingly – boasts gloriously powerful vocals.

Produced by the band's long-standing collaborator Stephen Street, *In The End* is 100% Cranberries, with all that the brand name promises. Not only were we not expecting it – we weren't even entitled to think it could be this good. But it is.
***In The End* album review by Jackie Hayden, April 2019**

"We weren't even entitled to think it could be this good. But it is."

Above: The Cranberries bring their famous sofa to Puerto Morelos, Mexico by Andy Earl.

ÉIRE N

OH MY DREAMS
IT'S NEVER QUITE
AS IT SEEMS
THE CRANBERRIES

GREAT IRISH SONGS | MÓR-AMHRÁIN NA hÉIREANN

2019

CAN I LICK IT? Yes, you can! The Cranberries' 'Dreams', Luke Kelly's 'On Raglan Road', Count John McCormack's 'Danny Boy' and U2's 'With Or Without You' are all featuring as part of An Post's *Great Irish Songs* collection, which is being released on May 2nd. The stamps will be available individually, as a mint collectors' four-pack and as a nifty looking first-day cover.

Hot Press **Newsdesk, April 2019**

RELEASED IN APRIL **2019,** The Cranberries' final album *In The End* has now earned a Grammy nod for 'Best Rock Album'. It marks their first-ever nomination at the prestigious awards.

Also nominated in the same category are Bring Me The Horizon, I Prevail, Cage The Elephant, and Rival Sons.

In The End peaked at number 3 in the Irish album charts and was called "an unexpected gift" by *Hot Press*' Jackie Hayden. In his review, he said, "*In The End* is 100% Cranberries, with all that the brand name promises. Not only were we not expecting it – we weren't even entitled to think it could be this good. But it is."

The album is based on fresh demos by the band, and features vocals recorded by lead singer Dolores O'Riordan before her tragic passing in January 2018. The surviving members of The Cranberries – guitarist Noel Hogan, bassist Mike Hogan, drummer Fergal Lawler – restarted work on the album later that year after much deliberation and with the support of Dolores' family.

With the songs at various stages of completion they turned to Stephen Street – who had produced four of their previous albums including *Everybody Else Is Doing It, So Why Can't We?* and *No Need To Argue* – and built the sounds around Dolores' vocals from those original demos. The resulting album blends rock, alternative and catchy almost pop-sounding melodies to deliver a classic Cranberries sound.

"We wanted to finish this album for our dear friend and bandmate Dolores," Noel Hogan says. "It's a tribute to her, the band and our fans for the past thirty years. Being honoured with this Grammy nomination has made this whole process even more special."

Dolores' mother Eileen O'Riordan adds, "Dolores would be so happy with this, she put her heart and soul into her songs and music. For us as her family it's kind of bittersweet, we're immensely proud yet saddened that she isn't here to witness and enjoy this, although I feel that she is in spirit."

The 2020 Grammy Awards will be hosted by Alicia Keys and are set to take place at the Staples Center in Los Angeles on January 27, 2020.

Hot Press **Newsdesk, November 2019**

Word On The Street

No Cranberries lieutenant was as trusted as Stephen Street, the A-List producer who helped them hone their sound in the '90s and was on hand to ensure that their final album was the perfect bookend to *Everybody Else Is Doing It, So Why Can't We?* Interview: Stuart Clark

PORTRAIT: MAX KNIGHT

When Dolores tragically died in January 2018, it was to Stephen Street they turned to decide whether they should finish off the *In The End* album they were in the early stages of making at the time. The man who sprinkled sonic fairy dust on *Everybody Else Is Doing It, So Why Can't We?* (1993), Stephen did the honours again on the gazillion-selling *No Need To Argue* (1994) before The Cranberries opted for a change of producer on *Bury The Hatchet* (1999), but returned to the fold for *Wake Up And Smell The Coffee* (2001) and has been their go-to man ever since.

Before, during and after contributing wholesale to The Cranberries' multi-platinum success, Streety as he's known to his friends, also earned a variety of metallic discs working with The Smiths, the solo Morrissey, Blur, Sandie Shaw, The Pretenders, Catatonia, Suede, Kaiser Chiefs, New Order and The Zutons. And that really is just for starters.

When we track him down to his London layer it looks like Stephen's on the bridge of the USS Enterprise such is the array of hi-tech equipment engulfing him.

Asked about that first "what should we do?" conversation with Noel following Dolores' death, he pauses for a moment and then says, "There was always this fear that we'd be accused of being insensitive to Dolores' passing, which the guys would have done anything – not making the album included – to avoid. My take on it was the same as Noel's: 'There can't be any digging at the bottom of the barrel. It has to meet a certain standard and not destroy the band's legacy. In fact, as a tribute to Dolores it has to be as good as anything The Cranberries have previously released.'

"So," Stephen continues, "I said to Noel, 'Just give me all the things that you've been doing with Dolores, I'll go through them and report back.' What he sent me ranged from mere little sketches to properly formed demos she'd done in America with session musicians. Obviously it had to be a Cranberries record, so bar one or two little keyboard touches we liked, we removed all the session stuff and just kept the vocal."

At this point technology proved to very much be The Cranberries' friend.

"The great thing about the format we work with now, ProTools, is that it's so easy to edit and cut and paste and move things around," Stephen explains. "If it had been on tape it would have been a much more difficult scenario. So, I tidied up the vocals – some had been recorded in her bedroom in New York so the quality was kind of suspect – and added a click track for the guys to come in and play to. It was emotional for them because Dolores' vocal was there as usual, but she wasn't."

As tough as those Bunker and Kore studio sessions

Telly time: Fergal, Dolores and Stephen (right) chilling with the *Everybody Else...* studio crew. Photo by Anne O'Connor.

undoubtedly were for Mike, Noel and Ferg, the payback from them was almost instant.

"The moment I heard the boys playing to her voice it sounded like The Cranberries," Stephen reflects. "I knew after that first day of tracking we were onto something and should see it through."

Were there a lot of songs to choose from?

"Some things were just too rough to use, so I said to the guys, 'Looking back over the past 30 years or so with CDs, people have been making albums that are far too long. Let's think of this as a vinyl record with five tracks a side, total playing time no longer than 45 minutes.' It was an old school approach that worked I think."

In The End's subsequent Grammy nomination – The Cranberries' first – for Best Rock Album suggests that it did. The lads got tuxedo-ed up for February 2020's awards ceremony in Los Angeles but weren't called on to give their acceptance speech, which doubtless would have thanked Stephen for his decades of steering them in the right direction. That said, there were those who questioned whether he'd been the right man for the *Everybody Else Is Doing It, So Why Can't We?* job in 1992 when it was recorded.

"It was completely ignored at first so as producer a finger was pointed at me – not by the band I hasten to add – for not giving us a record that's good enough for radio," he recalls. "There was a real apathy towards them in the UK, which

was a slap across the face. I knew we'd made a good album together but for all sorts of reasons good albums don't always get into the Top 30.

"The Cranberries wanting to work with me was mainly down to them being such massive Smiths fans and me being part of that. Island called me into a meeting where the guy who'd signed them, Denny Cordell, said, 'Let's do a session and see how it goes.' It was a case of 'If we like what comes out of that we'll give you the go-ahead to do the rest of the album.' The band had gone through a little bit of a bad experience with their previous producer who'd done their recording in Ireland, so the label were playing it safe, which was totally understandable. We really connected from day one and halfway through that session I was confident I'd get the rest of the album, and that's what happened. We did four or five songs, which Denny loved."

Were The Cranberries as naïve as the British music weeklies, and *Melody Maker* in particular, tried to make out?

"Yeah, you could tell they were kind of green and hadn't done a huge amount of playing live," Stephen proffers. "To a certain degree they were still mastering their instruments, but there was a natural charm and chemistry there. And that's the thing about bands; there has to be the right chemistry. If you had four Damon Albarns in Blur, it would be a disaster. You need some people to be strong-minded and others to be a bit mellower. Dolores was quite feisty, but the Hogan brothers were very mellow and Fergal somewhere

"It was emotional for them because Dolores' vocal was there as usual, but she wasn't."

in the middle.

"Making their debut album is scary for a band," he continues. "It's exciting but at the same time you don't think you've got the standing to say to the record company, 'This is how we want to do things'. You feel a bit like a kid at school trying to please teacher. I've got a pretty good reputation for working with bands on their debuts and being sympathetic to what they want to do. It was a Cranberries album we were making, not a Stephen Street one."

As much as he liked 'Linger' and 'Dreams', it was another song that stood out during those initial sessions.

"I wouldn't say 'Linger' and 'Dreams' sounded jaded but they'd been demoed a bunch of times before and I wanted to do something that felt really fresh and spontaneous," he explains. "At the end of a busy afternoon in the studio I said, 'Do you have anything else for me?' and they played 'Pretty' which was something they'd only done before in rehearsals. Straight away that was the key track for me."

Apart from feisty, how did he find Dolores?

"I had to win her confidence, but once I had we got on better and better," Stephen says. "One of my favourite Cranberries memories was going over to New York for the weekend to do what were supposed to be demos and having an absolute blast in and out of the studio. The tracks were so good they ended up being used on the second album, *No Need To Argue*."

How did Dolores measure up to the other singers – Chrissie Hynde, Damon Albarn, Cerys Matthews and Morrissey – Stephen's heard through his headphones?

"As good as any of them," he shoots back. "I loved what I called the 'Gaelic-isms' of their early music, which were largely down to Dolores. You could tell she was inspired by the church, but it was completely different to gospel music. There was something magical about the tone of her voice, which came from where and how she grew up. I wanted to keep that kind of Irishness without going down the trad band route. The mission with *Everybody Else Is Doing It...* was to make a record that was polished enough to compete with all the other indie alternative stuff that was out there but kept

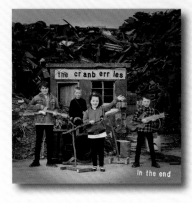

the particular charm they initially had."

Stephen only recently told Noel Hogan that it was bumping into Graham Coxon at a Cranberries gig in the Marquee that lead to him producing *Modern Life Is Rubbish*.

Noel's subsequent jokey reaction being: "Basically, he was two-timing us going between Blur and The Cranberries." Is Stephen guilty as charged?

"I didn't know Graham was going to be there, so it really was a chance meeting," he pleads in mitigation. "I'd done a few bits with them before but bumping into Graham put me back on the Blur radar. It's the random nature of the business we're in. Two great albums came out of that one night, and probably altered the course of my career."

And both Blur and The Cranberries' careers as well. Armed with the songs they'd already nailed in New York, Stephen and the band reconvened in November 1993 to record what turned out to be the biggest album of their career. The first indication that *No Need To Argue* was going to change their lives came when its flagship single, 'Zombie', hit number one on the US Alternative chart. Stephen would obviously have been aware of the general anti-war and violence theme, but did he appreciate it was Dolores' impassioned response to the Warrington bombings in particular?

"When I'm working with a singer I always ask for the lyrics so I can make my notes next to each line. My lead vocals are often compiled from different takes so I need to know them inside out and had picked up the deeper meaning 'Zombie' had in terms of the bombings. A lot of the time Cranberries songs would have been more about love and growing up – 'Twenty-One' is a favourite of mine from *No Need To Argue* – so it was nice to do something a bit more political, and which instead of nice finger picking allowed the boys to let rip. I didn't think, 'Oh, this is going to be a single', it was just the rock track on the record. My job is to pick the best eleven or twelve songs and let other people decide, 'This is the million-seller from it.'"

Stephen mentioned multiple vocal takes; how many did

"I'm really pleased you hear elements of the first album on *In The End* because that was a very conscious effort on my part."

Dolores need?

"Four or five, and that was just to sort out what I call the 'black spots', things that need a little bit of work done on them but nothing wholesale. She was a real pro in that respect."

Was it apparent when Stephen returned to the Cranberries fold in 2001 after seven years away that the rigours of rock 'n' roll life had taken their toll on Dolores?

"There was pressure on her all the time in the background as well, because at this point she was a mother," Stephen replies. "Dolores was juggling a family life, which flitted from Canada to Ireland with being in a band and making a record. My job was to say, 'When you're in the studio can we just really focus on this?' We had some great heart-to-hearts sitting on the floor in the area where she did her vocals with lit candles spread around. I was always going to her, 'Don't feel like you have to have this big message for the world. Try to draw them in using charm and nuance rather than declaring things all the time.' We did a bit of that on *Wake Up And Smell The Coffee* and some more on *Roses*, which I always thought was a very overlooked album. There were

some fantastic moments on it, but it was at the point where they weren't signed to a major label and it didn't get the push it deserved. I'm really pleased you hear elements of the first album on *In The End* because that was a very conscious effort on my part."

While his tenure as Cranberries producer is over, Stephen still checks in regularly with the guys.

"I feel very close to them," he concludes. "There's a chemistry there and we had great *craic* with each other over the years. I love them like brothers, really. Mikey is the funniest man on the planet and I'm just so sorry for them that it's over. I remember the guys coming in to listen to a playback of the last track we did, which appropriately enough was 'In The End' itself, and them being so forlorn. Normally you'd be looking forward to playing your new songs live but that wasn't going to be happening. As a farewell to Dolores and their fans, I don't think they could have done a better job."

· **Stephen Street interview by Stuart Clark, September 2021**

"I remember the guys coming in to listen to a playback of the last track we did, which appropriately enough was 'In The End' itself, and them being so forlorn."

The Legacy

Once they'd made their big 1990s breakthrough, no Hollywood blockbuster or smash hit TV show was complete without a Cranberries song or three helping to soundtrack the action. Time has cemented their position as international cultural icons who, post-Dolores' tragic death, continue to touch lives – Miley Cyrus, Erin Quinn and Peter and Lois Griffin's among them – with their music.

Opposite photo: Miguel Ruiz

WHEN YOU'RE GONE

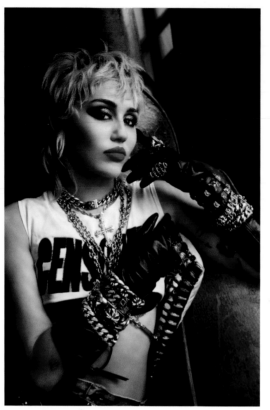

Covered in glory: Miley Cyrus by Mick Rock.

A superstar singer with punky peroxide hair belting out 'Zombie' with gale force gusto.

Cranberries fans will have done a double take on October 18th, 2020 when Miley Cyrus' cover of The Cranberries' anti-war anthem started going viral.

Performed by her at Los Angeles' legendary Whisky A Go Go venue as part of the online #SaveOurStages initiative, 'Zombie' had been a favourite song of Miley's since childhood.

Catching up on events 5,122 miles away in Limerick, Fergal, Noel and Mike liked what they heard.

"We were delighted to hear of Miley Cyrus' cover of 'Zombie'," they immediately tweeted. "It's one of the finest covers of the song that we've heard. We think that Dolores would be very impressed!"

Written by her in response to the IRA's February 26th, 1993 bombing of Warrington in England, which resulted in the deaths of three-year-old Jonathan Ball and 12-year-old Tim Parry, and the injury of 54 other people, there's no doubt that couplets like *"Another head hangs lowly/ Child is slowly taken/ And the violence caused such a silence/ Who are we mistaken?"* resonated in Trump's America too.

In the wake of Miley's reading of it, Spotify streams of the original 'Zombie' surged past 497 million, adding to the one billion-plus YouTube views the accompanying video has received.

Whether it's Lois and Peter discussing the addictive qualities of 'Ode To My Family' in *Family Guy*; Erin and the rest of the *Derry Girls* shedding a tear to 'Dreams'; or Aisling Bea and Sharon Horgan doing the worst version of (that song again!) 'Zombie' ever in *This Way Up*, The Cranberries continue to be as omnipresent on TV and cinema screens as they were in the 1990s when they helped soundtrack the likes of *Beverly Hills, 90210, Mission: Impossible* and *You've Got Mail*.

"Oh man, Aisling and I were genuinely heartbroken when Dolores died," Sharon Horgan tells us. "We always knew that if we did something together we would be murdering a Cranberries song at some point. When she passed I deep-dived into all these videos and interviews with her. That beautiful face Dolores had and her little downturned mouth. It was really affecting."

The BAFTA-winning Channel 4 series finds Horgan playing second fiddle for once to Bea who she says "cracks me up even when she's trying to be serious, which isn't very often. The dynamic of the two sisters, Áine and Shona, isn't far off what we have in real life. It was incredibly hard keeping a straight face doing 'Zombie'. I can't remember the exact number of takes, but it was enough for the crew to stop finding it funny. It was the earnestness of it that kept cracking us up."

Dolores' memory also lives on through the €4,000 Dolores O'Riordan Music Bursary, which is awarded each year to a Limerick band or solo artist of outstanding merit.

The first recipient in November 2019 was Emma Langford, a singer-songwriter of considerable pedigree who was also crowned RTÉ Radio 1 Best Emerging Folk Act earlier that year.

Part of the Irish Women In Harmony collective who did such a great job of covering 'Dreams' in aid of SAFE Ireland, her 2020 album, *Sowing Acorns*, is a tender, heartfelt collection of songs that you suspect Dolores would love.

"Growing up in Limerick, it was virtually impossible to get away from The Cranberries, but I have no issue with that – they are sensational," Emma says. "I was actually born the year Dolores joined the band, 1989. She even went to the same school as me, Laurel Hill. She was always there in my life, all over the radio and the telly. No matter what area you wanted to go into in life, to hear about someone like that, who came from your area, was really inspirational.

"She was totally Limerick – she really seemed to hold on to a sense of herself," Emma continues. "I can't imagine that was terribly easy, being thrown into the limelight and that kind of celebrity status at such a young age. She embodied an Irishness, a sense of where she came from in her music and that's what made her special. I love 'Dreams' and 'Linger', both songs have so many memories tied up in them. However, one of my favourites is 'Why', a song she wrote for her late father.

"I didn't expect to be hit as hard by her death as I was. I put The Cranberries on shuffle and that's the first song that came up and it's even more poignant now. To me, the music is timeless, it was something unique, but their themes are so universal – from relationships to politics. People will always listen to this music and feel something."

We couldn't have put it better ourselves. The 2020 Dolores Bursary went to Fox Jaw, a pop rock outfit whose *Breathe In The Strange* is also worthy of a place in any self-respecting album collection.

On September 6, 2019, the quartet were part of the musical line-up that gathered in her home parish of Bruff, Co. Limerick to celebrate what would have been Dolores' 48th birthday.

"We want to celebrate Dolores and her memory," her brother Brendan said of the inaugural Dreams Festival. "I have spoken to so many people who she inspired with her music. Her songs helped them cope through the dark times and encouraged them to write and play. Many of them

Under the influence: Emma Langford by Conor Kerr.

"She embodied an Irishness, a sense of where she came from in her music and that's what made her special."

performed over the weekend. People in rural Ireland are often isolated and music helps bring communities together and that's what we aim to do on Dolores' birthday."

While unable to take place in 2020 and '21 due to the Covid-19 pandemic, Brendan and the rest of the O'Riordan family are looking forward to staging a second Dreams Festival when the pandemic hopefully recedes.

It was fitting – but totally coincidental – that on the same day The Cranberries received their first Best Rock Album Grammy nomination, a stunning mural of Dolores was unveiled in Limerick close to King John's Castle.

The person responsible is Aches, the Dublin street artist who overlaid three separate images of her doing her rock 'n' roll thing on stage.

It's become a fitting place of pilgrimage for Cranberries fans from all over the world who, armed with Google Maps, can also take-in where Dolores went to school; the shop that supplied Noel and Mike with their first guitars; and venues like the Glentworth Hotel and the Theatre Royal where they played gigs that are now etched into local lore.

Dolores is sadly no longer around to walk them, but the streets of Limerick will forever reverberate with the sound of The Cranberries.

· **Stuart Clark, October 2021**

IN PERFECT HARMONY

'Dreams' was number one again in Ireland in July 2020 when
Ruth-Anne Cunningham organised a charity version of the song, which underlines just how
influential Dolores has been in her own country.

Having first struck in China's Wuhan Province just before the New Year, Covid-19 made its unwelcome arrival in Ireland on February 29, 2020 when a male student travelling back from a skiing trip in Italy had to be rushed to hospital.

Within three weeks of this, Covid-19 cases had been confirmed in all 26 of the Republic's counties.

Following a fortnight of partial lockdown, which scuppered the usual St. Patrick's Day celebrations, the then Taoiseach, Leo Varadkar, imposed a stay-at-home order on March 27th banning all non-essential travel and contact with people outside of one's home.

As the death toll mounted so did the job losses and fears that Ireland, along with the rest of the world, was heading for one of its worst ever recessions.

By the time that first lockdown was eased on June 4th, An Garda Síochána – the Irish police – had announced a 25% increase in domestic abuse cases nationwide, with 107 people prosecuted for offences in one fortnight period alone, it turned out, the same thing was happening all over the world.

Among those horrified by the statistics was Ruth-Anne Cunningham, the Dublin singer and writer of mega-hits for the likes of JoJo, One Direction and Britney Spears.

Acting on an idea that had been percolating in her head since before lockdown, Ruth-Anne contacted some of her fellow female Irish artists to see if they were interested in collaborating on a song to raise awareness and money for SAFE Ireland, the independent organisation dedicated to the protection of vulnerable women and children.

She had a sales pitch prepared but barely had to use it as, one after another, 36 people said "yes" to her plan for a communal cover of The Cranberries' 'Dreams', which would be recorded by each of them remotely and then knitted together by Ruth-Anne in her London home studio.

Asked what it was that attracted her to The Cranberries and 'Dreams', Ruth-Anne says: "First of all, the standard of songwriting. Then it's her voice, that uniqueness. Dolores

"Watching Dolores break out of her country and being global makes you dream bigger."

inspired in me the idea that I could sound like myself. Watching Dolores break out of her country and being global makes you dream bigger. Because she did it, it makes me inspired to do it.

"For quite some time I'd been wanting to get together with the females in Ireland to collaborate or write," she continues. "Just before lockdown I'd been messaging a few of them. When I was in lockdown, I was seeing so many things for charities happening, and noticing that there were a lot of males, and not very many females on the line-ups for things. I started reaching out to Erica Cody and Aimee and Soulé. They all loved it, and the idea started spreading like wildfire. They were like, 'Let me get this artist involved, and you should email this person.'"

Deciding on Irish Women In Harmony as their collective name, Ruth-Anne found herself engaging in some MacGyver-like improvisation.

"The string section all played into a phone, and I had to pull the audio for the video," she laughs. "Making it sound radio-worthy was very challenging. I didn't want anyone to sound the same, but I wanted it blended."

While her sleep suffered, Ruth-Anne found this way of working liberating.

"It definitely showed us that you don't need these big, expensive studios. I just feel proud that all the women were so on top of it. I didn't have to nag anyone for parts. I didn't have to beg. I was sent everything I needed really quick."

For her, the project was one of incredible fulfillment, and shattered the myth that women can't work together.

"This is about the collective, not any one person standing out," Ruth-Anne reflects. "All of them were so on board. There aren't as many opportunities for females as there are for males – and so sometimes it can make you feel competitive. But with this project, it's made us realise that we're stronger when we join together as a community."

Released on June 19th, Irish Women In Harmony's joyous reworking of 'Dreams' has to date been streamed 3.5 million times and raised close to €250,000 for Safe Ireland.

Tackling such an iconic song was a high-risk strategy, but in terms of both the money raised and the talent showcased, Irish Women In Harmony's cover of 'Dreams' is something that you just know that Dolores O'Riordan would be proud of.

"We had Dolores, we had Sinéad O'Connor, but who do girls have to look up to today as new emerging female talents?" Ruth-Anne concludes. "It's important that these women are highlighted because Irish women are doing amazing things around the world."

Amen to that!

· **Ruth-Anne Cunningham interview by Lucy O'Toole, June 2020**

WHAT *Dolores* MEANT TO US

LILLA VARGEN

"She was an incredible songwriter and a powerhouse frontwoman. I have looked up to her for many years for creating an undeniably unique sound and for unapologetically making music that she wanted to make. Dolores made me feel like a career in music was possible and that being honest in my songwriting is vitally important."

PILLOW QUEENS

"Dolores made our dreams of becoming musicians attainable in our minds, because not only were we hearing a woman's voice in rock music, but that voice also had a gorgeous Limerick accent. The fact that 'Zombie' was the first YouTube video by an Irish artist to reach a billion plays proves that female musicians are not just here to tick a box."

SOULÉ

"Dolores O'Riordan let her artistry do the talking. She is remembered for her voice and her lyricism. She wrote from the heart, and that's why many of her songs will stand the test of time. As women in the music industry, a lot can be thrown at you, but she kept fighting to create an amazing legacy. She never lost sight of her art, it's something I admire about her."

LYRA

"Dolores had a massive influence on my singing style and gave me the confidence to sing in my own accent, which is something I've held onto. Her music and unique voice will always be remembered."

ORLA GARTLAND

"She's the ultimate figurehead of strong Irish women in music. Her spirit is unparalleled – she certainly didn't strike me as someone who would have let her gender hold her or her career back in any way."

UNA HEALY

"I was a huge fan of Dolores and The Cranberries. Her lyrics and music were so powerful and inspiring to me growing up as a singer-songwriter, empowering me as a woman."

WHAT *Dolores* MEANT TO US

AILBHE REDDY

"Dolores had such an incredible vocal style. Hearing her sing in her own accent is so amazing still. As someone who was aspiring to be a musician it was incredible to have a trailblazer like her lead the way. I didn't realise how lucky I was to be able to look up to The Corrs, Sinéad O'Connor and Dolores O'Riordan."

MOYA BRENNAN
Clannad

"It's hard to come out with something new, but Dolores certainly did that. Two things always struck me about her. How she was proud of being Irish and a woman in the music world. I loved her for that alone, and her strength of conviction."

WYVERN LINGO

"Growing up hearing an Irish woman's voice on the radio was something we took for granted then. But it definitely gave us confidence in making music from a young age. My big sister was obsessed with The Cranberries and I remember being transfixed in the back of the car the first time I heard 'Ode To My Family.'"

FAY O'ROURKE
Soda Blonde

"Dolores has been a hero and a style icon of mine since I was a kid. She brought politics into my life through the female voice, which ultimately has had a huge part to play in the way I write music."

RÓISÍN O

"Growing up, it wasn't often you'd see a woman fronting a rock band, and I was hugely influenced by her. Her 'no shits given' attitude and unique vocal style was totally awe-inspiring."

ERICA CODY

"Her voice was so unique, sweet and gritty all in one. Especially being the frontwoman to all-male musicians can only leave you feeling inspired, not only that but also her songwriting capabilities. 'Dreams' has always been one of my favourite Irish songs."

LISA McGEE *On The Cranberries*

ZOMBIELAND

There was only one band whose music was going to bookend the first series of *Derry Girls* and that was The Cranberries. Show creator and real life Erin, Lisa McGee, tells us about the special place Dolores occupies in her and young Miss Quinn's hearts.

PHOTOS COURTESY OF CHANNEL 4

"The guys in the band probably won't be too pleased about this, but my introduction aged 14 to The Cranberries was a copied tape of *No Need To Argue,* which was doing the rounds at my school. I'd been looking for something that felt very Irish but contemporary and they blew me away. As a kid you're always searching for yourself in music, TV and cinema and I was like, "Oh, this is it! This sounds like modern Ireland." I remember lying outside on one of the rare sunny days Derry has in the summer and getting goosebumps listening to the music. Then I fell in love with the lyrics and, like Erin, had The Cranberries as the soundtrack to my teenage years.

Serious rock critics were a bit sniffy about the *"tanks..."* part of 'Zombie', but we totally related to its simple message of ordinary innocent people being the main victims of war. You often felt that you were forgotten in Northern Ireland and nobody cared, so Dolores singing about *us* was amazing.

I'm not sure why because I love loads of them, but 'Ode To My Family' is my favourite Cranberries song. It's an amazing piece of storytelling, which only somebody like Dolores, who had a great innocence but also a great worldliness, could have written.

When we were thinking about what the sound of *Derry Girls* should be, 'Dreams' said everything about that time. You know, the hopelessness and the poetry and the drama of it. Everything is kind of big when you're a teenager.

The Cranberries songs' feel very cinematic; there's such a scale to them. I wanted a very strong Irish woman at the start of the show, so the first thing in the script is going into Erin's bedroom and seeing a poster of Dolores and The Cranberries next to her bed.

Because I was very young when I got into them, she just seemed like this cool older girl, but you forget how young Dolores was herself when all this was happening. It must have been pretty intense.

I had the self-awareness to know I wasn't cool enough to copy her style. She was such an incredibly beautiful woman that she could get away with very tight haircuts and I couldn't have. I knew my limits!

The opening scene which 'Dreams' soundtracks was quite silly, so as a bookend to that we thought we'd use it again at the end of Series One when it bleeds from the gang dancing on stage at school to Madonna's 'Like A Prayer' into Mary, Sarah, Gerry and Granda Joe hearing the awful news about the Omagh bombing on the telly.

That episode went out on February 8, 2018, which was just after Dolores died, but the adding of 'Dreams' to that scene – it took us ages to get it exactly right – had been done months beforehand.

I remember someone from Channel 4 emailing to tell me the news and feeling this weird sensation because so much of what we'd been doing in the edit suite had involved Dolores' voice. I was shocked by her death and the stuff that had been going on for her personally, which I hadn't known until I started reading about it in the obituaries.

We always ended up hanging our big hooky moments on a Cranberries song. In Series Two, we initially play out on Enya's 'Caribbean Blue' before cutting again to 'Dreams'.

I was delighted to hear that Noel Hogan's latest song is with a real live Derry girl, Bronagh Gallagher, who we're hoping to get to do a bit on Series Three. Bronagh is a force of nature just like Dolores was."

· Lisa McGee in conversation with Stuart Clark, July 2021

"When we were thinking about what the SOUND of *DERRY GIRLS* should be, 'Dreams' SAID EVERYTHING about that time."

Remembering Dolores

Noel, Mike and Fergal marked what would have been Dolores' 50th birthday on September 6th, 2021 with a Limerick livestream event that conjured up wonderful memories of their musical adventures together. "Life is short; enjoy it," Dolores told us in the brand new found-footage video for 'Never Grow Old', a fan favourite song that proved to be eerily prescient. Those same fans will hopefully take some solace from her boyfriend and D.A.R.K. bandmate Olé Koretsky revealing how happy and artistically fulfilled she'd been, living between Limerick and New York. Dolores' mother, Eileen O'Riordan, also recalls the magic moments they shared.

Opposite photo:Kip Carroll

"DOLORES WAS REALLY ON FIRE"

As well as reconvening with The Cranberries to record *Something Else,* 2016 saw Dolores O'Riordan hooking up first musically and then romantically with D.A.R.K. bandmate Olé Koretsky. He talks about the precious time they spent flitting between New York and Ireland, and the creative roll she was on when she tragically passed away.

PHOTOS: JEN MALER

While her passion for The Cranberries remained undimmed, Dolores was also loving being a one-third shareholder in D.A.R.K., the category-defying outfit founded by New York DJ and producer Olé Koretsky and Smiths bassist Andy Rourke as Jetlag and renamed when she decided to hook up with them in New York.

What was supposed to be a side-project quickly became a way of life as Dolores simultaneously fell in love with the city and Olé who, having clubbed his way round all five of its boroughs, was ideally placed to introduce her to both the excitement and the anonymity the Big Apple had to offer.

"My friend, partner and the love of my life is gone," a grief-stricken Olé messaged shortly after Dolores' death in January 2018 while in London working on the second D.A.R.K. album. "My heart is broken and it is beyond repair. Dolores is beautiful. Her art is beautiful. Her family is beautiful. The energy she continues to radiate is undeniable. I am lost. I miss her so much. I will continue to stumble around this planet for some time knowing well there's no real place for me here now."

Three years later Olé is back making music – no self-respecting record collection should be without his *MMXX* EP – but clearly still mourning the woman he adored.

"Probably for the only time in my life I fell in love with the girl," he tells me when we hook up in his Brooklyn apartment.

"There wasn't a day she didn't make me laugh. Everything about my life changed in 2018. I'm still really struggling."

Born in the former Soviet Union, Olé arrived in Brooklyn aged nine with his small but precious record collection.

"During the immigration process I was in Italy in the late '80s and bought Elton John's *Sleeping With The Past,* John Lennon's *Double Fantasy* and a bootleg Beatles Best Of... from one of the street markets they have there," he recalls. "That lead me on to The Kinks and Pink Floyd: the standard classic stuff, which never sounds old. Once I was in New York, house and hip-hop became a big part of my life. Getting my hands on my first drum machine in my teens was a massive moment. Up till then I had no concept of how you made a record – I still think that way about filmmaking. You have to be in something to understand all the moving parts. So, I started obsessively messing around with this four-track drum machine and an acoustic guitar, building bits upon bits until I had something vaguely resembling a song. Being a Brooklynite, it was impossible not to draw inspiration from the Beastie Boys – *Check Your Head* was one of the ones I ran to the store to buy."

It was eighteen years after being wowed by Mike D, MCA and Ad-Rock that a wonderfully random series of events lead to Olé meeting Andy Rourke.

"This is a weird story," he laughs. "I wound up going to Washington D.C. with my DJ bag because I thought I hada

"There wasn't a day she didn't make me laugh.
EVERYTHING ABOUT MY LIFE CHANGED IN 2018."

*

D.A.R.K. life: (l-r) Dolores with Olé Koretsky and Andy Rourke in New York.

"When we were in a restaurant or a shopping mall together she'd always chuckle if The Cranberries came on, which they do all the time in America."

gig at a Britpop-themed night there. Usually I'm into beat matching and electronic music but, y'know, it was a few quid. I didn't realise D.C. had different licensing laws regarding what time places have to close and turned up at the venue when people were clearing out. There'd been a miscommunication between the promoter and myself, so I started talking to this Mancunian fellow and moved on with him to the pool in the Hilton where we hung out all night and well into the morning. He said his name was Mike but it wasn't until he mentioned playing with Buzzcocks and PiL after leaving his other band that the penny dropped and I realised it was Mike Joyce from The Smiths.

"I was in bad shape physically," Olé continues, "and he sent me up soaking wet to Rourkey's room to get a sleeping tablet. After explaining who the hell I was and why I was banging on his door, we hit it off. Andy and myself hung out all day playing music and kept in touch, so much so that when he was deciding whether to move to Los Angeles or New York he chose here and we started Jetlag."

Before we get to hear how Dolores entered into the equation, does Olé remember the first time he heard a Cranberries song?

"Jesus, yeah, that voice!" he reflects with a sad smile. "Back then I was in awe every time I heard it, but now I'll go to the grocery store and get very emotional because there's one of her songs playing. Although Dolores didn't like to listen back to her recordings, when we were in a restaurant or a shopping mall together she'd always chuckle if The Cranberries came on, which they do all the time in America."

Having written *Bury The Hatchet*'s 'Desperate Andy' with The Smiths very obviously in mind, it might be deemed fate that twenty years later Dolores ended up being in a band with their bassist.

"It's a synchronistic kind of thing," Olé agrees. "The lyrical meaning is something else – the Andy in question is not Rourkey – but musically, yeah, it was Dolores paying homage to The Smiths. I was a big fan of theirs in high school and thought I knew all the lyrics, but she really dug them big time and was able to tell Andy stuff about The Smiths he'd forgotten."

It was through Andy Rourke that Olé and Dolores first got to talk.

"Andy and I had just been working and working and working

"I eventually got it that she loved the songs. A miracle because only my mammy and Dolores liked my voice!"

on stuff – he lived upstairs from me and I had the studio in the basement – without really ever getting anywhere. Anyway, he calls me one day and says, 'Do you know who Dolores O'Riordan is?' I'm like, 'Yeah, course I do' and he goes, 'I ran into her and Smiths fan and all, she wants to hear what I've been up to. Do you mind if I send her our stuff?' I'm like, 'Sure, nothing's happening with it anyway. Maybe there's something in the files she could use even experimentally.' I emailed her the tracks – I didn't have time to isolate the instrumentals so my voice was on them – and thought no more about it until three months later when I was on the ferry over to see my mom. It was nice weather so I was on the upper-deck by the engines, which are very loud. I got a phone call from Dolores whose first words to me were 'Are you the boy singing?' She'd thought it was Andy but discovered then that it was someone else. I was struggling to understand her because of the noise and her accent, which was really thick, but I eventually got it that she loved the songs. A miracle because only my mammy and Dolores liked my voice!"

Asked whether he was nervous about working with somebody who'd sold upwards of fifty million albums, Olé admits, "Oh, yeah. I just felt, 'Jeez, I'd better pull my weight now!' I have issues with the record; there are a lot of mistakes I made. I've quite a few technical skills, but I'd never produced an album before. It was really interesting because for the first few months Dolores and I would be coming up with vocal harmonies and parts and working through lyrics via long sessions on the phone. When it came to the mixing, the mastering, the clearing of samples and just making a record though, I was in over my head. It was a lot of fun and a huge learning curve, but I can't listen to it anymore because of what's happened."

Olé is being extremely harsh on himself with 'Curvy', an electro rock banger par excellence, and the Kraftwerkian 'Gunfight' taking Dolores out of her musical comfort zone with spectacular results.

Talking about his becoming a New York resident in the 1990s, David Bowie said, "People here are very decent about their interactions with well-knowns. I get the occasional 'Yo, Bowie' but that's about it. My only rule is to avoid tourist areas. But if I weren't known, I'd still avoid 'em. In London, the saying goes, life takes place behind doors. Here it's on the street."

The impression I get is that Dolores felt the same way about The Big Apple.

"This is a well-to-do, low-key neighbourhood with lots of families and buggies," Olé reflects. "Nobody here bothers you. I moved to it from the Lower Eastside, a completely hipster downtown club area where Dolores would occasionally get stopped for a photo. How she reacted depended on the approach. If it was, 'Hey, I know who you are, you're cool!' she was okay with it. I remember being in a restaurant and Andy, who's a massive fan, going up and introducing himself to Jim Jarmusch. That's one thing, but people get weird. Another time I was outside a pub where I was DJ-ing having

a cigarette. I didn't realise that the actor Adrian Brody was standing next to me until these girls, who'd just got out of a taxi, surrounded him saying, 'You're famous!' They didn't know him or his films yet they were in his face to the point where the guy had to run away."

It wasn't long before Dolores was taking Olé back to Limerick to meet the mammy and all her siblings.

"We were over and back constantly because I wasn't a resident there and she wasn't a resident here," he explains. "I was talking earlier about Dolores' accent being thick, well, it's a sticky one too, as I discovered when I first went to Ireland and immediately started picking it up. She'd try and get me to do different ones – 'Are you from Kerry, boy?' – and cracked up at my attempts. She also laughed every time I got an Irish pronunciation wrong, which was quite often."

What a lot of people don't know about Dolores is how sidesplittingly hilarious she could be.

"God, yes!" he nods. "It's only recently that I've been able to look at photos and videos of us and in virtually all of them she was fooling around. It was always, 'Hey, Koretsky!' Dolores only called me Olé when the conversation was a serious one. You'd have to have seen it to find it funny, but she did this really exaggerated 'I'm off to work' walk/march. She had that physical comedy thing going on too."

There was also – in the nicest possible way – a toughness about Dolores, which probably came from having five elder brothers.

"Jeez, I felt safe with her," Olé admits. "She felt safe with me

> ## "I knew Dolores had my back. Instead of freaking out I'd be like, 'Okay, what's the next adventure?'"

too but in a different way. On the last few Cranberries festivals and tours, we'd end up walking for ages – in Barcelona it was nine, ten hours straight. I'm borderline agoraphobic but even in sketchy places like Peru where there are no traffic lights and the traffic's coming at you from every angle, I knew Dolores had my back. Instead of freaking out I'd be like, 'Okay, what's the next adventure?'"

It was Dolores who again lead the way when Olé made one of the most important trips of his life to Eastern Europe.

"When I met Dolores she'd just lost her dad, which was a big deal for her," he explains. "She was having a hard time with it. I was born in Odessa, which used to be in the Soviet Union but is now the Ukraine. When Dolores found out that my dad was still there and that we hadn't seen each other for a long, long time, she took it upon herself to reconnect us. Once that had happened, Dolores made sure I was out there at least once a year and came with me. She loved Odessa. I was like, 'Jesus, I'd be afraid...' but she was, 'No, no, no, I know where the park is, I know where the beach is, I've got this city locked down. Don't worry about me, you sit with your dad here.' It was the

same with me in Limerick; I just thought it was wonderful.

"I fell in love with Ireland immediately but when we lost Dolores it turned from a magical place into a dark place for me."

Olé got a chance to see her in arena rock mode when, under the D.A.R.K. banner, himself and DJ Wool opened for The Cranberries on their final *Something Else* tour.

"We did about a dozen dates before the rest of the tour was cancelled because of Dolores' back thing – we ended up in the hospital in Bristol," he recalls. "I really didn't want to play but I had a conversation with Noel who was like, 'Hey, someone's coming out with us so it might as well be you since you're going to be with Dolores anyway.' I was a little intimidated, especially by the arenas although the theatres where you've got people sitting looking at you were scary too. I loved seeing the camaraderie between Dolores and the rest of The Cranberries.

"Meeting the guys in L.A. after the Grammy thing popped off, I was wondering how's everyone thinking and feeling but it was so easy to pick things up with them. I can see how they were able to sometimes take years off and then get

Olé, Olé, Óle: The Cranberries with D.A.R.K. supporting them in May 2017 at the Bord Gais Energy Theatre, Dublin. Photos by Karl Leonard.

straight back into it. The personalities within the band were all amenable to that. No airs and graces, no big heads, just down to earth guys."

Olé and Dolores' New York City neighbours included Kinks legend Dave Davies who in an obituary piece he wrote for the UK *Observer* newspaper revealed that, "We had a mutual respect. We talked about writing together – I had an idea for a song called 'Home', about being home again, and she understood what I was trying to say. But we never sat down to do it, and that makes me really sad. She was very kind to me, too. We said we'd meet when she was next in London and that was that. It was an honour to get to know her. The world's a poorer place without her."

"To have a legend like him say that about Dolores is amazing," Olé smiles ruefully. "It was Dave's missus who recognised Lo-Lo and, yeah, he was all about it. The problem was time. There was a renaissance happening with myself and with Dolores; the volume of work we were doing together was crazy. Jeez, I hope some of this music sees the light of day. Youth was to mix it. With the D.A.R.K. album, the acoustic Cranberries record and the tour, it was like pop, pop, pop.

Dolores was really on fire."

It's some small consolation that, after her much publicised travails, Dolores was in a good place again when she died.

"Yes, I think so," Olé nods. "Shortly before she passed, Dolores was thrilled that Eminem, an artist she admired and thought was really cool, sampled pretty much the whole of 'Zombie' on his album. She'd never met him but said to me, 'He's got the dirty mouth, but I've a feeling he's a good guy.' Dolores had her own strong beliefs but she wasn't judgmental at all. If religion or politics ever came up in conversation it was a 'Koretsky, how do you feel about this?' sort of thing rather than her just being angry and giving out. She wasn't a relativist – Dolores knew what was wrong and right – but she refused to paint people with a broad brush. She was proud of the fact that she'd sung for The Pope and that Princess Diana was there and they sung to meet. She knew she was loved and was able to give love back with interest."

There is no finer epitaph than that.

· Olé Koretsky interview by Stuart Clark, July 2021

"Her Music Lives On, So She's Not Really Gone."

No one knew Dolores better than her mother, Eileen O'Riordan, who shared in such celebrated moments as her singing with Pavarotti and meeting The Pope. She remembers Dolores' childhood, the pride she felt as The Cranberries conquered the world – and the comfort that fans of The Cranberries bring her.

PHOTOS: THE LIMERICK LEADER

"Dolores' father, Terry, played the accordion and I used to take her with me when I sang in the church choir. As a young one she'd sing along with me, so from the beginning she was surrounded by music. Dolores began singing in the choir herself and doing the readings, and when she was about ten or twelve started playing the organ in the church. In a way, going to mass was like having dinner: it was part of our lives.

It was a big family and they were all into their music: *Top Of The Pops* was a major thing in the house and Dolores would be glued to that. She loved Goth music and style, and had posters of Morrissey and The Cure on her bedroom walls. We all had part-time jobs, so with the church and the sport and everything else, life was busy.

Dolores went to the Gaelcholáiste at Laurel Hill, which meant all of her education was through Irish. She had a great passion for the language. All the boys and girls in the family went to Irish dancing lessons too. Dolores was a good little dancer – she was at Féile a few times and won medals. When The Cranberries played their first big Limerick gig in The People's Park, she wore her dancing uniform, which had a lovely Celtic design on it.

Dolores also started having piano lessons - she was professionally trained - when she was in her early teens with a lady, Miss Lenihan, who had a Georgian townhouse in the city-centre. She passed all her London School of Music exams and could read music perfectly.

RECORD DEAL

I was married at eighteen and spent most of my time after that at home with the children, so I didn't really know what was involved when Dolores said she was auditioning for a band.

Anyway, she went into town to meet the boys and came back with a rough version of 'Linger' that the boys had given her on a tape. I remember her being down in the small little bedroom she had and after a while saying to me, "Have a listen to this." She'd been writing the melodies and the lyrics for the song on the keyboard I'd bought her a few years earlier while I was stood there in the corridor, and I thought, "This is really good!" That was like a revelation to me.

Then I got to hear her sing it in front of an audience in this little venue in the basement of Cruise's, a gorgeous hotel in Limerick city, which has now sadly been knocked down. It was all a little above my head, but everyone was clapping

"I still get letter after letter saying,
'I wouldn't be here if it wasn't for Dolores' music.'"

*

"I felt very proud when I first heard 'Ode To My Family', which Dolores didn't tell me about until it was ready. It was a lovely surprise."

along and I really enjoyed it.

When Dolores said she wanted to go travelling with the band I was like, "Well, you can't because you've got college." As far as I was concerned that was that.

She went, "How about I make you a promise? Let me take a year out and if I'm not a success at the end of it, I'll go to college then." And sure, within a year they had their record deal with Island Records.

When Dolores had her first child, Taylor, I went on tour with her to mind him – so I was there with Simon Le Bon and everyone else when she sang with Pavarotti. Afterwards I was sat at the table when Dolores went up to talk to Princess Diana. She said to her, "Let's go to the bathroom and have a chat" and Diana was like, "Oh, I can't" – because her security would have had to tag along with her. It was bad enough for Dolores not being able to go shopping or out into the street, but Diana had no life outside of her royal duties.

I was also there with Dolores in The Vatican when she met The Pope. We had a lady with us who was going to mind Taylor, but as the car was waiting we changed our mind and dressed him up quickly to take him with us. When we got there it was such a small little crowd, I'd say about sixteen people. The Corrs were there the same day.

Pope John Paul was an old man by then, but I'll never forget his piercing blue eyes and how he put his arm around Taylor and sat him on his knee.

I probably saw more of the places The Cranberries were playing in than Dolores did, because I'd be free during the day when she'd be going off to soundcheck. Sometimes when they were touring, we'd have a little apartment in the hotel for five or six weeks, which I stayed in and Dolores flew back to whenever she could. I'd put all these pictures up to make it feel a bit homely.

PEOPLE ARE SO GOOD

The kids are doing great now, which is wonderful to know. Taylor is 23. Molly, who's home now for the summer of 2021, is 20. And Dakota, the baby, is 16.

I got sick myself for a while after Dolores died and then Covid happened, but everything now is nearly back to normal with us being able to see each other.

I haven't been able to listen to any of The Cranberries' songs on my own since she died, but 'Daffodil Lament' is my favourite. Then there's 'Joe', which was dedicated to my father. I felt very proud when I first heard 'Ode To My Family', which Dolores didn't tell me about until it was ready. It was a lovely surprise.

It's great how her songs, and records by The Cranberries, still get played everywhere. I was at the All-Ireland hurling final in 2018 when Limerick won, and got very emotional when they started singing 'Dreams'. The fella next to me asked, "Are you Dolores' mother?" He turned out to be a Redemptorist priest from Limerick who's Chaplin to the Travellers. I felt like Dolores had sent him there to mind me. His name's Teddy Kelly and we've kept our friendship up since.

I still get letter after letter saying, "I wouldn't be here if it wasn't for Dolores' music." And, "I felt like she was singing about me." Somebody sent a lovely Mass Card the other day addressed to, "Dear Eileen O'Riordan, mother of the late beautiful Dolores O'Riordan, RIP, Limerick." That got to me. People are so good.

I know we don't want to talk about sad things, but she was so sick. When she died, I knew she was at peace. Her music lives on, so she's not really gone."

• Eileen O'Riordan in conversation with Stuart Clark, September 2021

Viva Las Vegas: Dolores on a September 28th, 1993 visit to Sin City's Huntridge Theater by Phill Nicholls.

HAPPY BIRTHDAY DOLORES

On the day that Dolores would have turned fifty, her bandmates took part in a special
online event, which included the unveiling of a new Spotify playlist and video.
Stuart Clark joined them for what was both a sad and joyous occasion...

PORTRAIT: KIP CARROLL

I've been back in Limerick for precisely two minutes when walking down from the railway station I bump into Cathal O'Neill, the hairdresser who once tended to Dolores and her Cranberries travelling companion Breffni's tresses when they were back in Limerick.

He recalls all the laughter, storytelling and wine-drinking that went on when the two old friends were in the salon.

Our conversation takes place opposite Pery's, AKA The Glentworth Hotel, where Dolores and the lads went to watch bands – The Golden Horde, Fatima Mansions, The Stunning and The Fat Lady Sings among them – and played a couple of times in their indie-minded D-Club.

Round the corner from the Pery on Cecil Street is the Theatre Royal, scene of The Cranberries' triumphant December 1993 homecoming show. Fun Trivia Fact: the Royal is also where the Eurovision episode of *Father Ted* (*"My lovely horse, running through the field..."*) was shot.

Plastered onto one of the pillars is a photocopied photo of the band playing that Christmas to a crowd who – short of jumping on stage and giving them a communal hug – couldn't have been more adoring.

A good few of the thousand people lucky enough to have bagged tickets would have knocked back a pre-gig pint (or four) in the nearby Costello's Tavern, a favourite haunt of Noel, Mike and Ferg's but not Dolores, who found it a bit too testosterone-y.

Head right and you come to the People's Park where in July

1991 The Cranberries appeared on the same 2fm Lark In The Park bill as Colors, Those Stilted Boys, They Do It With Mirrors, The Blue Angels and An Emotional Fish.

Turning left, and left again, brings you to Savin's, the music shop where Mr. and Mrs. Hogan bought their little boys Noel and Mike their first guitars.

I could go on like this till the proverbial cows come home. Suffice it to say that The Cranberries are now a part of Limerick's DNA. This stroll down rock 'n' roll memory lane is compacted by the fact that today is what should have been Dolores' fiftieth birthday.

To commemorate the occasion her bandmates have taken over the sixth floor of the Strand Hotel, which is at the top end of the Ennis Road, where Noel and Mike grew up and still live, albeit in their own homes.

I've been invited to host the livestream *Remembering Dolores* event, which is beaming out around the world via their Facebook at 7pm. The plan is to introduce the Spotify playlist of lesser-known Cranberries songs that the lads, Dolores' son Taylor and the extended O'Riordan family have compiled; premiere the new found footage video for 'Never Grow Old'; and then pack as many memories and yarns as we possibly can into the remaining 45 minutes or so.

Before heading over the Sarsfield Bridge to the Strand, myself and *Hot Press* snapper Miguel Ruiz head up to Castle Street which, since November 2019, has been home to Aches' stunning 'glitch graffiti' mural of Dolores giving it loads live.

My "why's there a feckin' fence in front of it?" rant ends

A tour of The Cranberries' Limerick: (clockwise from top) The People's Park, Theatre Royal and Costello's Tavern, and the band reminiscing in the Strand Hotel. Photos by Miguel Ruiz.

"From the very beginning she was like one of the boys. Growing up in a house full of brothers... we were the next step up from that!"

when I'm informed that it's there to protect the wild flowers that have been sown in front of it. Dolores, who got seriously into her native flora and fauna while living on her Kilmallock stud farm, would doubtless approve.

"You'd forget it was there and then be really startled – in a good way – driving past it," Ferg says an hour later when I tell him how myself and the boy Ruiz have spent our afternoon. He's just about recovered from his Friday night appearance on Ireland's *The Late Late Show* with Dolores' mum, Eileen O'Riordan, who we agree is a force of nature like her daughter.

"I've been doing this for over thirty years now but I still get nervous when a camera's pointing at me," Ferg explains.

To be found, naturally, on YouTube, the *Late Late...* segment featured an orchestral mash-up of 'Linger', 'Dreams' and 'Zombie' featuring the voices of Dolores O'Riordan Bursary winner, Emma Langford, and her fellow Shannonsider, Kellie Lewis, who Dolores mentored on the Irish version of *The Voice*.

The mood in the Strand's City View Suite as we wait to go 'live' is somewhat sombre at first but soon lightens as we start swapping favourite Dolores memories and, my goodness, there are lots of them.

Everyone agrees that she would publicly have professed to being horrified by the fuss being made of her fiftieth and privately been delighted!

Fears that we're going to be talking to ourselves for the next hour are allayed when just before getting the "5-4-3-2-1, you're on!" countdown we're told that there are close to five thousand people in the waiting room.

There's no beer but otherwise it feels like we're in the pub as we reminisce about that heady night in Oberhausen with AC/DC and the Rolling Stones; being totally awestruck going for dinner with U2; running round North America with Duran Duran; and the time opening for R.E.M. when Michael Stipe squeezed into Dolores' pink rubber mini-dress with spikes.

"The two of them were giddy, laughing and giggling, and she took Michael off to the dressing-room, to try on loads of outfits," Fergal grins. "He had some kind of belly-top on as well. He looked pretty cool in it!"

As Noel notes: "Under it all, Dolores more than anybody was up for a laugh the whole time. From the very beginning she was like one of the boys. Growing up in a house full of brothers... we were the next step up from that!"

The elder Hogan kicks off a double-whammy of good news for fans with confirmation that work on a major Cranberries documentary will soon be resuming.

"We had started filming bits, and doing interviews for it," he tells us. "At the time we were rehearsing for a tour. So, we put it on 'hold' when we went on the tour and then, unfortunately, Dolores passed away. So the stuff was sitting there. Then it became obvious after a while that we should really do a documentary about the band from start to finish. We started working on that a little bit more then, and fleshing that out.

"Unfortunately, the world changed – something happened a year and a half ago, to stop everything! – but now things are starting to move again."

While the timeline on that is somewhat fluid – if I were a gambling man, I'd say expect the doc sometime in 2024 – the 25th anniversary edition of The Cranberries' third album, *To The Faithful Departed*, will be with us at some point in 2022.

"We managed to find three demos that everyone had forgotten about," enthuses Ferg who's overseeing the reissue. "It just came to me one day that we'd done them in the middle of a tour in Paris with Tim Palmer, who produced Tears For Fears and a few other bands, before we worked with Bruce Fairbairn. They sound great, but because we ended up going in a heavier direction on the album we re-recorded them."

Heading into the home straight, Noel tells us how the new 'Never Grow Old' video we're about to see for the first time was assembled.

"It's mainly from the extra B-reel footage that was shot when we were making videos. Somebody went through all the tapes that have been gathering dust for years. Some of it I remember like yesterday, other bits I'm like, 'Where's that and who are they?' I don't have any recollection at all. It really captures Dolores' playful side and the *craic* we had together. We love it and I think fans will too."

The 200,000-plus views in a week suggest that they do. As Dolores explained to us in 2001, the song came from the most personal of places.

"'I wrote 'Never Grow Old' with no music whatsoever," she recalled. "I was walking outside here, with my little baby in a pram with me and I started singing: *I have a dream/ Strange as it may seem/ This is my perfect day.*' I ran home

and tried to get down the chords on the piano but didn't because I was distracted. The baby was crying! So I lost it. But the next day I woke up and it came back to me so I wrote it at the piano, then played it with the lads."

So fresh is the video from the editing suite that the lads have only seen it once and yours truly not at all, which means I'm totally unprepared for the bit at the end when Dolores' looks into the camera and says, "Life is short; enjoy it. Take care, see you soon."

This explains the lump in the throat, the wobble in the voice and the tear in the eye as I join Noel, Mike and Ferg in the final act of wishing Dolores, doubtless looking down at us with great amusement, the happiest of fiftieth birthdays.

The silence after the floor manager says, "We're off air…" is broken by Dolores' brother PJ who shouts from the back of the room, "Lads, you did her proud!"

The same is true of the tens of thousands of Cranberries fans who'd ensured that throughout the day Dolores had been trending on social media. Mike, who spent a couple of hours scrolling through them, says that they're a great comfort to the band.

She may no longer be physically with us, but Dolores Mary Eileen O'Riordan will live on forever through her music. I feel truly blessed to have known her.

· **Stuart Clark, September 2021**

A river runs through it: (l-r) Noel Hogan, Mike Hogan and Fergal Lawler at the *Remembering Dolores* event in Limerick. Photo by Miguel Ruiz.

REMEMBERING DOLORES PLAYLIST

'Never Grow Old'
Wake Up And Smell The Coffee

'Schizophrenic Playboy'
Roses

'The Glory'
Something Else

'What You Were'
Everybody Else Is Doing It, So Why Can't We Super Deluxe Reissue

'Daffodil Lament'
No Need To Argue

'I Will Always'
Everybody Else Is Doing It, So Why Can't We?

'This Is The Day'
Wake Up And Smell The Coffee

'Joe'
To The Faithful Departed

'Pretty'
Everybody Else Is Doing It, So Why Can't We?

'I'm Still Remembering'
To The Faithful Departed

'You And Me'
Bury The Hatchet

'Waiting In Walthamstow'
Roses

'Everything I Said'
No Need To Argue

'Why'
Something Else

'Twenty One'
No Need To Argue

the cranberries

REMEMBERING DOLORES

 HOT PRESS BOOKS

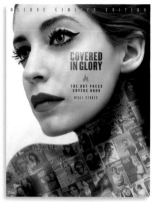

COVERED IN GLORY: THE HOT PRESS COVERS BOOK
By Niall Stokes

Packed with history-making covers, this remarkable book offers a marvellous trip through the past 40 years of music history-in-the-making. Comes in lavish Platinum, Limited Edition hardback format that is hand numbered and signed by *Hot Press* editor Niall Stokes; and superbly produced Gold Edition.

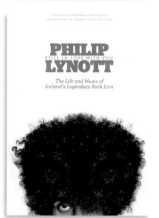

PHILIP LYNOTT: STILL IN LOVE WITH YOU
By Niall Stokes

Available in your choice of two formats, this is an exceptionally beautiful book that tells the unique story of Ireland's original black rock star and leader of Thin Lizzy, Philip Lynott, in a remarkable documentary style. This powerful work is a must-have for fans of Irish rock and fans of the man they called 'Philo'.

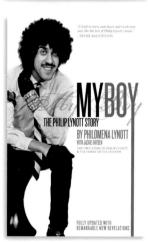

MY BOY
By Philomena Lynott and Jackie Hayden

My Boy is the extraordinary, No.1 best-selling memoir in which Philomena Lynott tells the story of the unique relationship she had with her son, the Irish rock icon Philip Lynott of Thin Lizzy. Deeply moving and hugely revealing, the book has been optioned for a movie by rising UK production house, Shy Punk Productions.

For all Hot Press Books, posters, magazines and merchandising, go to **hotpress.com/shop**